"The conservation of buildings is messy and complicated. The philosophically led decisions that seemed easy to make in the office are almost always harder to implement when the project becomes a live building site. I welcome this book because it embraces those challenges and shows how a thoughtful architect can find practical solutions that remain true to the original design principles. It also demonstrates that the tenets of conservation philosophy proposed by William Morris remain valid today if we choose to care for our heritage in a way that puts people at its heart."

– **Sara Crofts**, *CEO, Institute of Conservation*

The Production of Heritage

In this important book, the authors unpack the theoretical and practical issues around the development of heritage sites, critically dissecting key conservation benchmarks such as the ICOMOS guidelines, BS 7913 and the RIBA Conservation Plan of Work to reveal the mechanics of heritage guidance, its advantages and conceptual limitations.

Underpinned by an active understanding of the conservation philosophy of William Morris, the book presents five case studies from the UK and North and South America that speak about different facets of heritage value, such as urban identity, commodification, authenticity, materiality and heritage as an intellectual and ethical framework. Heritage is never neutral; its definition is privileged yet its influence is political. Art, landscape and archaeology all offer examples of how the operational ideas of adjacent disciplines can influence an integrated idea of heritage conservation, and how this is communicated in order to determine significance and share in its custodianship.

This book provides insights into how to identify and challenge these limitations, expanding inclusion by describing tactics for changing how people can relate to and build on the past. Clearly written for all levels of readership within the conservation professions and community custodians of heritage buildings and places, the book provides strategies and tactics for understanding the heritage significance of materials, their fabrication, detail and use. The narratives that historic fabric contains can help shape the meaningful involvement of local people, providing a roadmap for those navigating the double-bind of using the past to underpin the future.

Alan Chandler is a founding director of the architectural practice Arts Lettres Techniques with Luisa Auletta, working consistently on the interface between contemporary design and conservation since 1993 when, as students at the Architectural Association, concrete casts weighing several tonnes were poured into flexible moulds taken directly from Hawksmoor's St George's Church in Bloomsbury using paper pulp, hessian and bitumen to create a site-specific installation in the portico. This early engagement with questioning material and heritage value has persisted, with expertise in conservation accreditation and award-winning projects in the UK and Chile maintaining a focus on how politics and cultural perception connect with material and philosophical conservation.

Examining for the RIBA Conservation Register began at its inception in 2011, followed by membership of the RIBA Conservation Committee and Steering Group, has allowed a perspective on the culture of professionalism, the criticism of which in this book should be balanced with a genuine respect for the knowledge and commitment of many professionals within the field, and an acknowledgement that the RIBA has made a genuine investment into conservation practice, supported by dedicated and intelligent staff within the organisation. The aim of the dissection is to discover what is missing, not what is wrong. He is a reader in architecture and currently leads research in architecture, computing and engineering at the University of East London.

Michela Pace is a researcher at the IUAV University of Venice in the field of urbanism; she has previously worked and collaborated with universities including UEL London, PoliTo Turin and PoliMi Milan, UH Hasselt and Tongji University Shanghai. She studied the rising centrality of the 'heritage' rhetoric within processes of urban financialization worldwide, and the use of notions of memory, legacy, patrimony and tradition inside city marketing. Heritage in particular was observed in relation to real estate activities and the phenomena of land privatisation and gentrification in Western and Eastern global cities. At the same time, as an architect, she deepened her experience of community-based research, collaborating with a different spectrum of partners and clients for the making of local projects. These include local communities and schools, councils and policymakers, international NGOs, charitable foundations and private clients. Merging the observations of 'heritage' promotion and protection at the global and local scale has the ability to disclose those mechanisms able to promote an idea of city, and the language and the rules able to distribute it. What is at stake is not only the concept of past and the power of history, but also the collective ability to imagine alternative futures.

The Production
of Heritage

The Politicisation of Architectural Conservation

Alan Chandler and Michela Pace

Routledge
Taylor & Francis Group

LONDON AND NEW YORK

First published 2020
by Routledge
2 Park Square, Milton Park, Abingdon, Oxon OX14 4RN

and by Routledge
52 Vanderbilt Avenue, New York, NY 10017

Routledge is an imprint of the Taylor & Francis Group, an informa business

British Library Cataloguing-in-Publication Data
A catalogue record for this book is available from the British Library

Library of Congress Cataloging-in-Publication Data
Names: Chandler, Alan, 1966– author. | Pace, Michela, author.
Title: The production of heritage : the politicisation of architectural
    conservation / Alan Chandler and Michela Pace.
Description: New York : Routledge, 2020. | Includes bibliographical
    references and index.
Identifiers: LCCN 2019028283 (print) | LCCN 2019028284 (ebook) |
    ISBN 9780367078003 (hardback) | ISBN 9780367078010 (paperback) |
    ISBN 9780429022869 (ebook)
Subjects: LCSH: Historic preservation—Political aspects. | Historic
    preservation—Case studies.
Classification: LCC CC135 .C42 2020 (print) | LCC CC135 (ebook) |
    DDC 363.6/9—dc23
LC record available at https://lccn.loc.gov/2019028283
LC ebook record available at https://lccn.loc.gov/2019028284

ISBN: 978-0-367-07800-3 (hbk)
ISBN: 978-0-367-07801-0 (pbk)
ISBN: 978-0-429-02286-9 (ebk)

Typeset in Sabon
by Apex CoVantage, LLC

Contents

Overview

Heritage and building conservation are increasingly attracting public and professional conversations – few major urban regeneration schemes fail to utilise its rhetoric to establish the credentials of the proposal, sell its unique qualities or bolster notions of establishing a grounded 'public realm'. But how well is this resurgence in 'heritage' understood or debated? Who produces the definition of heritage? How is it produced? Having produced heritage, who does it belong to?

We are entering a political-social moment where the role of the State in underwriting heritage protection is disengaging from the physical reality of heritage sponsorship, maintenance and development. From public bodies such as the National Trust to local initiatives running and maintaining parks and amenities, heritage custodians are increasingly reliant on voluntary or community support to sustain themselves and their 'assets'. However negative this shift appears, there is also the opportunity to reconsider how communities engage with their inheritance and how that built inheritance can meaningfully contribute to its locality and social fabric. The heritage industry is a global phenomenon, as we demonstrate through case studies, utilised to underwrite redevelopment even as it secures preservation. As with any industry there is a business model, a means of production, shareholders and the production of surplus that frequently gains ascendancy over the rights of the individual, the community and its identity.

The key question is how communities can become engaged in the complex set of issues around heritage significance and how professionals can inform this understanding. This spans across social identity, cultural awareness and tolerance, inclusivity, common history, technical conservation and capturing grant funding. How are these facets of heritage related within an easily communicated set of ideas that can empower not simply preservation or resistance to change, but the development of heritage as a social benefit? As such, this book is aimed at two constituencies – the community and the heritage professionals. The fact that one can identify two constituencies rather than one is for the authors the key issue:

For communities whose environment has a built history that does – or could – play an increasingly important role in their identity and everyday activities there are no publications that support their understanding of the value heritage brings to a place, and how that value can be articulated to form the basis for inclusion and sympathetic development.

For professionals, heritage is usually treated as either a technical exercise, frequently assuming that historic buildings require 'curation' as though they were museum objects. Another, equally technocratic view is in the role 'sustainability' plays in historic buildings – the mechanics of 'retrofit' and energy efficiency. For us this is a partial, exclusive reading of the issue, missing the cultural context and participation that is increasingly vital to sustain the role of historic buildings and places in society.

Heritage is defined and produced legally through international charters, codes of practice and protection frameworks under national and international law; technically through accredited training in material performance and technique; educationally via specialist programmes transferring knowledge from technical and legal agencies to interested parties – an exclusive circle. What is not defined is how social responsibility in building conservation is enabled, or how conservation decisions are actively informed by community engagement. Do practitioners and their clients who invariably steer heritage-based development understand and nurture its intangible potential or simply enact technical 'protection' of negotiated pieces of built fabric as part of a financial development? How easy is the generally accepted notion of history as a 'common good' open to exploitation for other motives?

The following research identifies how the production of heritage is not a neutral process, with the professionalisation of heritage contributing to the separation of significance from use. The advanced understanding and connoisseurship of heritage value (both culturally and financially) by professionals and their clients creates, in its mildest form, a lack of community engagement in what ought to be a collective history and at its worst acting as a mechanism to enable gentrification and allow profit-led 'regeneration' to co-opt heritage under the brand of collective identity. We explore these issues through the lens of philosophy, ethics, analysis, design and material craft – the convergence of these separate fields of enquiry within a discourse on the practice of architectural conservation is a unique approach to a unique moment in history. The aim is also to provide 'roadmaps' to navigate this double bind of using the past to underpin the future.

The context of the book is the absence of conservation, traditional construction or heritage knowledge within the criteria framing the education of architects in the UK (and across Europe and the US incidentally), leaving architectural students with no experience of the pre-1914 buildings that make up 40% of the UK's architectural projects annually. Post qualification, the educational development for professionals engaging with heritage focuses on techniques of investigation, methodologies of reporting and adherence to core principles of significance. This technical emphasis, we believe, misses the critical conversation with communities for whom the buildings and places under scrutiny 'belong to' in terms of cultural significance, and this lack of socio-political empathy illuminates a critical absence in an architects training – community engagement. Without the tools to develop their own understanding of the localised social significance of heritage, how can architects and heritage professionals communicate an awareness of social significance to the communities who are ultimately their clients? If this responsibility to communicate heritage value falls to others to develop, who then are the real clients – the inhabitants for whom the buildings and places matter, or investment interests far removed from the everyday that created our built legacy in the first place?

We reflect on the meaning of 'fabrication' (of the city, memory, identity, value) within the neoliberal city, in particular how the retreat of centralised heritage management leaves a vacuum of custodianship that communities are increasingly having to fill – but with little support. When policymakers or communities choose to remember, do they preserve historic architectural evidence as a form of cherished redundancy, or actively participate in the physical traces of previous activity and identity? We ask if our cultural identity is founded on what we no longer do, or what we continue to achieve? The danger present here is that the role of custodian becomes adopted by agencies of development that redefine heritage in their terms, for their benefit, leaving communities to look on as their surroundings radically change, while staying strangely familiar. The guidance published on Heritage Area assessment and value building is critically dissected, the presumption in favour of development is challenged – not to challenge development *per se*, but to question the nature of its benefit, and for whom. Understanding how to read guidance and reveal assumptions is vital for professionals and communities alike.

William Morris and John Ruskin philosophically underpin a series of critical case studies that discuss alternative models for how heritage can be produced, and to whom it belongs. There is a widespread belief that the defensive, protectionist stance of Morris stifles the ability for historic buildings to respond to contemporary needs, however our reading of Morris fully acknowledges his committed social and political agenda which saw buildings as social documents that live through their inhabitation, engage people in their meaningful adaptation and repair, and resist commodification by emphasising the value of community use. The case studies inform a forensic review of the underpinning frameworks for conservation in the UK and beyond, tracing the connections between the underpinning philosophies of conservation and contemporary practice in order to acknowledge critical gaps in both – not to undermine architectural conservation, but to build a more socially engaged and informed practice. We look in detail at the conservation and redevelopment of the Palacio Pereira in Santiago de Chile and Battersea Power Station; the role of community in the destiny of Covent Garden; the relation of technical understanding to philosophy in the conservation of St. Pancras Church; the clash of ideologies of the 'past' at Clandon Park, the transformation of social significance through the history of the Whitechapel Art Gallery; the integration of art, archaeology and architecture at Altab Ali Park; the communication of heritage and social issues within art projects at the Courtauld in London and the 'Ferramenta' project from Chicago. These case studies collectively demonstrate the importance of understanding 'significance' in material, historical and social terms, advocating the necessary synthesis of all three in the development of meaningful heritage projects. Each case study speaks about a different facet of heritage value – as urban identity, as a commodity, as a technical construct, as an intellectual and ethical framework that can underpin community involvement in shaping historic environments for contemporary participation. What do we 'inherit'? What is its value to us? Is that value universal or culturally conditioned? How can communities articulate their defence of historic places in a way that secures their role in future development?

Book structure

To orchestrate the case studies, the book is divided into six chapters, each of which explores different experiences of heritage conservation at both small and large scale. The primary focus is London, whose policies and foundational thinkers inspired conservation practices here and abroad. The introduction presents the intellectual approach to the understanding and handling of heritage, while a glossary accompanies each chapter, providing selective and provocative definition of key terms able to orientate the reading. That language frames thinking is no longer debatable – since George Orwell's polemical exploitation of this idea in *1984*. Being critical of how we phrase ideas and the inclusivity or exclusivity of the meaning we give has never been more important. Throughout this book statements and concepts are unpicked and words are interrogated to reveal imprecision and ambiguity that passes for certainty and authority. This task is necessary to establish what matters, and where power relations are disguised behind language(s) of inevitability that require challenge.

Chapter 1 – Introduction presents the notion of heritage as complex, proposing some tools for reading and opening a dialogue on the themes it entails. 'Heritage' developed and was conceptualised thanks to a number of institutional, intellectual and popular contributions during the last two centuries and it has always been linked to the production of narratives. With time, heritage became increasingly linked to legal practices (for example in the production of charters and protocols for the statutory protection of buildings); to technicalities (informing practices of conservation and the standards linked to them); and to education (reinforcing the linkage of legislation and technical knowledge). Taking inspiration from the contributions of William Morris to the notions of history, protection and restoration of ancient buildings, we argue that the practice of heritage is now distanced from a social dimension. Surely, the most shared rhetoric linked to heritage is that it belongs to everybody (Merriman, 1991; Smith, 2006; Waterton and Smith, 2009) as it is a 'public good' (McGimsey, 1972; Fowler, 1984), a depositary of 'public interests' (Cleere, 1989). According to this vision, heritage would have an 'otherworldly' quality (Douglas & Isherwood, 29) therefore incommensurable in economic terms. However, many approaches emphasise the economic value of heritage to be simultaneously relevant from an economic and cultural point of view (Mason, 2008). What can be noticed is that heritage is being increasingly appropriated by the neoliberal system of space promotion and production that exploits the notions of culture, memory, legitimacy and continuity normally attributed to heritage in order to promote economic gain. This introduction discusses the power of heritage narratives, the concept of history as an unfolding process as opposed to the rectifying preservation of historic elements, and the role of profession in relation to these two opposed approaches to conservation. Moreover, it introduces the frameworks that currently underpin conservation and questions how these universally accepted principles actually frame our understanding of history.

Chapter 2 – The Production of Heritage focuses on the active material history of our heritage buildings, intended as a reflection on and engagement with the accumulated physical evidence of everyday life over time. The case study is the Palacio Pereira (2012–2019), Santiago de Chile, chosen by the Chilean Government as one of two heritage projects to commemorate/articulate the Bicentenary of the Chilean republic. The author was invited to collaborate on a competition entry for the restoration and repurposing of the building and, given the status of the project, the approach to heritage conservation at a national level. This case study contains a series of strategic context documents as well as verbatim responses to conservation issues that arose after winning the project, consolidating the working strategy, and work on site. In presenting the correspondence in this way, we aim to show how the issues and inconsistencies around language and meaning were negotiated within a project context, and more importantly, how influential the intangible, often unspoken value systems that underpin stakeholders' understandings of heritage, and how a perspective on the legacies of conservation philosophies around identity, integrity and value can shape the technical responses to a highly significant, fragile building.

Chapter 3 – Place: material and the urban imaginary targets the relationship between real estate dynamics and the inclusion of cultural references. Often regeneration projects targeting historic structures in culturally significant neighbourhoods are characterised by narratives that build on the legitimising presence of history. A critical review of the redevelopment processes of Covent Garden (1970 ca.) and Battersea Power Station (1980 onwards) reveal how the concept of heritage, intended as a narrative, has evolved. These case studies reveal how the process of significance selection has been made, and who is the final beneficiary of a certain interpretation of heritage. Moreover, they show how the preservation and promotion of heritage elements is considered not only as a final outcome, but also as a form of sustenance for the policies that generated the regeneration. They acknowledge the valorization of heritage as a complex process: the patrimonialisation of these historic places as objects, commonly referred to as the practice of urban conservation. The shift from centralised redevelopment for the 'public good' in Covent Garden has transformed into a quasi-privatised process of place based profit, however certain key indicators remain consistent – a rhetoric of public benefit, the monetary value of heritage, the definition of 'significance' as an historical evaluation not a contemporary social phenomenon, aligned to optimised redevelopment.

Chapter 4 – The memory of surfaces talks about value of recognising the imperfections of our surroundings rather than overlooking or overwriting them in order to preserve the ideal past. Often, the role that surface plays in our comprehension of time and identity in a historic building is the defining element. However, every surface is also linked to a more ephemeral dimension: the one of use, social relationships and events that characterised layered pasts. Critically, when we modify an existing building we need to be conscious of the fact that we are handling both material and social history and that intervention has the power to highlight or erase part of the story, as the writer of any narrative can do. *'The Memory of Surfaces'* installation, created throughout the historic Somerset House, together with the National Trust's Clandon Park, partially destroyed by a fire in 2015, are the subjects of observation. How and why surfaces are revealed or concealed is an argument often played out with conservation authorities, we rehearse and reflect on this argument here.

Chapter 5 – History and material significance explores the relationship between meaning and surface and investigates how official narratives linked to originality and authorship are increasingly excluding communities in the definition of their own heritage. Craft, manufacture, material specificity and social appreciation are some of the topics we will deepen, revealing that aesthetics is not simply appearance (Pye, 1968) and functionality is not simply technical (Benjamin, 1936). The case studies presented here, the Grade I listed church of St. Pancras (1819) and the Whitechapel Gallery in London (1901), will reflect on the practicality of art and the fetishisation of craft technique. Their stories are representative of how the changes that always concern architecture have material and social consequences born out of selection and constraint and affect the way we understand and engage with place.

Chapter 6 – Tactics for a way out of the heritage trap looks at the role of 'Conservation Plan' as the pre-eminent tool for understanding heritage and determining what is done with it. Through its observation and de-layering we aim to redefine the mechanics of conservation empathy, and address other possible ways to include community inputs, beyond the current constraints of the profession. In order to do so, we analyse one built project in London and two art installations: Altab Ali Park (2012) in London by MUF art/architecture, the 'Peoples Landscapes' project for the National Trust (2019), and the Prada Foundation art installation *Ferramenta* (2018) by American artist Theaster Gates. These projects help to refocus our attention on familiar landscapes as a means to re-evaluate how we know the place we live in. In particular they use the philosophy of 'as found' to inform projects that reflect on contamination and layering of meaning. All of our case studies explore the benefits of these techniques for those who share the use and the memories of them.

The chapter closes with a consideration of 'custodianship' over 'ownership' and the change in relations that ordinary people can have with the historic fabric that they occupy through a critique of the developing financialization of our collective past. In response, we summarise 'tactics for getting out of the heritage trap' that include public engagement (learning from art and archaeology) and lessons from landscape practice (accommodating inevitable change and revising meaning long-term not short term). The 'statement of significance' needs to acknowledge that social rights and political shifts are intrinsic to our historic environments and identity, rather than become the developers' justification for stasis, smoothness and affluent tranquillity as promised by the CGI rhetoric of heritage led regeneration projects.

References

Benjamin, W. (1936) *The Work of Art in the Age of Mechanical Reproduction*, Arendt, H. (ed.), New York: Random House.

Cleere, H.F. (ed.) (1989) *Archaeological Management in the Modern World*, London: Unwin Hyman.

Fowler, D.D. (1984) 'Ethics in Contract Archaeology', in Green, E.L. (ed.), *Ethics and Values in Archaeology*, New York: Free Press, pp. 108–116.

Mason, R. (2008) 'be interested and be aware: joining economic valuation and heritage conservation', *International Journal of Heritage Studies 14* (4), pp. 303–318.

McGimsey, C.R. (1972) *Public Archaeology*, New York: Bantam Books.

Merriman, N. (1991) *Beyond the Glass Case: The Public, Museums and Heritage in Britain*, London: Leicester University Press.

Pye, D. (1968) *The Nature and Art of Workmanship*, London: Cambridge University Press.

Smith, L. (2006) *Uses of Heritage*, London: Routledge.

Waterton, E. and Smith, L. (2009) *Heritage, Communities and Archaeology*, London: Duckworth.

Acknowledgements

The following have kindly donated images and permissions to bring our text to life: The Prada Foundation in Milan for releasing images of the artworks of Theaster Gates; Ken Jacobson for kindly providing a copy of John Ruskin's beautiful 1849 daguerrotype from Venice; the National Trust for agreeing the use of our photographs of Clandon Park; the Covent Garden Community Group for opening access to documents from the events of the 1970s, the Society for the Protection of Ancient Buildings for a copy of an early manifesto and perspective of St. Pancras Church; Helen Howard for providing her scientific examination of the original decoration at Somerset House; and MUF Architecture/Art LLP for documents and images from Altab Ali Park. My colleagues and friends Alberto, Cecilia and Paula in Santiago de Chile merit a special mention, firstly for inviting me to participate in the reclaiming of the Palacio Pereira and then asking me to maintain a supporting role as this incredible project has unfolded. Their support for this publication is gratefully acknowledged. I would like to personally thank Luisa Auletta for enabling our practice to sustain its work in parallel to teaching and research, without which half the chapters in the book would be empty, and Michela Pace for extending and sharpening the scope of the entire book in what has been a great collaboration.

Chapter 1

Introduction

The fabrication of history. Heritage conservation in a capitalist culture

Approach

Our approach develops a critical overview of conservation, identifying two key and recurrent positions that run throughout the approaches to the conservation of the heritage environment in the UK, with relevance to practice in Europe and beyond. In the 19th century Eugène Viollet-le-Duc and William Morris formalised two different, if not antithetical visions of restoration, reuse and adaptation of existing buildings. These approaches have been selected here with the precise intent to explore the understanding of the built and cultural legacies in our cities and because they are a recurring point of reference for contemporary conservation practice. The philosophy of Viollet-le-Duc establishes a scholarly reconstruction of history that confirms our expectations of materiality, style and value, as opposed to Morris's prioritisation and preservation of the marks of time, wear and age as the cultural evidence of human use. William Morris in particular is our primary reference point throughout the book. A social activist associated with arts and crafts movement and founder of the Society for the Protection of Ancient Buildings (SPAB) in 1877, Morris was concerned with the reading of a building as an historical text, its fabric evidence of both material and social marks of time. Viollet-le-Duc, however, practised restoration using historically informed conjecture to recreate the impression of a particular moment in time, reversing the damage of both weather and the events of history in order to present an informed, but culturally privileged viewpoint for civic consumption. The evidence of historical events – often revolutionary and socially significant (such as the destruction of sculptures on the façade of Notre Dame of Paris in the revolution of 1793), are consequently erased from the building in the name of education, in this case Viollet-le-Duc's reinstatement of copies of the missing sculptures as though the Revolution hadn't happened. Editing history through seamless restitution becomes a form of cultural correction that George Orwell took to its logical conclusion in *1984*, but that Morris as a social revolutionary was already sensitive to in 1884.

Both Morris and Viollet-le-Duc are intellectually woven into the charters and standards that frame heritage policy, pedagogy and practice and the unravelling of these very different philosophies becomes increasingly urgent given the role and status of history in an increasingly populist political arena where collective identity is assumed rather than understood. This chapter provides an overview of the origins of 'conservation' and the political context that it is bound to; the significance of heritage within its practices is explored through the role of narratives, which have the ability to select from our past and determine what is relevant for our present. We explore William Morris's thought, especially when social engagement as a form of history is concerned, and the use that current charters make of both language and philosophical approach to conservation. Finally, we offer a reflection on the role of professionals within the definition of heritage, with the intention of opening the discussion on heritage to a larger public. By recalling key thinkers from the last two centuries, presenting best practice and provocative examples, the aim is to reflect on matters of selection, inclusion and readability in order to orientate the reading of the chapters that follow.

1.1 Heritage as narrative – the value of selection

References to the past are increasingly used to orientate construction and to build place significance. This trend brought some specific terms into fashion. 'Heritage' is one of them and has been largely promoted as a 'value' linked to local specificity and national character. In a short time it has become a buzzword, with projects worldwide including references to it in their marketing materials. Its use involves slippery concepts such as culture, memory and identity, which are fundamental to the political and social discourse at the local and global scale. What needs to be clear is that heritage in itself is not a thing. Rather, "heritage is about the process by which people use the past – a 'discursive construction' with material consequences" (Harvey, 2008: 19 see Smith, 2006). This means that heritage is a selective concept that does not necessarily involve history, as history would entail a more careful observation of the facts and their implications (Scrivano, 2017). Heritage doesn't do the same work as history. It can be easily isolated and rearranged to inform a bespoke narrative. At heart, heritage refers to "the ways in which very selected past materials and artefacts, natural landscapes, mythologies, memories and traditions become cultural, political and economic resources for the present" (Graham and Howard, 2008: 2). Present concerns, therefore, are the temporal dimension of heritage. Its construction is closely linked to the notion of 'memory' that, unlike history, seeks an uncritical relationship with the past (Nora, 1989).

More than this, memory is extremely selective and therefore concerned with the celebration of a certain account of the past (Kearns and Philo, 1993). By giving significance to a selected portion of the narrative, memory prevents it from fading but also alters its meaning in relation to the wider historical process that created the context in the first place (*ivi*). The risk is that the historic dimension is excluded. This allows the selection of interpretations and representations to inform an idea of the present and, in turn, to imagine the future. It follows that "heritage is less about tangible material artefacts or other intangible forms of the past than about the meaning placed upon them and the representation that can be created from them" (Graham and Howard, 2008; Graham, Ashworth and Tunbridge, 2000; Smith, 2006).

Of special interest in the dissection of 'heritage' is the use and misuse of the terms 'tangible' and 'intangible', confusing an understand how and for whom certain buildings, landscapes or social contexts are significant. This ambiguity is often employed in the narrative strategies used to support economic, political and social programmes and teaches us that we should observe communication as another form of construction. The tendency is to refer to 'intangible' heritage to mean cultural aspects linked to traditions, habits and practices that exist beyond the single building, and sit in relation to a context or to a wider landscape. Although this is certainly true,[1] we should pay attention to the deviations that abstract narratives can bring, especially when the notion of heritage is exploited by commercial operations.

By defining heritage as 'intangible' our physical response to that place can be and is unconstrained – the history that it contains becomes a convenient narrative that both confers status by association but presents no physical constraints to future development or investment return. Quoting an invisible history is intrinsic to the 'heritage game' played out in the financial exploitation of both place and commodities. The changing use of urban fabric and the evolving communities within it surely alters the context of place, producing physical alterations behind renovated façades that are fixed, although local people's ongoing presence in that place is not. The question is how to respond to the presence of individuals, events or beliefs where their significance is not documented and understood. The risk is that both people and urban fabric become an easy material to be renewed through 'heritage' informed regeneration, rather than considered within the concepts of protection and conservation projects that could or should involve protecting and conserving livelihoods, ways of life and community footholds in a place.

What do we really mean by tangible and intangible heritage? Real places can, through the way that they are handled, create fiction from fact – one example is the Foundling Museum in Coram's Fields, London. The museum tells the exemplary history of the Foundling Hospital, and of the artist governors who supported the children's charity with their work. The actual building seen today was erected in 1935–7, and while the pastiche treatment of the exterior gives an ambiguous sense of the historic, the building contains three original 18th-century Rococo interiors salvaged from the demolition of the original hospital in 1926 – the *Picture Gallery*, the *Court Room* and the *Committee Room*. Within these original rooms that once hosted Hogarth, Gainsborough and Reynolds, who all donated their artworks to raise money for the hospital, their paintings hang and Handel's musical instruments lie thanks to the Gerald Coke Handel Collection that reinstated the residency of objects belonging to the great composer and philanthropist. The building is therefore a large replica vitrine containing preserved but decontextualised spaces within which original artefacts sit. The tangible history of the building is a misconception because its interior and its exterior purport to be seamless, when in fact two centuries separate them; the presence of Handel's possessions within rooms where he performed bring the intangible value of his personal presence into a building he never entered but rooms that he did. The issues around tangible and intangible are critical when considering the significance and value of a building or place, and how we reveal or conceal historical fact within heritage fiction. If the tangible can be allusory and illusory, and the intangible actually an integral part of the ongoing changes that have continually shaped a place, greater accuracy is needed in the way we acknowledge significance and actually what is being understood and evidenced.

If we assume that heritage is "a contemporary use of the past" (Graham, Ashworth and Tunbridge, 2000: 2) we should think that heritage is then used or 'consumed'. "What is consumed, however, is not so much the heritage itself, in the form of, for example, a building or a cultural landscape, but its representation in the form of historical narrative" (Groote and Haarsten, 2008: 181). It is then easy to understand how the construction and appreciation of heritage becomes a matter of communication, susceptible to the nuances of meaning that the author determines.

*Figure 1.1
Foundling
Museum,
London.*

*Source: Picture by
the authors, 2019*

Heritage is therefore a mechanism able to create meanings (Hall, 1997: 197), a process of selection that needs to be considered in relation to a wider economic, political and social context. Communication strategies never transport notions of memory and identity innocently.

The concept of heritage, its invention as such and its refinement as a mechanism of communication and selection is a product of European culture and its origins can be traced to the 18th century (Hernandez Martinez, 2008). At that time, the term was used to address ruins and monuments. From there it gradually extended to include urban centres, traditions and natural landscapes. The reason for the rise of a 'heritage consciousness' was a perception of the need for conservation. The discipline of restoration initiated in those years, aimed to safeguard precious relics and was the result of a long process that started with the Renaissance. Simultaneously with this fascination for the ancient, history began to be used to inform bespoke narratives. The construction of a mythical past allowed the rewriting of history, providing new legitimation to those in power. Notions of memory, legacy and tradition started to invade the fields of knowledge and arts, as much as the field of politics, and heritage started to be associated with values of identity and legitimacy. The British Empire offers a direct example: all empires absorb their conquests but risk losing shape unless some form of politically controlled cultural legibility is defined and imposed. Thus, they provide limited local identity re-scripted into a 'natural' relation with the clear, overarching authority.

The link between power, geography and identity grew stronger in the 19th century, when the idea of 'national heritage' was fundamental to the definition of the nation states. Mainly, national and universal pasts were mobilised and monumentalised to give meaning to the present and to envision the future socially, politically and culturally (Huyssen, 2003). Later, after the second half of the 20th century, the notions of identity and representation associated with heritage became more complex, as the subjects able to define it became increasingly detached from the traditional frameworks of nations, ethnicity, class and kinship (Graham and Howard, 2008). Heritage started to be part of narratives linked to local characters and vernacular elements especially in the 1960s, evolving one decade later into so-called cultural planning (Mercer and Grogan, 1995). As early as the Second World war, the importance of global relationships in the definition of local policies and spatial attitudes significantly affected the way heritage was perceived. With the crisis of nation states, national 'heritages' once linked to specific geographies were reframed as sites and practices of global significance. In the era of great pacifications, the concept of 'world heritage' started to be promoted by international bodies such as UNESCO. Heritage became one of the internationally acknowledged sources of value, progressively shifting its significance from cultural to financial. In the globalised era of economic investments, heritage continues to be a mechanism of communication and selection, but the meaning of territorial affection is less bound to social and community reasons than it was in the past and is increasingly related to financial appropriation. Patrimonialisation has appropriated many symbols from the architectonic, urban and territorial landscape while becoming progressively linked with market operations (Olmo, 2018).

If we assume that heritage is necessarily linked to the making of present narratives, it is clear that there is a need to explore the language of heritage in order to understand underlying concepts and bias. Language, as evidenced in the often contradictory definitions in the glossary, is not neutral; it codifies cultural and political positions and part of this book's project is to open up the ICOMOS[2] concept of 'reading' a building or monument, asserting that our perspective on the language we use actively influences what we understand. Our language is not neutral and neither is the knowledge that it frames. To explore this observation further we reference the writing of George Orwell and his masterful dissection of language. *Politics and the English language* (1946a) identified a staleness of imagery and a lack of precision as key factors in the use of language to obscure meaning rather than invite understanding and participation. The use of jargon creates hierarchies of those who understand and those who do not. The reverse is equally effective, where language is characterised by easily understood generalities that allow those who do not understand to think that they do.

> As soon as certain topics are raised, the concrete melts into the abstract and no one seems able to think of turns of speech that are not hackneyed: prose consists less and less of *words* chosen for the sake of their meaning, and more of *phrases* tacked together like the sections of a prefabricated hen-hous.
>
> (Orwell, 1946a: 105)

Language may be politically motivated, it may be used in innocence, but what is clear is that contemporary language around conservation employs a range of words, notions and definitions that are anything but common knowledge. The word 'heritage' is exemplary – frequently used to discuss a cultural aspect or tradition that has been passed down through generations, it is also applied to buildings, objects and things. Its use implies important relations between the past and the present, but seldom specifies what those relations are and for whom they are important. 'Heritage' generalises community-specific knowledge that ought to be meaningful rather than meaningless – a concept rather than a specific inheritance, its use becomes a signal requiring respect rather than an opportunity to learn.

It is useful, at this point, to deepen some of the thoughts that characterised the conceptualisation of heritage in the last two centuries. We chose to adopt the perspective of William Morris (1834–1896), selecting key themes from his conservation thinking:

- Physical fabric is the tangible record of intangible human action – not the other way around.
- Revising the physical revises meaning and depends on the viewpoint of the revisionist for its truth or otherwise.
- The humble and the epic are equally deserving of protection – human history is present in a palace as it is in a dry stone wall.
- Craft is not a specialist practice but one that all can engage with and benefit from – beauty is democratic.
- Contemporary life requires contemporary expression.
- Sympathetic use is vital, intervention respectful, imitation is folly.

First and foremost, William Morris's attitude towards history acknowledged the power of narrative that buildings entail as layered texts, set against Viollet-le-Duc's view that privileged a rectifying approach to historic elements. Heritage is viewed as an evolving narrative versus heritage as a fixed image, an opposition that recurs throughout the book.

1.2 History as an unfolding process – style or substance

Is history the result of human action or the context for human action? Do we frame our future with the defining frame of the past, or is history simply the residue of our daily activity? This is more than a question of semantics; it is a question of priorities. The determination of the role history plays is fundamental not only to cultural identity, but to what that cultural identity achieves in the future. The origins of architectural conservation as both philosophy and practice illustrates this diversity of approach.

In the Manifesto for the Society for the Protection of Ancient Buildings (1877), William Morris defined two acute observations on what he perceived to be a crisis of attitude towards the artefacts of built history. Two potential, and potentially conflicting, strategies for working with ancient buildings sit side-by-side within the Manifesto: to continue to develop buildings as living enclosures of human endeavour, or to maintain them as the artworks they are and to house our endeavours in the new:

> Strategy 1. The need for "protection in the place of restoration" and the folly of imitation. Put another way, the definition of repair means to do as little as is necessary, and when you do, to do it without pastiche.
> Strategy 2. History is a living process that registers its passing upon the built environment, and that process is a testament to a genuine art of the everyday without affectation and artifice.

These ideas are complementary, but in essence offer very different conclusions that we must work through. When committed to only repair, which through protection and preservation from wear and weather maintains the building as an artefact for future study, we therefore have only a 'curatorial' role in our historic environment and can read its accumulated history of use up until the point at which we may only repair. The implication of this idea is that the history that shaped the building as artefact is now over, engagement other than its conservation is withdrawn – "to resist all tampering with either the fabric or ornament of the building as it stands; if it has become inconvenient for its present use, to raise another building rather than alter or enlarge the old one" (Morris, 1877). At the time of his polemic, Morris was faced, as we are now, with a situation where contemporary intervention is overwhelming the "bygone art" of making unaffected, crafted and locally relevant architecture with its language, its demands and its materiality, and is destroying the readability of historical continuity. From appearance to chemistry, contemporary building can be considered incompatible with ancient fabric, so from this point onwards we should interpret but we should not elaborate. The conclusion is that the 'curatorial' role is intellectually active but physically passive, implying that history becomes considered as academic rather than actively produced. This aspect of the Manifesto is defensive – better to withdraw from interference than ruin through ignorance – and is borne of Morris's conviction that the connection between an industrialised and pre-industrialised society is broken.

However, as is clear when considering Morris's second strategy, this is not where his ambition lies. The notion of a curatorial future runs counter to Morris's own idea of history as an unfolding process of creative change, and against his own experience of craft as a constant activity of making. This is encapsulated within his own counter argument:

> A church of the 11th century might be added or altered in the 12th, 13th, 14th, 15th, 16th, or even the 17th or 18th centuries; but every change, whatever history it destroyed, left history in the gap, and was alive with the spirit of the deeds done midst its fashioning. The result of all this was often a building in which the many changes, though harsh and visible enough, were, by their very contrast, interesting and instructive and could by no possibility mislead.
> (*ibidem*)

Architecture is a celebration of change over time, of legibility without artifice. Both building and dwelling are an invitation to adapt sympathetically to the needs of the time, "of necessity wrought in the unmistakable fashion of the time" (*ibidem*). The real issue is defining how change is wrought so that it is "alive with the spirit of the deeds done midst its fashioning" (*ibidem*). How can architectural judgements be attuned to the balance between the endeavour to be housed and the house itself such that the essential nature of the activity is expressed, yet maintains and enhances the presence of the house through the very act of alteration? We will evidence how this line of thought can underpin a complex conservation strategy in Chapter 2.

Fundamental to any discourse on heritage, its production or even destruction requires us to look critically at how we deal with history. Karl Popper published *The Poverty of Historicism* as a book in 1944, defining historicism as: "an approach to the social sciences which assumes that historical prediction is their principal aim" (*ivi*: 4).

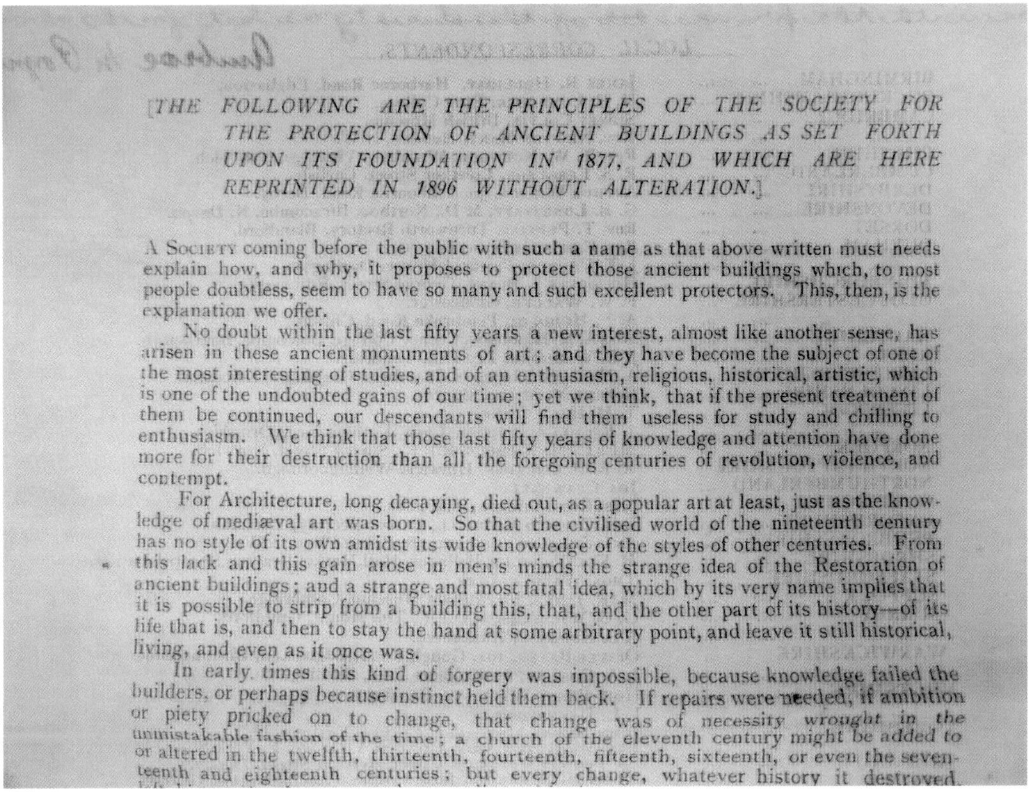

Figure 1.2
The oldest existing version of the 1877 founding principles of the Society for the Protection of
Ancient Buildings (SPAB) c.1924.
Source: Courtesy: SPAB

"The belief . . . that it is the task of the social sciences to lay bare the law of evolution of society in order to foretell its future . . . might be described as the central Historicist doctrine" (*ivi*: 105–106). However: human history is a single unique event. Knowledge of the past therefore does not necessarily help one to know the future. "The evolution of life on earth, or of human society, is a unique historical process. . . . Its description, however, is not a law, but only a singular historical statement" (*ivi*: 108).

It is interesting to consider Popper's treatise on historicism – not within the context of social science, rather architectural conservation. As an alternative to historicism Popper offers "piecemeal social engineering" that describes small scale, localised social changes that are perceptible and effective. The unpredictability of the future, he argued, makes the effect of any larger changes untraceable and unspecific, so only incremental adjustments generate 'real' change rather than perceived change. This concept is remarkably close to Morris and the SPAB concept of sympathetic use and maintenance, and the rejection of the restoration of ideologically important historical moments or the freezing of a building's evolution that precludes active social participation or denies the role of a building as an active ongoing documentation of human labour and life.

However, we cannot deny that the very concept of heritage is contentious, and disparity between values of conservation drive very different ways of approaching, dealing with and discussing heritage. Because of its representational powers, heritage was and is often seen as an image of history, privileging the iconographic meaning it demands and an academic approach to significance recognition. The development of history as image has a long heritage of its own. The early Victorians utilised increasingly modern technologies such as iron frames, concrete and industrial masonry; however, debate around how these technologies were aesthetically orchestrated created fundamental questions about how we identify with architecture, and how we decode its language. To connect their commercial enterprise to an architectural and cultural language of power, historic styles were co-opted and utilised, echoing the way the Romans adopted and adapted the classical language of Greece. Archaeology became an increasingly significant and influential practice throughout the 19th century, as we explain in Chapter 5, and was as much about the culture of the collector and tastemaker as it was the collection of cultural knowledge. The excavation and theft of antiquities in the 18th and 19th centuries underpinned a conceptual gap within the idea of heritage – cultural significance. When the custodians of historic places are disregarded, the artefacts and places significant to their original culture become 'knowledge commodities'. With knowledge comes privileged access to it, connoisseurship creates narratives for intervention at several removes from locality and community.

So prevalent was the rebuilding and 'improving' of ancient European buildings through the kind of historical connoisseurship mastered by Viollet-le-Duc that writers, artists and thinkers around John Ruskin developed critical and, in the case of William Morris, political alternatives for conservation practice. This conversion of artefact and meaning into a knowledge commodity was not reserved for the archaeological discoveries of classical civilisation. European history was equally the victim of cultural imperialism, which fused an academic disregard for local cultural ownership with a disinterest in the physical antiquity of both architecture and place.

Morris, like Marx, was capable of the most exquisite writing when describing the dynamics of social exchange and interaction. His call in the Manifesto to leave historic buildings 'as found' is a hymn to appropriate adaptation which enables a continuity of use that established buildings as the physical documentation of our social history in its widest sense. William Morris addresses this directly in order to call a halt to making historic buildings into spectacle by asking us "to resist all tampering with either the fabric or ornament of the building as it stands: if it has become inconvenient for its present use, to raise another building rather than alter or enlarge the old one" (Morris, 1877). Morris articulated this position when confronting the 'corrective conservation' of Viollet-le-Duc, where the connoisseurship of the visual language of history completely dominated any appreciation of the material reality. Morris advocated the readability of history as the trace of ongoing human endeavour, directly contradicting the practice of restoration, "where the partly-perished of the ancient craftsmaster some unoriginal and thoughtless hack of today" (Manifesto, 1877). Le Duc aimed for the symbolisation of history, the use of history as spectacle and its reinforcement through addition and alteration to serve a clearer, less compromised notion of the past as a culturally legitimised backdrop to the present.

Morris on the contrary articulated a set of principles that bear some relation to cultural practice in Japan, which Morris was familiar with. The aura of original fabric – unlike the Japanese practice of renewal as continuity, however, shares the reverence on craft practice and the social status of the maker as a core concept. Morris actively challenged the monumentalisation of historic buildings, identifying 'history in the gaps' between layers of alteration that linked history intimately to action, rather than inaction. He proposes the idea that common culture inhabits the space between fixed areas of knowledge. Preservation and maintenance of these assets leaves space for our contemporary contribution, executed with material and craft that creates an equivalent to the original, but avoids imitation. The work that creates tomorrow's history is as much a social act as it is an economic one, the human value of meaningful work is the participation in the making of place and therefore the making of shared meaning. Buildings are documents that allow social and cultural history to be read in order to support the activities of contemporary culture.

A very particular 20th-century perspective on 'the existing' informed two post-war generations of intellectuals who created critical responses to tangible history through a sensitivity towards ephemeral information, elaborating on how a complex set of meanings (about use, production, consumption and significance, for example) are deposited onto everyday objects. A number of architects and artists developed a new culture of memory starting from the vernacular and the 'found' as a form of built and cultural heritage.

> The vernacular architecture was embraced by many modern architects as a reference able to clarify and elaborate on constructive and artistic techniques. It started an intense debate on techniques, and was often intended as a sustainable approach to the city; and eventually assumed as expression of regional and local identities and as an alternative to the Modern Movement.
>
> (Secchi, 2005: 154)

Figure 1.3
Altab Ali Park landscape, London.

Source: Courtesy: MUF architecture/ art 2012

Architects Alison and Peter Smithson, artist Eduardo Paolozzi and photographer/artist Nigel Henderson played a significant role in elaborating the ideas around valuing 'the existing' that Ruskin and Morris articulated almost a century earlier, but within a post–World War II context centred on contesting the direction of reconstruction and challenging how a society forgets conflict. Operating within the Independent Group was a loose affiliation of young practitioners linked to the Institute for Contemporary Arts in London. The most notable early manifestation of their thinking on the value and role of the existing came in the exhibition *This is Tomorrow* at the Whitechapel Gallery in September 1956. Revisiting post–World War I Dadaist tactics[3] involved both an acceptance of the consumerist society of aspiration and waste, the Smithsons, Paolozzi and Henderson determined what they saw as permanent value within the physical evidence of a contemporary society that could articulate new social and artistic relationships.

The Independent Group utilised both found materials and found situations to frame a critical position towards a pre-war modernist orthodoxy that they saw as re-establishing itself post-war within the rhetoric of comprehensive reconstruction and renewal. Paolozzi's work engaged with Kurt Schwitter's recycling strategies, creating three-dimensional figurative collages that through the process of bronze casting made new formal possibilities for sculpture. The Smithsons and Henderson used building and photography in a manner more akin to Georg Grosz's approach to painting, whereby the identification of subjects and elements become re-composed according to the rules of artistic discipline in order to undermine or overthrow that very discipline. Where Dada and the Independent Group collide with Morris is the radical position taken to the 'found'. In placing a previously unimagined value on the physical evidence of human interaction with ordinary material, through found objects, archetypal architectural forms such as the patio or the pavilion, or the photography of working communities going about their daily life, the simplistic assumptions of capital processes of production, consumption and replacement are challenged, as is our relation to those processes. This combination of valuing the residues of the everyday, acknowledging commonly held identification with familiar architectural form and the embrace of the everyday redirects our attention onto what our inheritance actually is. Paolozzi's early reworking of scrap into sculptures always remained within the comprehensible canon of sculpture – the bust, the statuary of saints, but "he was seeking a conflation of artefacts and material phenomena in the world he inhabited – one whose modernity manifested itself in a culture where modern machinery jostled with archaic imaginings". (Potts, 2010: 42)

Crinson and Zimmerman (2010) have argued that the Smithsons were profoundly influenced by Wittkower as they sought to establish a revised discourse for modernism, utilising their interest in photographic imagery and the post-war proliferation of advertising as a means of exploring the process of building, its description and reality. The layered, almost informal photographs of the construction site of their first building, the Hunstanton School (1953) in Norfolk by the Smithsons' collaborator Henderson reveal an intense interest in the muddy reality of the building process as much as the outcome. Even when the building was finished, the photographs of the completed spaces were taken with the furniture removed from view; this act rendered the completion incomplete as it still requires human inhabitation. Through their considered image-making and theoretical storytelling, the Smithsons considered the building to be a framework for activity, both acknowledging and undermined the notion of 'architect as author' and refuting the building as a spectacle by leaving the document of it incomplete, with occupants to have the last, undocumented word. The role of gatherer, instigator and enabler is a recurring one in the recent history of architectural practice but is a marginal one. The discipline of architecture is framed by assumed roles with the resulting products reflecting the determinism of the architect, developer or both. Buildings are elaborate collaborations requiring negotiation and compromise, but are presented as unified, absolute solutions in the popular consciousness. The Smithsons and their Team 10 colleagues such as Aldo Van Eyck actively attempted to undermine architectural solutions that illustrate an architectural vision in favour of an empathetic and responsive practice based on the patterns of use 'as found', acknowledging their value and enabling their continuity rather than their replacement.

The set of principles Morris generated through the SPAB the came to inform the 20th-century contribution to conservation – the charters. We will observe some of them here, including ICOMOS, Venice Charter and Burra Charter, in order to clarify the intellectual platform that conservation practice operates within, and to consider how the social custodianship advocated by Morris is challenged by the technically scholarly artifice of Viollet-le-Duc.

1.3 Frameworks for heritage, education and training

What are the frameworks that currently underpin conservation? How do these universally accepted principles actually frame our understanding of history – given that history is a negotiable idea rather than a law?

An historic building is, according to the Venice Charter, "imbued with a message from the past". An ostensibly clear reiteration of Morris's core message on the value of readability in the preservation of all stages of historic development, this could be seen as a clear victory over the 'school of restoration' and its advocacy of the rewriting of cultural narratives. The relationship between Morris and the Venice Charter requires analysis however, as the nature of the 'message' defined in 1877 but articulated as an international framework in 1964 is ambiguous.

The Venice Charter understood these 'messages' as cultural and historical values that are conveyed by the physical presence of a building together with its setting. This emphasises the value of technological knowledge and the skill by which it has been executed, which is the core, genuine communication that needs to be safeguarded. Morris influenced the Venice Charter not only with the idea that buildings communicate, but also that they need to communicate changes to their fabric over time. As such the concept of 'authentic' does not necessarily mean 'original'. Article 11 asserts that all periods of the building contribute to its significance and deserve respect since the unity of style is not the aim of conservation. The building 'as found' therefore constitutes 'its authentic state, not its original formal concept'. Following this line of thought a 'test of authenticity' was adopted by the World Heritage Committee in 1977, with inclusion in the World Heritage List needing to meet the test of authenticity in design, materials, workmanship or setting (UNESCO, 1988). However, as with any criteria the 'test of authenticity' can be challenged, with cultural and practical issues around the interpretation of 'the test' requiring the World Heritage Committee to undertake a critical re-evaluation in 1992. Almost simultaneously, the 'test of authenticity' was followed by a further re-evaluation of how that test was put into practice. The General Assembly of the International Council on Monuments and Sites (ICOMOS), which met in Colombo, Sri Lanka in 1993, recognised that many different professions need to collaborate within the common discipline of conservation in the process and require proper education and training in order to guarantee good communication and coordinated action in conservation. The fourteen points they determined underline a set of common requirements that underpin recognised accreditation processes in conservation across the world:

> The aim of this document is to promote the establishment of standards and guidelines for education and training in the conservation of monuments, groups of buildings ("ensembles") and sites defined as cultural heritage by the World Heritage Convention of 1972. They include historic buildings, historic areas and towns, archaeological sites, and the contents therein, as well as historic and cultural landscapes. Their conservation is now, and will continue to be a matter of urgency.

> a   read a monument, ensemble or site and identify its emotional, cultural and use significance;
>
> b   understand the history and technology of monuments, ensembles or sites in order to define their identity, plan for their conservation, and interpret the results of this research;
>
> c   understand the setting of a monument, ensemble or site, their contents and surroundings, in relation to other buildings, gardens or landscapes;
>
> d   find and absorb all available sources of information relevant to the monument, ensemble or site being studied;
>
> e   understand and analyse the behaviour of monuments, ensembles and sites as complex systems;
>
> f   diagnose intrinsic and extrinsic causes of decay as a basis for appropriate action;
>
> g   inspect and make reports intelligible to non-specialist readers of monuments, ensembles or sites, illustrated by graphic means such as sketches and photographs;
>
> h   know, understand and apply UNESCO conventions and recommendations, and ICOMOS and other recognized Charters, regulations and guidelines;
>
> i   make balanced judgements based on shared ethical principles, and accept responsibility for the long-term welfare of cultural heritage;
>
> j   recognize when advice must be sought and define the areas of need of study by different specialists, e.g. wall paintings, sculpture and objects of artistic and historical value, and/or studies of materials and systems;
>
> k   give expert advice on maintenance strategies, management policies and the policy framework for environmental protection and preservation of monuments and their contents, and sites;
>
> l   document works executed and make same accessible;
>
> m   work in multi-disciplinary groups using sound methods;
>
> n   be able to work with inhabitants, administrators and planners to resolve conflicts and to develop conservation strategies appropriate to local needs, abilities and resources.
>
> (Guidelines for Education and training in the conservation of Monuments, Ensembles and Sites, 1993)

The language and phrasing of ICOMOS was, whether deliberately or unthinkingly, directed towards a professional audience caring for monuments rather than working buildings, the reader being the heritage protagonist who is required to accomplish the act of reading and defining heritage. We argue that cultural significance resides not only within the building, but within the community that uses it. A document sets out what has happened, but there is a significant shift needed to interpret that 'text' and determine the future of places. That shift requires a contextual investigation that is not necessarily physical. Identifying the identity of a building is as clear or vague as writing history. History as a concept attempts to communicate unambiguously the factual legacy of a given situation. However, we know that every narrative implies a point of view and acts of selection, included history. What can be noticed is an increasing shift from history to histories, where the agenda of those writing influences what is written and what is read. The fourteen technically informed points within ICOMOS are self-justifying – they are concrete and formalise many of Morris's entreaties to respect material and craft, maintain and conserve historic fabric, investigate and understand the building as a document. Other entreaties, however, are missing, most significantly in the role of ordinary people.

Point g is interesting and frequently overlooked in its requirement to make the reporting of knowledge to be in an intelligible manner readable by all. In practice, the specialist language of conservation work makes this point challenging to comply with. Specialists in niche areas of work require specific skills to communicate to a lay audience. The language of point seven is ambiguous – is a 'non-specialist reader of monuments' a member of the public? The last point (n) is perhaps telling in the assumption that preparedness is needed to resolve conflicts when preparing conservation strategies – clearly this aspect of the work is problematic. Concluding with the recognition that strategies must be appropriate to local needs, abilities and resources could be understood as implying a community focus; but it could also be a requirement to maintain fiscal responsibility by not specifying what cannot be delivered. If such a list of points underpins all conservation accreditation schemes in the UK and many more overseas, having such latitude in interpretation is more of a weakness than an asset.

In the section *Organization of Education and Training*, point 12, the ICOMOS *Guidelines* continue:

> Education and sensitization for conservation should begin in schools and continue in universities and beyond. These institutions have an important role in raising visual and cultural awareness – improving ability to read and understand the elements of our cultural heritage – and giving the cultural preparation needed by candidates for specialist education and training. Practical hands-on training in craft-work should be encouraged.
>
> (*ibidem*)

This latter phrase makes for an exceptionally interesting point – the development of educational awareness in all schools is a far-sighted ambition to create an involvement that will shape the future citizens' attitudes towards built cultural heritage. This is an ambition that is laudable, but how strong are the connections between this ambition, stated within one sentence of one paragraph, and the fourteen points as a whole? This educational ambition begins as wide ranging but concludes as being necessary as a cultural preparation for specialist skills training – as though that were the ultimate goal of this awareness. If education on heritage and its value is given to all, then the awareness of historic fabric and its relevance creates a climate where maintenance, custodianship and engagement – identified by Morris as vital – requires far fewer emergency repairs to make or campaigns to save. The fourteen points are a partial realisation of core conservation values, but in effect their underlying focus is on monuments rather than buildings, consolidating commemoration rather than sustaining or promoting active use. An overlay for participation is a necessity to reconcile the preserved historic monument with the protected historic building. This would help to outline the engagement needed with users and the ability to educate and mitigate around contemporary conflicts between activity and preservation.

The relationship of habitual life with the material aspect of our built environment has a political and social aspect. William Morris's radical socialism found a correspondence in his redefinition of the historic building as a social document, the material technologies of these buildings being for him an artistic and cultural construction. Sharing the craft skills required to care for old buildings was seen as a collective effort, a counter position to the capitalist division of labour, and saw the significance of historic buildings not simply as emblematic, but as a working backdrop to people's daily lives. For Morris, work was craft, and craft was social engagement. A key differentiation from the socially informed language of Morris towards the technically informed language of Viollet-le-Duc came with the re-evaluation of the term 'workmanship' and its adoption into the *Operational Guidelines* of the UNESCO World Heritage Convention. Craft assumed a constitutive role of the 'authenticity of processes' necessary to prove the value of a building. This semantic shift was partly a welcome de-gendering of a term, but importantly it placed the notion of 'authenticity' firmly within the act of making that 'workmanship' merely implied. The preamble to the Venice Charter (1964) when talking about ancient monuments as a common heritage, states "it is our duty to hand them on in the full richness of their authenticity". Is this authenticity of the original fabric, or the authenticity of a process that delivers a carefully made and recognisable copy? Authenticity is a term inextricably linked to heritage, but as we focus on 'authenticity' and 'significance' in Chapter 2 through a detailed project narrative, we show how the inherent ambiguity in their definition opens up questions about how we realise conservation projects, and what they mean.

1.4 The professional landscape – how is heritage framed for the architects who frame heritage?

For Morris, the ongoing, sympathetic use of heritage is a social goal. Social and cultural value is an evolving process, corroborated by Popper, and is by definition incomplete. Where Morris said "every change, whatever history it destroyed, left history in the gap" (Morris, 1877), we as architects see in those gaps opportunities for change. The management of physical change is comprehensively addressed through ICOMOS, but the social change that Morris describes as being intrinsic to the historic building – how is that dealt with in the conservation training and accreditation frameworks of current practice?

Usually, a combination of standards, guidance and legislation form a safety net for historic environments, rather than attending to the cause of the issue. Given frameworks of evaluation have the obvious advantage of being generally applicable but often unspecific and rarely adaptable, accreditation is a system for built environment professionals to establish, through peer review, their credentials for conservation practice. The RIBA has a tiered scheme called the *Conservation Register*[4] based on the ICOMOS criteria, which is comparable to other internationally recognised accreditation schemes, giving some form of parity in the global heritage marketplace. Alignment with acknowledged standards allows funders and clients some degree of certainty as to the acuity of their chosen specialist, although at a detailed level no system based on considered opinion can ever claim infallibility. The technical bias within ICOMOS underpins its own absences – the management of change materially and socially lacking balance. The difference between data and use is fundamental, the ability to amass and process the former can have no direct relation with the latter, allowing a schism between cultural knowledge and cultural practice that returns consistently throughout the case studies within this book, and within the global historic built environment generally. We should acknowledge that a common understanding of heritage issues is in deficit because it stopped recognising the changing relationship between people and buildings as a relevant part of built history. Does contemporary conservation practice formally acknowledge this relationship, and if so, how is it evidenced?

British Standard 7913 is a *Guide to the Conservation of Historic Buildings* and was published on 31st December 2013.[5] At present, it is the only UK–wide standard on conservation derived from industry professionals and subject to public consultation. How 'public' the consultation was is questionable, given that heritage is public in the widest sense of society and the public that participate in detailed technical consultations are usually related closely to the field of those who are conducting the consultation. British Standards are by definition post-facto consolidations of knowledge that may or may not fully embed, grasp or value the depth of understanding of the field to which the Standard refers. The conservation field has broadly welcomed the BS 7913. John Edwards, writing in the IHBC bulletin (September 2015) discussed its value as a lever to ensure compliance with not only basic technical good practice, but with conservation philosophy. It should be noted that in his view the majority of people who deal with historic buildings are not the previously noted 'public', but are property managers:

> one must bear in mind that the majority of people who deal with historic and traditional buildings are not experts, and come from the mainstream property and construction industry. They typically will not refer to, say, the English Heritage 'Principles of Conservation', because they probably do not even know they exist. But they will have heard about British Standards and will hopefully follow BS 7913: 2013. This means that they will get to understand Conservation philosophy, including 'significance' and how it is used.
>
> (Edwards, 2015: 45–46)

Edward's view is that BS 7913 consolidates knowledge effectively, and notes that there are already numerous standards across Europe that already do this. This does not necessarily provide the reassurance that the formalising of other 'standards' in the format of a new 'standard' is inherently a correct thing to do, merely that another standard has been written, priced at £198 per copy. It is interesting to look beyond the 'standard' at the organisation that underwrites it, and the context within which it operates. It is worth nothing that this strategy of unravelling how hitherto accepted frameworks were constructed and why underpins not only this book, but any project involving aspects of cultural inheritance.

The British Standards Institute (BSI) adopted its name in 1931 after receiving a Royal Charter in 1929 as a governmental organisation to underwrite engineering codes and codes of practice. In 1998 a revision of the Charter enabled the organisation to diversify and acquire other businesses, and the trading name was changed to BSI Group. BSI has diversified into new fields such as smart cities, nanotechnologies, cell therapy and Building Information Modelling (BIM). The BS 8901 for sustainability management systems underpinned events such as the 2012 Olympic games. "As a result of these strategic moves, and through more than a century of growth, BSI now delivers a comprehensive business services portfolio to clients, helping them raise their performance and enhance their competitiveness worldwide" can be read in the BSI presentation (website, no date). This corporate, globalising rhetoric matters because the operation of standardisation is intrinsically linked to a particular model of supply chain. The requirement to comply, usually enshrined in a procurement system that is intrinsically risk-averse, has the effect of self-selecting those businesses or individuals who maintain the standards, thereby creating a virtuous circle of compliance that very easily excludes those who do not or cannot keep pace with the revisions that both maintain best practice and ensure membership to the club. This is far from freely accessible information (as we have noted), and the ability for the BSI Group to withdraw it with no notice, or to revise it whenever deemed necessary, ensures that it sustains its publishing business in parallel to promoting best practice.

The *Standard* has a value in being able to gain support for sympathetic building practice in the case of normative modern technical solutions, and BS 7913 clearly makes useful technical points, such as promoting the reduction of damp that exacerbates heat loss and material deterioration at the same time, advocating appropriate maintenance. However, through what it omits it discourages other practices which, ironically are all also compliant with (other) British Standards. In section 0.1 it notes "British Standards that are applicable to newer buildings might be inappropriate" (Edwards, 2015: 45–46). How effective is a Standard that overrides/consolidates other standards but that carries no more authority? While exemptions from modern standards are envisaged as flowing from BS 7913, this is far from certain and generates more judgement requirements than it provides.

Section 7 emphasises a cautious approach to conservation work: "The removal of historic fabric and patina should be avoided as far as possible to retain authenticity" (www.designingbuildings.co.uk/wiki/BS_7913). As has been noted, the understanding of authenticity is far from clear, and while at face value this advice appears straightforward, there is a wider set of considerations to take account of. Significance and authenticity are intrinsically linked, the former frequently triggering the latter. Significance is described in detail in sections 4.1–4.4, reinforcing the importance of this notion and the way in which it is defined: "Those directing the works should have an understanding of the significance of the historic building" (section 7.1). The notion of significance from the Venice Charter returns. Defining a statement of significance for an historic building is effectively a 'sliding scale' of importance that facilitates an argument for what can change and where it can happen. This relation between the technically provable and the emotionally understood is poorly delineated, yet hugely influential to the outcome of projects involving historic places.

The spaces within the building identified as of significant cultural value are invariably the areas requiring expensive specialist expertise, techniques and materials to simply consolidate the existing. The new is more cost effective to build and gains monetary or operational value faster. There is an open question as to how *Statements of Significance*, commissioned by the developer, objectively deal with this simple fact. With all listed buildings requiring *Heritage Statements* to accompany applications for consent to make alterations, there is a mechanism for oversight. However, with local authorities lacking funding to provide appropriately qualified officers numerous enough to work effectively, and with one authority working in isolation from the next, there is huge consistency issue in how significance is recognised and authorised. If or when the policing of listed building consent devolves to specialist professionals, this situation could become even more questionable.

The publication by RIBA of a *Conservation Plan of Work* (Feilden, 2017) can be seen as a significant moment. It is the primary acknowledgement by the professional body that conservation is a substantial practice requiring particular areas of awareness and understanding to operate. Working with an historic building changes and limits the role of the client and even more of the 'user' (often not the same), and conditions what the architect knows, does and operates. The mismatch between the eight work stages of new-build (0 through to 7) and the demands of particular forms of practice such as heritage conservation or zero carbon sustainability has been acknowledged. This has resulted in the RIBA recognising that 'overlays' are required to focus the vagueness and highlight where the detailed description of operations required from the architect in each stage is either missing or misleading. It is useful to review the *Conservation Plan of Work* to gain an understanding of how it overlays a conservation bias onto the standard model, and what kind of model of practice it advocates. Its author, architect

Figure 1.4
Perspective
corrected
elevation of the
Palacio Crossing,
2014.

Source: credit:
© Felipe Fontecilla

Hugh Feilden, sets out how the generic can become reasonably specific. How does this 'overlay' translate ICOMOS, and importantly does it bring the societal aspect of conservation into the Plan of Work?

Stage 0 of the Plan acknowledges the identification of 'spirit of the place' and does not actively preclude community engagement but clearly such engagement activity could be argued as substantial to gain such an identification. It appears to have no specific place or time/fee allocation beyond the conventional client/architect arrangement, perhaps tacitly acknowledging how unpopular this would be with client bodies. That the critical establishment of the strategic brief is given 0 as a number, and that historically when fees were apportioned to work stages by the RIBA this stage was simply left to negotiation or hourly rates, which says something about the way the grounding of a project in a place and the input of its users has always been marginal to the process of building delivery. Practices that undertake serious community engagement at strategic briefing stages are extremely rare beasts within the architectural jungle.

Stage 1 similarly lacks the option of engagement – there is an assumption, understandably, that there are readily available sources to understand significance. Archives and records as well as on-site investigation provide excellent data; however, the relationship between locality and heritage 'asset' appears to exist as a record of the past, rather than facts of the present that the project engages with. Clarification on the role of the briefing process includes the explanation/interpretation of heritage assets, but within the context of client documentation rather than wider social understanding. Identifying opportunities for inclusive access is similarly technical in that it relates to the physical accessibility of people with impairment in relation to the building regulations, rather than social or cultural inclusion, which is not a matter of technical compliance. Stakeholder contribution to a conservation plan or heritage statement is noted, but only with reference to Historic England or the local authorities.

The discussion of the production of the *Draft Heritage Statement* in Stage 2 provided an opportunity to redefine the scope of what aspects of a project are included and how that evidence was gathered, but guidance towards tangible, physical evidence of heritage significance is the priority. In our view, the addition of an 'engagement' supplement for public projects is required for the early part of the process – current advice on engagement from Historic England, is explored in detail not on stage 0–3 but on stage 6. Page 63 notes testing concept design within the design team as well as with "external stakeholders". How this is done outside of statutory stakeholders such as planning authorities is not specified.

Feilden notes on the subject of 'Significance and Sensitivity' that whereas 'significance' is essentially intangible and can be seen as a social/theoretical construct, 'sensitivity' is generally quantifiable and relates directly to the historic fabric in question. Feilden brings an interesting angle to significance here, almost as an aside that deserved more exploration. The liberation of significance from purely technical or historical worth and its openness to include social significance and use significance informs much of the work discussed within the following chapters.

> Understanding the difference between significance and sensitivity is important, as fabric can be sensitive without being significant. Indeed it can be difficult to attach significance to historic fabric specifically, except for obvious standalone items such as memorials, fireplaces, doors etc. This is particularly true when significance is given to social or community value which attaches to

the activity associated with the building as much as to the design or technical
innovation of its fabric, which may be perfectly ordinary.

(p. 27 PoW)

This is an exceptionally important point, and problematises the desire to minimise risk
when commencing work on relatively unpredictable historic buildings. Significance
has become an overriding concern for conservation. This is logical when attempting
to justify alteration or preservation, but since 2018 the assumption that significance is
a fact, like interstitial condensation or dry rot, is becoming questioned.

Feilden establishes a clear fracture in the 'significance' discussion, asking how significant a wall is when wanting or needing to cut a door through it. Significant to
whom? How significant does building fabric need to be before it achieves protection?
Planform is often quoted as inherent to the legibility of historic buildings, both in terms
of resisting the alteration of internal walls within a listed building, but also a requirement to put new walls into altered spaces so as to 'reinstate' the planform previously
lost – a common position adopted by local authorities when assessing proposals in
historic buildings. This phenomenon extends the understanding of heritage significance
into the conjectural and the restitutional, breaking ties with the idea of historic fabric
documenting change over time and applying it to an historic organisation of space that
has been lost. The lack of clarity about significance of what exists, or what existed,
what we do and what was done, what we value practically or symbolically makes
working on heritage projects both fascinating and fraught. As Feilden helpfully notes,
"considerable confusion is caused by the use of the same or similar wording in different sources of information, but with different nuances or sometimes even different
meanings" (Feilden, 2017: 36). Our use of glossaries in conjunction with the dissection
of ideas and assumptions about heritage provides a basis for effective interrogation
and the role that a social agenda could and should play in what is an overwhelmingly
technical heritage discourse.

Conclusion

The 'production of heritage' is a truism – history is made consecutively and collectively, now becomes then, the everyday becomes rare, and rarity becomes desirable
and attainable at a cost. This process becomes politicised when we look at heritage
either as a product or as a process that can and is constantly adjusted and adapted
according to requirements. As with any product, we have to ask what it is for, who
does it serve, how much will it cost and what benefit does it give. This seemingly
obvious set of questions are, however, very poorly answered when considering heritage. 'Authenticity' and 'significance' as words already lack precision, as we see in
the glossary of terms that we include at the start of each chapter. These terms are
accepted definitions, but also provocations to our habitual acceptance of words and
their meanings. If significance is only understood by consultants, authorities and
developers via the ambiguities of a specialised language of standards and protocols,
then that ambiguity is open to manipulation, particularly if the rhetoric around their
use is exclusive rather than transparent. The Yamato Declaration (UNESCO, 2004)
considered the interdependence of tangible and intangible forms of heritage, with
Article 12 exhorting national authorities "to explore and support investigations of
strategies and procedures to integrate the safeguarding of tangible and intangible

heritage, and to always do so in close collaboration and agreement with the communities and groups concerned". The attitudes to participation are developing at high level, but how far does the profession follow through?

We believe that the communities who are interested users of historic places are the source and custodians of 'significance', the chapters that follow explore this assertion, concluding with snapshots of how this can be realised in practice.

Notes

1 Intangible Heritage is a term used to describe historical association not necessarily evidenced in the materiality of a place. In 1972, the World Heritage Convention attempted to define an understanding of heritage that was both natural and cultural, influencing the way heritage was thought about, developed and protected at both national and international levels. Subsequently the UNESCO Convention for the Safeguarding of the Intangible Heritage (2003) framed more specifically the practices and policies associated with intangible cultural heritage. Cultural Heritage, as intended by UNESCO, is meant to include "not only monuments and collections of objects" but also "oral traditions, performing arts, social practices, rituals, festive events, knowledge and practices concerning nature and the universe or the knowledge and skills to produce traditional crafts" (UNESCO, Intangible Cultural Heritage). However, Smith argued (2006) that an 'authorised heritage discourse' has underpinned the majority of UNESCO's heritage policies, determining what is authorised, recognised and validated as valuable expression of cultural heritage, often favouring a Western-centered approach (Smith and Akagawa, 2017). The need of re-theorizing intangible heritage was explored by a number of authors, focussing on heritage as a cultural practice (Harvey, 2001) or as "a body of knowledge and as a political and cultural process of remembering/forgetting and communication (Urry, 1996; Dicks, 2000; Graham, 2002; Peckham, 2003; Smith, 2006)" (Smith and Akagawa, 2017: 6); the definition of 'intangible' values (Blake, 2001; Brown, 2005), the safeguarding and managing of evolving cultural heritages (Nas, 2002; Arizpe, 2004) among the other topics.
2 ICOMOS (International Council On Monuments and Sites) is an international, professional association that works for the conservation and protection of cultural heritage places around the world. Now headquartered in Paris, ICOMOS was founded in 1965 in Warsaw as a result of the Venice Charter of 1964, and offers advice to UNESCO on World Heritage Sites. (https://en.wikipedia.org/wiki/International_Council_on_Monuments_and_Sites). For more information visit: www.icomos-uk.org/icomos-uk-home/.
3 Dada was an offshoot of surrealism that surfaced in Weimar Germany – a reaction to the political framework that generated the First World War and the subsequent political failings in its aftermath. Schwitters, Hausmann, Grosz and Dix among others used artistic tactics of the absurd and a radical re-use of socially produced ephemera and waste to reclaim what meaning meant in art, and how a society can use art to create a mirror to reflect itself. Dada created work that was both a rearrangement of the existing – Kurt Schwitters created abstract, non-figurative collage constructions and assemblage from found waste that started as framed collages but grew in scale and complexity to inhabit entire rooms – termed 'Merz'; Georg Grosz and Otto Dix utilised 'found' conditions and characters from the human collateral damage that Weimar Germany otherwise turned a blind eye towards – disfigured and disabled war veterans providing subjects to convey the political failings of the time; Raoul Hausmann developed photomontage to splice photographic sources into politically charged satire on the decadence and ineptitude of political elites and the rise of National Socialism.
4 RIBA Conservation Register is divided in three levels of competence – Specialist Conservation Architect and Conservation Architect which are accredited, a Conservation Registrant which is an apprentice level pre-accreditation stage. For more information visit: www.architecture.com/knowledge-and-resources/resources-landing-page/find-a-conservation-architect
5 British Standard 7913, webpage: https://shop.bsigroup.com/ProductDetail/?pid=0000000000 30248522

* The definitions of the glossary are often but not always freely based on a number of dictionaries' definitions including Oxford Dictionary, Merriam Webster, Collins Dictionary, LaRousse and institutional definitions and legislations provided by ICOMOS, Venice Charter, Historic England, The Institute of Historic Building Conservation, the Localism Act, or professional ones as Building Conservation, Technical Preservation Services then elaborated in relation to the personal view of the authors and the contribution of other authors, hereby mentioned.

Bibliography

Arizpe, L. (2004) *Intangible Cultural Heritage, Diversity and Coherence* Museum International, Vol. 56, Issue 1–2 Blackwell: Oxford.

Benjamin, W. (1936) *The Work of Art in the Age of Mechanical Reproduction*, Arendt, H. (ed.), New York: Random House.

Blake, J. (2001) *Developing a New Standard-Setting Instrument for the Safeguarding of Intangible Cultural Heritage: Elements for Consideration*, Paris: UNESCO.

Brown, M.F. (2005) 'Heritage Trouble: Recent Work on the Protection of Intangible Cultural Property', *International Journal of Cultural Property*, 12: 40–61.

Cleere, H.F. (ed.) (1989) *Archaeological Management in the Modern World*. London: Unwin Hyman.

Crinson, M. and Zimmerman, C. (eds.). (2010) *Neo-Avant-Garde and Postmodern: Postwar Architecture in Britain and Beyond*, New Haven, CT: Yale Center for British Art and the Paul Mellon Centre for Studies in British Art in association with Yale University Press, pp. 29–54.

Dicks, B. (2000) *Heritage, Place and Community*, Cardiff: University of Wales Press.

Edwards, J. (2015) 'Why Building Conservation Needs BS 7913', in *Context 141*, The Institute of Historic Building Conservation, September, pp. 45–46.

Feilden, H. (2017) *RIBA Plan of Work 2013 Guide Conservation*, RIBA Publications: London.

Fowler, D.D. (1984) ' Ethics in Contract Archaeology', in Green, E.L. (ed.), *Ethics and Values in Archaeology*, New York: Free Press, pp 108–116.

Graham, B.J. (2002) 'Heritage as Knowledge: Capital or Culture?', *Urban Studies*, 39 (5–6): 1003–1017.

Graham, B.J., Ashworth, G. and Tunbridge, J.E. (eds.) (2000), *A Geography of Heritage: Power, Culture, Economy*, London: Arnold.

Graham, B.J. and Howards, P. (eds.) (2008) *The Ashgate Research Companion to Heritage and Identity*, Franham: Ashgate Publishing.

Groote, P. and Haarsten, T. (2008) 'The Communication of Heritage: Creating Place Identities', in Graham, B.J. and Howards, P. (eds.), *The Ashgate Research Companion to Heritage and Identity*, Franham: Ashgate Publishing, pp. 181–194.

Hall, S. (ed.) (1997) *Representation: Cultural Representations and Signifying Practices*, London: Sage.

Harvey, D.C. (2001) 'Heritage Pasts and Heritage Presents: Temporality, Meaning and the Scope of Heritage Studies', *International Journal of Heritage Studies*, 7 (4): 319–338.

Harvey, D.C. (2008) 'The History of Heritage', in Graham, B.J. and Howards, P. (eds.), *The Ashgate Research Companion to Heritage and Identity*, Franham: Ashgate Publishing, pp. 19–36.

Hernandez Martinez, A. (2008) 'Conservation and Restoration in Built Heritage: A Western European Perspective', in Kearns, G. and Philo, C. (eds.), *Selling Places: The City as Cultural Capital, Past and Present*, Oxford: Pergamon Press, pp. 245–266.

Huyssen, A. (2003) *Present Pasts: Urban Palimpsests and the Politics of Memory*, Redwood City CA, Stanford University Press.

Kearns, G. and Philo, C. (eds.) (1993) *Selling Places: The City as Cultural Capital, Past and Present*, Oxford: Pergamon Press.

McGimsey, C.R. (1972) *Public Archaeology*. New York: Bantam Books.

Mercer, C. and Grogan, D. (1995) *The Cultural Planning Handbook: An Essential Australian Guide*, St. Leonards: Allen & Unwin.

Merriman, N. (1991) *Beyond the Glass Case: The Public, Museums and Heritage in Britain*. London: Leicester University Press.

Morris, W. (1877) *Manifesto for the Society for the Protection of Ancient Buildings*. [Online] Available at: www.spab.org.uk/about-us/spab-manifesto (Accessed: March 2019).

Nas, P. (2002) 'Masterpieces of Oral and Intangible Culture: Reflections on the UNESCO World Heritage List', *Current Anthropology*, 43 (1): 139–148.

Nora, P. (1989) *Between Memory and History: les Lieux de Memoire, Representations*, No. 26, Special Issue: *Memory and Counter-Memory* (Spring): 7–24.

Olmo, C. (2018) *Città e democrazia. Per una critica delle parole e delle cose*, Milano: Donzelli.

Orwell, G. (1946a) *Politics and the English Language*, London: Horizon.

Orwell, G. (1946b) *Why I Write*. Reprint 2004, London: Gangrel.

Peckham, R.S. (ed.) (2003) *Rethinking Heritage: Cultures and Politics in Europe*, London: I. B. Tauris.

Popper, K. (1944) *The Poverty of Historicism*, London: Routledge.

Potts, A. (2010) 'New Brutalism and Pop', in Crinson, M. and Zimmerman, C. (eds.), *Neo-Avant-Garde and Postmodern: Postwar Architecture in Britain and Beyond*, New Haven, CT: Yale Center for British Art and the Paul Mellon Centre for Studies in British Art in association with Yale University Press, pp. 29–54.

Pye, D. (1968) *The Nature and Art of Workmanship*. London: Cambridge University Press.

Scrivano Paolo (interview), Senior Associate Professor of History, Theory and Criticism of Architecture, XJTLU Univeristy (Shuzou, China, 3 March 2003).

Secchi, B. (2005) *La città del ventesimo secolo*, Bari: Laterza.

Smith, L. (2006) *Uses of Heritage*, London: Routledge.

Smith, L. and Akagawa, N. (2017) *Intangible Heritage*, London: Routledge.

UNESCO. (2013) *Convention for the Safeguarding of the Intangible Heritage*, Paris: UNESCO.

Urry, J. (1996) 'How Societies Remember the Past', in Macdonald, S. and Fyfe, G. (eds.), *Theorising Museums*, Oxford: Blackwells.

Waterton, E. and Smith, L. (2009) *Heritage, Communities and Archaeology*. London: Duckworth.

Charters and other guidelines www.icomos.org/en/charters-and-other-doctrinal-texts

In particular:

Burra Charter. [Online] Available at: https://australia.icomos.org/publications/charters/

Guide to Conservation of Historic Buildings. [Online] Available at: https://unidoc.wiltshire.gov.uk/UniDoc/Document/File/MTUvMDQwMDQvT1VULDEyMDE3NDc=

Venice Charter for the Conservation and Restoration of Monuments and Sites. (May 1964) Venice: Italy. [Online] Available at: https://www.icomos.org/charters/venice_e.pdf

UNESCO Yamato Declaration (2004). [Online] Available at: https://unesdoc.unesco.org/ark:/48223/pf0000137634

Websites

British Standard 7913. [Online] Available at: https://shop.bsigroup.com/ProductDetail/?pid=000000000030248522

BSI Group. [Online] Available at: www.bsigroup.com/en-AU/About-BSI/Our-history/

Foundling Museum. [Online] Available at: https://foundlingmuseum.org.uk/about/the-museum/

Guidelines for Education and Training in the Conservation of Monuments, Ensembles and Sites (1993). [Online] Available at: www.icomos.org/en/component/content/article?id=187:guidelines-for- (Accessed: 30 March 2019).

ICOMOS. [Online] Available at: www.icomos.org/en/home-wh

Manifesto for the Society for the Protection of Ancient Buildings (SPAB). [Online] Available at: www.spab.org.uk/about-us/spab-manifesto

RIBA Conservation Register. [Online] Available at: www.architecture.com/knowledge-and-resources/resources-landing-page/find-a-conservation-architect

Society of Protection of Ancient Buildings (SPAB). [Online] Available at: www.spab.org.uk

UNESCO Intangible Heritage. [Online] Available at: https://ich.unesco.org/en/what-is-intangible-heritage-00003

UNESCO Convention for the Safeguarding of the Intangible Cultural Heritage (2003) Paris. [Online] Available at: http://portal.unesco.org/en/ev.php-URL_ID=17716&URL_DO=DO_TOPIC&URL_SECTION=201.html

UNESCO 1988: Operational Guidelines for the Implementation of the World Heritage Convention, pp. 79–86. [Online] Available at: http://whc.unesco.org/statutorydoc.

Chapter 2
The production of heritage
Philosophies of fabrication

Approach

The Entrepreneur, the Developer and the Investor are leading characters from Modernism and latterly Neoliberalism, and are defined by their ability to create 'something from nothing'. Conjuring wealth and change from thin air, however, has consequences. As Karl Marx (1848: section 1.18) wrote in the *Communist Manifesto*:

> All fixed, fast-frozen relations, with their train of ancient and venerable prejudices and opinions, are swept away. All new-formed ones become antiquated before they can ossify. All that is solid melts into air, and all that is holy is profaned, and men at last are forced to face . . . the real conditions of their lives and their relations with their fellow men.

'Something from nothing' has implications for relations, both personal and cultural, material and historical that are profound. As Marx identified, the 'ancient and the venerable' are conditions which are incompatible with the force of change, however Marx did not go on to discuss what 'something' made 'from nothing' looks like. Is perpetual change, wrought from the actions of modernity creating ever-newer languages, or, as was the case with so-called post-modernity is the 'ancient and venerable' the visual fuel with which to generate the acceptable face of change – a 'nearly new' trading on familiarity to provide security whilst simultaneously tearing our relational fabric apart? Philosophies of fabrication explore the philosophical context of the status of the 'ancient and venerable', discussing the sweeping away of actual, active material history and its replacement with its passive imaginary. Examples of critical resistance to this process of dematerialisation will focus on not only physical material but on how we understand and relate to that material to fabricate our future memories now. A means of resisting 'something from nothing' is, logically creating 'something from something' – achieved through the recognition that contexts have value, that what becomes of them through change also has value – a relational value. When the existence of 'nothing' is refuted, when everything is 'something', we are required to understand what there is, not only to know what we want.

An 'active material history' is the observation of, reflection on and engagement with the accumulated physical evidence of everyday life over time. This assumption derives from the practices of observation that formalised in the 19th and 20th centuries with the fundamental notion that urban environments are both historically and socially produced. The city would be a central place to observe the progression of history, its changes and the tensions that animate it. This possibility was clearly articulated by Mumford (*The City in History*, 1961) and Spengler (*The Decline of the West*, 1918), who registered the progressive stratification of the city as phenomenon historically determined, unitary and specific. In particular, *The City in History* opened to a critical observation of the urban environment and to the possibility of describing historical conditions starting from physiognomic observations.

Three pioneering authors, Simmel (1903), Kracauer (1963), and Benjamin (1940), worked on the concept of materialist historiography, counting on observation and description of common objects, everyday landscapes and single bibliographies. The reading of space would be, for them, the reading of a specific historic moment, because space becomes the terrain where history unfolds. This is distinct from an academic, archaeological or critical 'history of material' because it emphasises ongoing use as a core criterion of value. Why does this distinction matter? It matters because history, its man-ifestation and status have social and political consequences depending on how citizens engage with it. The inhabitation of and identification with built history is profoundly different to the classification of historic structures and spaces as information, entertain-ment or commodity. History is fabricated in the sense of being made socially; the key consideration is in how we define fabrication – as an authentic act of manufacture, or the making of a falsehood. As part of a wider exploration of the 'fabrications of memory', the opportunity to participate in the competition to 'restore' and repurpose the Palacio Pereira in Santiago de Chile required a reflection on the first significant moment of resis-tance to the fabrication of falsehood – the establishment of the Society for the Protection of Ancient Buildings by William Morris in 1877, how that resistance connected to a deeper intellectual heritage of 'English Empiricism' articulated by John Locke, and how its re-manifestation within the radical 'as found' practice of Alison and Peter Smithson in post-war Britain could inform a conservation strategy for the 21st century.

The first case study in the 'production of heritage' is the Palacio Pereira in Santiago de Chile. It deals with the conservation and transformation of a magnificent ruin and the pressures of oscillating between 'restore' and 'preserve'. The similarities and differ-ences in intent and execution clarify the consequences of particular ideologies down to the smallest detail. The reading and interpretation of William Morris was instrumental in the winning of the open architectural competition for the Palacio, instigated as one of two projects that commemorated the bicentenary of the Chilean Republic.

This case study contains verbatim a series of strategic context documents as well as detailed responses to conservation issues that arose after winning the project, consoli-dating the working strategy, and work on site. Inserted between the texts a contextual narrative positions the documents. In presenting the correspondence in this way, we aim to show how the issues and inconsistencies around language and meaning were negotiated within a project context. More importantly, we show how influential the intangible, often unspoken value systems that underpin stakeholders' understandings of heritage, and how a perspective on the legacies of conservation philosophes around identity, integrity and value can shape the technical responses to a highly significant, fragile building.

GLOSSARY

Anti Scrape: *phrase - origin: the need for an association (Morris letter to The Athenaeum, 10 March 1877).*

"What I wish for, therefore, is that an association should be set on foot to keep a watch on old monuments, to protest against all 'restoration' that means more than keeping out wind and weather, and, by all means, literary and other, to awaken a feeling that our ancient buildings are not mere ecclesiastical toys, but sacred monuments of the nation's growth and hope". The principle that occupation is additive not subtractive, and that layers of use are more valuable to the substance of a building than the re-presentation of one of those layers for the purposes of appearance or coherence.

Adaptation: *noun – origin: early 17th century from French, from Latin adaptatio (n-), adaptare (v) (Oxford Dictionaries, online).*

Modifying a place to suit the existing use or a proposed use. *Use* means the functions of a place, as well as the activities and practices that may occur at the place. The active adjustment to suit operational requirements that Morris identified as originating a readable 'history' left in the gaps between changes – negotiation between physical form and spatial operability. In conservation terms, any adaptation requires a commensurate degree of sympathy for the original when introducing the new activity, material or space.

Authentic(ity): *noun(adjective) – from the Greek 'authentikos' (of undisputed origin); 'genuine': also made or done in the traditional or original way, or in a way that faithfully resembles an original (Oxford Dictionaries, online).*

The common conception of 'authenticity' in a European conservation context concerns the maximum retention of the existing fabric of a building, in other words the persistence of the real. With 'authenticity' also defining something made or done in a traditional way, authenticity is *therefore the real thing, and the resemblance of a real thing, which is not the real thing but a simulacra (is this a quotation?)* – the use of the word within the language of marketing and persuasion means that the ethical and cost implications of either meaning become lost.

Compatible use: *phrase – Burra Charter 2013, Article 2, 1.11. "Compatible use means a use which respects the cultural significance of a place. Such a use involves no, or minimal, impact on cultural significance".*

The definition of 'compatible' becomes wider in response to the widening gap between historic and contemporary cultural practices. Article 6, 6.3. states "Policy development should also include consideration of other factors affecting the future of a place such as the owner's needs, resources, external constraints and its physical condition".

Craftsmanship: *noun – 1325-75 Middle English 'craftes man' – man of skill, from Old English 'cræftiga' workman with skill in a particular craft (Dictionary.com, online). Interesting link to the medieval latin word artificiarius or 'artificer' – an inventor/maker of artefacts but linked to artifice which defines trickery and guile and is the origin of 'crafty' implying cunning and deception.*

That a word associated with moral integrity is also inextricably linked to deception is ironic, in particular the contemporary associative use by individuals or companies and associations to trade buildings and objects that are industrially produced.

Demolition: *noun – origin: Mid 16th century, via French from Latin demolitio(n-), from the verb demoliri. (Oxford Dictionaries, online). The action or process of demolishing or being demolished. Informal: An overwhelming defeat (demolishing my opponent); Comprehensively refute (demolishing their argument).*

The application of destructive removal is both a neutral description of an action, but through informal use attains personalised, adversarial connotations. Demolition is a frequently contested action in heritage terms: any listed building can be demolished if a widely recognised public good is achieved – such as the construction of major public infrastructure ("substantial harm" in National Planning Policy Framework terms).

Intervention: *noun – origin: Late Middle English: from Latin interventio(n-), from the verb intervenire (see intervene) (Oxford Dictionaries, online). The action or process of intervening – altering a course of events; occur as a delay or obstacle to something being done – both precipitating change or preventing change – intervention is both negative/ aggressive and passive/supportive and requires circumstances and context to justify.*

When intended in positive terms as the support for vulnerability, its effectiveness entirely depends on the quality of evaluation that precedes it.

Patina: *noun – origin: 17th century, Italian from Latin 'patina' (a shallow dish) (Merriam-Webster Dictionary, online).*

A tarnish on the surface of bronze or similar metals, produced by oxidation over a long period; a gloss or sheen on a surface resulting from age or polishing; the impression or appearance of something; something that makes someone or something seem to be something that they are not, which may be positive or negative depending on context.
   'Patina' becomes (mis)applied to the tarnish of age that occurs without use, but also the polished surface that is made shiny with use, it refers to an unadulterated aged surface but is also applied to someone or something that presents itself dishonestly. Like 'authentic' the word contains its opposite.

Significance: *noun - from Old French, or from Latin 'significantia', from 'significare' (to indicate, portend). The quality of being worthy of attention; importance; the meaning found in words or events (Oxford Dictionaries, online).*

In conservation terms significance is a key word that is established through the use of a 'Statement of Significance': identifying the relation between the site and wider events or associations either current or historical. Significance is reflected in the listed buildings framework where three grades of significance are used to reflect heritage importance, however significance requires judgement based on evidence, but judgement invariably brings interpretation and evidence is relative – it is therefore questionable when a term is used as a benchmark when it is in fact a sliding scale.

Splendour: *noun – origin: Late Middle English: from Anglo-Norman French 'splendur' or Latin 'splendor', from 'splendere' (to shine, be bright). Magnificent and splendid appearance; grandeur (Oxford Dictionaries, online).*

Synonyms: magnificence, sumptuousness, grandeur, luxury, opulence, gloriousness lavishness, richness, new, unspoilt, perfect – the implication for applying this to an historic building has implications if not used with qualification. New work can achieve this perfect state – but that state implies timelessness, however our idea of time and the consequences of its operation are separate and antagonistic realities.

2.1 Palacio Pereira, Santiago, Chile – questions of authenticity and sensitivity

In 2012 the author was invited to collaborate on a competition entry for the restoration and repurposing of Lucien Ambroise Hénault's neoclassical Palacio Pereira in Santiago, chosen by the Chilean Government as one of two heritage projects to commemorate the Bicentenary of the Chilean republic. The brief asked for a new approach to heritage strategy making to identify new directions for conservation in Chile. The reconstruction of the empty parts of the site, which covered most of a city block, in parallel with the consolidation and conservation of the historic building was due to start on site in 2016.

The author provided this strategy for the project team, composed of architects Cecilia Puga (lead architect), Alberto Moletto (project architect), Paula Velasco (project architect), conservation consultants Nuno Castro Costas, Patricio Mardones, Gabriela Villalobos, Rebecca Emmons, Daniel Rodríguez, Francisca Navarro, Fernando Perez with Luis Cercós and engineer Pedro Bartolomé. The project carefully articulated a position on conservation as opposed to restoration, contextualising the charters on conservation of monuments (such as Venice Charter, 1964; the Appleton Charter, 1983; the Burra Charter, 1988/1999; the Nara Document on Authenticity, 1994; the World Heritage Convention, 1972), defining the relevance of the intellectual positions of Morris and Viollet-le-Duc to establish a clear framework for evaluating how age, use marks, decay and repair can contribute to the readability of history without artifice, whilst acknowledging the human expectation for the new. As part of the process of developing a strategy into tactic and details the author engaged with politicians and heritage stakeholders in a series of presentations and public debates, the substance and process of which is described here.

The work on adaptation and conservation brought to light collaborations between politician, academics and professionals highlighting the importance of this operation at many levels. A series of photographs by the authors explore 'fabrication as making' and 'fabrication as falsification', testing Morris's philosophy of conservation and critique of restoration within a contemporary built context. This case study is described through a series of chronologically arranged texts that accompanied the development of the project from the competition entry through the presentation of an elaborated strategy after winning the project, correspondence on the developing design and finally a series of observations from the construction site as the project nears completion in 2019. These pieces of text are used in their entirety and are not edited together. The reason for this is to show to the reader how the ideas and arguments either developed or remained consistent, with the report on the site work clarifying how this train of thinking became real. The links between thought and practice evolve, and this aspect of working with architectural heritage is worth highlighting. For all the methodological, technically justifiable preconditions of heritage work, the ideas are what galvanise projects, grow confidence in funders, persuade authorities of virtue, bring the public behind the scheme, frame the re-inhabitation and direct the conservation even during the project implementation. 'Significance' is not a rigid determinant but a principle to guide.

Figures 2.1
and 2.2 Palacio
Pereira
courtyard and
anteroom –
proposed CGI.

Source: Puga,
Moletto, Velasco,
2012

Figure 2.3
Palacio Pereira
competition
entry panels 1.

Source: Puga,
Moletto, Velasco
with Chandler,
2012

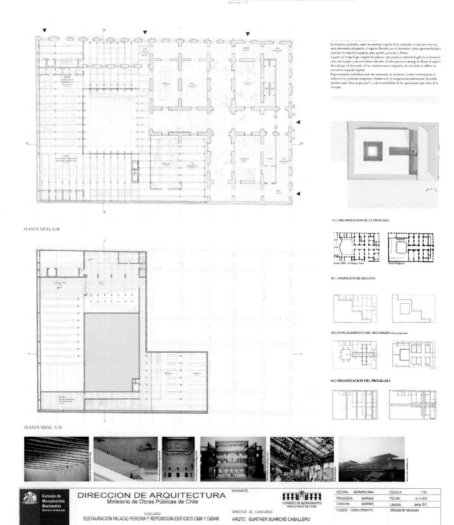

The competition – November 2012

> Head of State, President, Sebastián Piñera said of the Palacio Pereira project "it is a very important Bicentennial Legacy Project, to recover, renew, and deliver the project as an inheritance or legacy to future generations." He reiterated the project strategy to "save all you can, but additionally construct a building that integrates what was, is and will be the Palace, which will be home to the Dibam and Monuments Council National, and will be open to the public with an exhibition hall, a gallery, a cafe and an auditorium". Magdalena Krebs, director of the Dibam, said the project winner, "which will become the face of cultural heritage institutions, is the best project to collect the past to build the future.
>
> (DIBAM, 2012 translated from Spanish)

The involvement of the Directorate of Libraries, Archives and Museums and the National Monuments Council ensured that the competition brief (Government of Chile, 2012) was highly specific, and defined what was termed 'Intervention Criteria' that framed the submissions:

2.0 Objectives

The Recovery and enhancement of the historic monument Palacio Pereira, as official headquarters of the Directorate of Libraries, Archives and Museums and the National Monuments Council, which must establish itself as a public cultural space, enhance the building and its environment, and transform this property into a reference to the country's heritage Institutions. In that sense, this competition aims to:

- An emblematic response intervention in equity that highlights one of the most representative buildings of the housing stock from the late nineteenth century in our country, declared Historic Landmark.
- A contemporary intervention response is raised with respect for the building historical, yet innovative, using materials, technology and contemporary language.
- An answer consistent with the role of the main institutions responsible for the country's heritage, the Directorate of Libraries, Archives and Museums and the National Monuments Council.
- A response that values the presence of this building in the urban space, by rescuing the heritage asset associated with public use, open to the community.

The competition therefore needed to deliver a hybrid, a 'utility monument' requiring privacy while being public, a contemporary institution but also national emblem. It was within the *General Guidelines* that challenges arose and assumptions about the value of one part of the fabric over another were made clear, along with the prioritisation of the original sequence of spaces and external composition and how the new-build elements were to be realised in a contemporary way using contemporary materials. Five grades of intervention were specified covering five areas of the building: Grade 1: Restoration façades and Great Gallery; Grade 2: Interior of the historic building;

Grade 3: Courtyard; Grade 4: New building; Grade 5: Demolition. Recognising the planform as being a departure from the European model and therefore an important Chilean model was critical to the building's cultural status. The materiality associated with the façades and the gallery were highly significant.

> "For this reason, the Grand Gallery should be returning a historic restoration of the building in this space all original splendour. There are vintage photographs and mapping, which allows this type of intervention" stressed the brief. "Decoration and ornamental elements shall be subject to restoration (cornices, fascias, pilasters, plinth, antetechos, etc.), and must repay those elements as fences, balconies, doors and windows that are stored and can be retrieved"
>
> (Palacio Pereira Competition Brief, 2012)

Restoration or conservation? This aspect of the brief was challenging; it went against Morris's philosophy and implied 'restoration' in the mode of Viollet-le-Duc, that is to say, accepting and reading the marks and degradations of use over time or the pristine recreation of a more-or-less accurate historical reconstruction. Confronting this part of the brief was therefore a risk.

The award

The project lead by Cecilia Puga was awarded in 2012.[1]

> For the Pereira Palace contest, 31 projects were presented and after 3 days of deliberation, the jury chose Cecilia Puga's proposal by consensus. According to Magdalena Krebs, director of the Dirección de Bibliotecas, Archivos y Museos (DIBAM), the proposal 'resolved in a very good way the levels of intervention that were demanded in the brief'. For the new building, a solution was devised that will recover the typology of the original building, in a contemporary language, looking for an adequate solution to the points of connection between the historical and the proposed building. This emblematic historical monument will be destined to house the central offices of the DIBAM, of the Council of National Monuments and of the patrimonial-cultural institutionality of Chile.
>
> (Pastorelli, 2012)

> In the framework of the XVIII Biennial of Architecture and Planning 2012 – which took place at the Centro Cultural Estación Mapocho was held on Tuesday December 4 the award of the International Competitions "Palacio Pereira" as part of the Bicentennial Legacy presidential initiative. The ceremony was led by the President, Sebastián Piñera, along with the ministers of Public Works, Loreto Silva; of Housing, Spatial Planning and National Assets, Rodrigo Perez; the director of the DIBAM, Magdalena Krebs; the executive secretary National Monuments Council, Emilio De la Cerda. President Piñera said that "countries with no history, zero memory countries, dreamless countries without mission are countries with no future. And so, every society has to try to pick up their own story and at the same time, a mission and a dream

for the future", and "what better way to introduce this new work as a Bicentennial Legacy". In this context, the National President of the Association of Architects of Chile, Luis Eduardo Bresciani, said that the winning scheme "works with an enabling, ethical background, historically proven".

(DIBAM, 2012)

The project

The following is the competition text from 2012, written by the author that, translated, accompanied the drawn scheme on three standard submission panels.[2] The desire to reframe the brief and its requirement to 'restore splendour' is intrinsic to the text, the use of Morris is explicit in underpinning the rationale for the conservation works and the interfaces with the new sections of the building that would fill the site where missing sections of the Palacio used to stand:

Art of negotiation: the Palacio Pereira

> A church of the 11th century might be added to or altered in the 12th, 13th, 14th, 15th, 16th, or even the 17th or 18th centuries; but every change, whatever history it destroyed, left history in the gap, and was alive with the spirit of the deeds done midst its fashioning. The result of all this was often a building in which the many changes, though harsh and visible enough, were, by their very contrast, interesting and instructive and could by no possibility mislead.
>
> (Morris, The Society for the Protection
> of Ancient Buildings Manifesto, 1877)

The negotiation between preservation (the building as historic artefact) and inhabitation (the constant adjustment between place and human needs) is perfectly identified by Morris at the birth of the SPAB. Morris celebrated the overlaying of social necessity, but his appreciation was underpinned by the way it was executed – the craft with which the adjustments were made are testaments to human artistry. "What is done" was intrinsically about "how it was done".

For the architects, the Palacio Pereira competition provided a starting point from which to attempt the reconciliation of two potentially antithetical positions – conservation and inhabitation. The character of assembly became crucial in communicating the life of the building where its ruination becomes wrapped up in, not an adjunct to its continued occupation. The two positions – modern and traditional – inevitably meet at a physical junction, and this aspect required the greatest care.

The "truth" of a construction is inherent in the vernacular construction beloved by Morris, yet the articulation of the importance of "truth" effectively became necessary when our ability to camouflage structure and material for ulterior motives became widespread. Lucien Ambroise Hénault's manipulation of the "truth" of construction at the Palacio is no less theatrical than John Nash's or Schinkel's, as material and constructional expression was purposefully orchestrated to achieve a theatrical backdrop to an elite society, not to express load-bearing masonry. If the Palacio is a stage set for the culture that commissioned it, how do we now appropriate its ruin and deal with the concepts of truth and history?

In selecting their material strategy, the architects sought to draw our attention to the complexity of inhabiting a ruin, prioritising neither the new intervention, nor the character of the elegant wreckage of the Palacio. The passage of time has given the building what Romanticism called 'the Sublime', where material effect gives the observer the direct understanding of the sensation of time inspiring awe and veneration, becoming associated in the Eighteenth Century with the aesthetics of the British enlightenment linked to natural processes and man's sense of wonder.

The condition of the Palacio is unique in Santiago, its faded presence is a mirror to the modern city, its aesthetic qualities a measure of social and cultural progress. What began as an inauthentic stuccoed brick expression that borrowed from the European cultural elite has, through time acquired the patina of truth through its use, misuse and abandonment, and as such that presence of material decay provides the buildings greatest asset – its place as a document of a genuine South American history.

The question of how to approach the materiality of the building as it is found is key to the competition. Through a combination of sensitive material repair, utilising modern techniques of analysis to deliver accurate specifications for lime, pozzolans and masonry, and where necessary super strength resin and stainless steel to pin and suture the building into a seismic-resistant whole, the ruins of the building are to be retained. This provides a built document within which new activities can dwell and responds to the call from Morris to continue adding layers of history to a site.

To facilitate the new inhabitation, the empty site provides the opportunity to reconstitute the original block planform, and to respond to the Beaux Arts symmetry to create a new whole. The structural principal of the new building is of its time and is crafted to a fine scale to allow its use within the footprint of the old Palacio to take floor loading away from the fragile walls. The use of the cross-shaped corridor as a winter garden mirrors the new corridor, reinterpreting the access space of the Palacio as a garden linking the heart of the building with the new courtyard as a social and environmental 'breathing space'.

Historic building work is a constant struggle to reveal and discover whilst refraining from disturbing or destroying. Yet without revealing and discovering, without accepting the radical change that discovery brings, there would be no interpretation. History elaborates our intellectual relationship to the past, but it is based on physical and material realities. Modernity is characterised by the standardisation of assembly and the tactics of components – a fine immaterial aesthetic in contrast to "traditional" construction based on craft that operates through keying, interlocking and the accumulated protection of soft materials with ever harder ones. The fusion of both kinds of materiality through painstaking attention to detail required at the Palacio questions the polarising of historic and modern – manufactured materials can key, interlock, and accumulate degrees of protection too, but require the craft that Morris demanded to do so in a manner that re-establishes an architecture "alive with the spirit of the deeds done midst its fashioning".

Description of the project

Overall, between' rebuilding' and 'start from what exists', we opt for the second alternative – adopting the space freed by the passage of time as an opportunity to understand the complex relationship between past, the present and the future. From the original typology of the palace that creates the relation between the cross-shaped gallery, the courtyard and its perimeter corridors the new building fills the space liberated by the collapse of the original buildings. Symbolically representing a network of scaffolding, the intervention emphasises the temporary condition and dynamics of asset recovery, alluding to a "work in progress", and the reversibility of the actions that are performed on it.

Levels of intervention – the project establishes 3 levels of intervention or strategies:

PLANFORM OF THE BUILDING

The first level of intervention considers the recovery of those spatial pieces that constitute the symbolic world of the Palace, such the cross-shaped corridor and the original façades towards San Martin Street and Huerfanos Street. It is proposed to restore the damaged areas, establishing strategies of continuity and consolidation of original architectural elements of the building. The project is a promenade of spaces, the uses defined partly from necessity, partly as a direct response to the character of the rooms.

FINE SCALE OF THE SURFACE

The second intervention strategy recovers the south and east halls and the internal façades in the first and second level, reconstructing the missing parts where vestiges of the stucco surfaces remain. In the manner of the Rachel Whiteread sculpture 'Ghost', the textural quality of the missing surfaces of the palace are replaced, but in a materiality that is clearly contemporary. This strategy allows the eye to follow contours and shadows that constitute a whole, but appreciate that modern bridges between historic fragments have been made. There are a range of scales for which this strategy is effective, it is for the team to determine the range of bridging texture that works on a case by case basis – beyond a certain distance one moves from a fractured historic surface repair to the making of a new wall with embedded fragments floating in a matrix. With hundreds of recovered plaster fragments available from the Palacio there is a question about the effectiveness of this floating fragment solution. The colouration and material quality needs careful determination, as Harrap suggested, the idea of commemorating the broken edge distracts from the quality of the fragment and becomes a design element of its own. When the idea is the reunification of the building, emphasising the breaks is self-defeating. Confident colourwork is required.

Leaving some of the ancient halls in the current naked condition, the masonry is left with an evocative power, establishing the truth of brick construction that was never previously visible. The beautiful proportions resulting from floor collapse creates new spatial possibilities. The brick is evidence and testament to ruination, but the porosity and effective thermal mass provide not only visual information, but actively shape the acoustic and thermal space. David Pye referred to the non-visual contribution of building mass and proportion that results in achieving "weather in the space" (Pye, 1968) – a perceptible atmospheric condition that supplements our visual understanding of a place. The careful organisation of the environmental performance of the building materials should enhance the characterisation of the spatial sequence. The use of plaster needs therefore to be judged not only on appearance.

Cracking and masonry failure require an entirely new strategy for repair. Built with lime-based mortar and wide, flat, low fired bricks, the Palacio relies on thickness and mass for stability. The flexibility of the lime matrix has undoubtedly contributed to its survival, however, Portland cement grout injections would introduce completely rigid veins in the wall structure that creates, rather than eliminates, crack propagation. Removal of the use of concrete becomes a task in itself, the correct methodology to adopt is to start with the performance of the brick structure itself, braced laterally with structural timberwork. Under analysis, the majority of seismic requirements will be met – only then are areas of vulnerability identified and techniques such as stitching using high tensile wire (such as the AIA approved helifix system) become appropriate. This technique uses the mass of the wall either side of the crack to maintain the integrity of the wall, the placement of the wires designed to create a tensile field within the wall to stabilise it as a whole, not only locally to the fracture. Perpendicular wall tying is also possible, as well as pinning loose stucco elements back to the brick.

COMPLETION OF THE SITE

Finally, the third scale of intervention refers to the new construction. Through the proliferation of structurally fine elements new construction fills the gaps left by the abandon of the place, to build a body of elements that also helps contain the empty cross gallery that is currently diluted by the absence of one of the quadrants that originally contained it. This "scaffolding" contains a clear singular space; a non-programmatic space that creates the relationship between the functions that surround it and establish a dialogue between the subtle and atmospheric cruciform gallery converted into internal garden and the new courtyard with vertical galleries.

(Competition Panels 'El arte de la negociacion', presented to the 'Cosejo de Monumentos Nationales – Ministerio de Educacion' in Santiago, Chile. Team: Cecilia Puga, Alberto Moletto, Paula Velasco, Alan Chandler)

Following the award of the project, a workshop to develop the ideas and respond to the clients' elaboration of their expectations was held at the Palacio in Santiago in March 2013. The Neues Museum renovation in Berlin by Harrap and Chipperfield (2009) emerged as the clients' key reference point for the project. This was useful in that it allowed the diverse members of the client body to have confidence that the approach we advocated was in some way achievable, even noteworthy. However, any museum is a spectacle, as befits a receptacle for viewing history as a collection of an often-plundered past, with the Neues Museum having the added aspect of being a spectacular relic of war itself. However, the Palacio Pereira was destined to be a workplace and a public space in a congested city, as well as the requisite monument and expression of national identity.

An evaluation of where Neues was helpful and identifying where it was divergent from the team's ideas was necessary and was presented to the client body by the author in March 2013 within the derelict Palacio in Santiago.

2.2 Defining the strategy

Lessons from Neues: a steer from the committee

Taking the 1964 Venice Charter as a starting point, the presumption is 'what remains will remain'. Overlaid on this is the political assumption that the patina of age is authentic in its expression of history. The presence of Morris and Ruskin is profound,

yet sets architects and archaeologists on some form of collision course. The preserva-
tion of a vessel or textile is a clear case of suspended animation, preventing further
decay to allow appreciation and study. One does not drink from a Roman cup, yet
we are asked to inhabit an historic building, requiring services, data management,
fire regulations compliance and environmental control. Clearly suspended animation
cannot logically determine a building conservation strategy.

The architectural technology integration within the Neues Museum (2009) is directly
comparable to the Palacio Pereira, and as with Neues a series of simple, high-level deci-
sions were required to frame a secondary layer of decision making that takes the spaces
on a case-by-case basis. If the top-level decisions are too detailed, the ability to work
within the spaces will be restricted and the resulting work clumsy; if the top level is
too loose and lacking in discipline, the work will become arbitrary. At Neues the team
determined to omit all false ceilings and surfaces. This created huge problems in thread-
ing surfaces through the building. Where an original ceiling remained in one room, it
was missing in another, making the linear laying out of pipework beloved by services
installers impossible. The mapping of routes vertically and horizontally became key.

The positive result is that the building conveys its integrity 'as a building' in every
room, at no point does it feel as though portions of it have been lost within plaster-
board voids and excuses.

At Neues, a cohesive tonality for repairs and a uniformity of language for 'new'
interventions was assumed. It was decided that techniques such as pointing brick-
work would 'learn' from the immediate surroundings rather than impose a uniform
solution – therefore minimising the obvious presence of new work but remaining
detectable on close inspection. New deep-set mortar followed where old deep-set
mortar existed, flush pointing where the mortar made a single surface with the brick.

The Neues team recognised that the refusal to 'restore' the building to a point in its
past would meet public and critical resistance. Decay and age are socially loaded states
that are negatively charged. The fact that reinstatement is a form of fakery, what Alois
Riegl termed the treachery of the false, that the point of history that one restores to
is arbitrary when buildings change constantly and in a way are never 'finished', and
that the materials we use now are only distantly related to those that survive are facts
that seem not to persuade a public that seeks reassurance that history will only ever
be benign.

The Neues project marked a creative step forward in relation to the two main Euro-
pean strategies for the re-inhabitation of the ruin, illustrated effectively by Carlo Scarpa's
Castelvecchio (1956–1975) and Sverre Fehn's Hedmark Bishopric Museum (1979). At
the Castelvecchio a crafted, continuous intervention weaves a whole out of the existing,
the fine detailing used throughout creating a tracery that binds the rough stonework,
so well in fact that the new work provides more visual fractures than are left within the
existing – visual and spatial reminders are required to reconfirm that one is in an historic
ruin. At Hedmark the ruin was less spatial, so the new construction effectively entombed
the ruin in a sympathetic but clearly modern materiality, used to orchestrate a sequence
of appreciation that makes the new architecture into a vehicle for storytelling.

Neues adopts both of these strategies, but avoids the smoothing out that Cas-
telvecchio achieves, and reserves the new structure used at Hedmark as an internally
expressed framework rather than an envelope. The use of concrete at Neues is always
as an element or support to the existing space rather than becoming a space itself.
At Neues the new spaces are identical reclaimed brick, and reticently complete old

volumes or reinstate key visual lines on elevations. Problematically, the new concrete work imports a new monumentality into the old monument, visually defying the original architects' efforts at weight reduction to combat the shifting Berlin sands. The ingenious adoption of Sir John Soane's characteristic vaulting and the use of the latest cast iron technology are sidelined in favour of the new architects' personal form language.

This 'in-between' strategy at Neues lacks the modern confidence of Scarpa or Fehn at one level, but is more intellectual at another, providing a nuanced solution that reveals its post-modernity in avoiding a single answer to a complicated question. It is irritating to find that the narrative around Neues is determinedly ambiguous about its master narrative – implying that there is one, when in fact the absence of a master narrative is such a valuable asset to the final project.

Where Neues fails is in the dialogue between the new work and the reality of the existing – a building built on silt on an island, the original architect deployed advanced techniques to lighten the dead weight of the building. Terracotta pots and vaulting min-imises floor depth and loading, iron columns replace stone and masonry. This technical context delivered a building that is at odds with the massive concrete monumentality of the new insertions. Regarding the work to conserve the existing, the plethora of finely made repairs retain a common principle known and understood by Morris – visible crafted repair, protection of historic fabric, avoidance of pastiche, adding to the visual and tactile narrative of the building to enable sympathetic (re)use. However, the sheer number of repairs and the visibility each offers creates a cacophony of repair that creates a museum of conservation rather than a conserved museum. The artefacts play minor roles, dressing the building rather than addressing the public. From a cultural perspective one can justify this as being akin to the original conception of the museum itself – a storehouse of looted artefacts from a colonial system designed to propel the narrative of political power. However, from our contemporary perspective does this historic fable retain its validity, or should the way we understand the museum throw a critical light on this concept?

(Transcription from the Steering Committee meeting, Santiago, March 2013)

Following the presentations in Santiago, the position of the project needed consolida-tion both philosophically and practically. That these two words can be considered as separate, even antithetical, is already an issue of language and habit requiring chal-lenge, as both words impact on the other and on the outcome. This involved going backwards to take stock of the competition requirements, re-mapping them against the competition-winning ideas in a way that supported our intuition about how to approach the building, but also questioning the ways those intuitions were being ide-alised within the design process. Ideas can attain the status of objects that display their own sense of permanence, realities that appear given rather than opportunities to re-evaluate the journey of ideas. 'Report A' was submitted to the Chilean authorities to advance the process. The report deals with the five grades of intervention noted in the brief: (Grade 1: Restoration façades and Great Gallery; Grade 2: Interior of the historic building; Grade 3: Courtyard; Grade 4: New building; Grade 5: Demolition) and considers, for each of them, the 'surfaces and fabrics' and the 'openings and the reorganization'.

Winning the competition without losing the building: April 2013

Report A – introduction

The "Intervention Criteria of the Property" is the primary context document for this report, which responds to the four 'grades' or areas of intervention: façade and great gallery, interior and courtyard. The new building is outside the scope of conservation strategy, however its interface with the existing fabric will receive attention in the relevant sections where it occurs.

Before referring to these 'grades' of intervention, an overall set of themes are elaborated which cover a number of areas. It is important to establish an overall thematic approach prior to closer definition, to ensure that there is a consistency of approach underpinning the various degrees of intervention and manipulation that are proposed. The themes are elaborated using the following headings:

Relevant standards and Charters: Structural works-establishing priorities Ornamentation-restoration and context

The themes were inherent in the competition strategy, elaborated at the Palacio Pereira workshop (the text of which is reproduced at the end of this report). The ideas are partly philosophical and applicable to historic buildings generally, partly derived from the particular situation of the Palacio. Some concepts are developed into requirements (to 'define . . . '), others are statements which the author asserts to be relevant and important. The requirements do not contain answers within themselves, rather their assertions open up debate about the definition of the architecture outlined in the competition.

The production of the report is from the basis of an informed opinion, but needs to be understood as a provocation to discuss and resolve, rather than impose a particular solution to a given context. The role of an assertion is to open up the intellectual gaps between aspiration and rhetoric which exists within all projects, but doubly so in projects where national significance is at stake. The emotional and intellectual are linked in such situations, and as the author is a cultural outsider, the disadvantage of ignorance is also the advantage of being able to ask the question everyone assumes doesn't need asking, but to which there are usually, and unexpectedly more than one answer. It should be noted at the outset that the Authorities have made an exceptional move in the rescue of the Palacio Pereira and committing its renewal to open competition. For any authority to reinvent its remit is a sign of a healthy democratic outlook.

Any recommendations to look to the UK for legislative for procedural ideas is in no way meant to underplay the quality or depth of knowledge available in Chile, rather it stems from a lack of familiarity with available Chilean practice on the part of the author. The UK spent the 18th and 19th centuries looking to the future, and has spent the latter part of the 20th and certainly the 21st looking to the past, and has an effective and quite current cultural debate on the historic built fabric underway. If some of this debate proves instructive and new to the Chilean context, so much the better.

Summary of key concepts

The workshop provided an opportunity to respond to the actual architecture of the Palace and map existing ideas onto the building 'as found'. Certain themes proved to be highly relevant, and the qualities of the detail and material required certain ideas to be modified.

These ideas were tested intellectually against an analysis undertaken by the author of a key reference for the Palacio – the Neues Museum renovation in Berlin by Chipperfield and Harrap – and formed part of a discussion about the extent of intervention, and the merits of trying to achieve coherence in the intervention. The ideas are summarised as follows:

- *Define enduring lines and volumes.*
- *Take a position on the relationship between colonial and Chilean architecture-history is not neutral.*
- *The authenticity of the building and the authenticity of the building strategy influences the authenticity of the new use.*
- *Durability is only ever in relation to use – fragility only matters when it is tested.*
- *Determining the horizons of use should determine the extent of intervention.*
- *Prototype wherever possible, determine tests that describe appearance but also process – a prototype educates the designer, the maker as well as the potential user.*
- *Each room must have an 'idea' linked to its identity. This 'idea' persists even when the rooms identity changes, influencing the manifestation of the new use positively.*
- *Different scales of rupture will demand different scales of repair – fine textural repair for mosaic and grain, median scale for cornice and string course, large scale repair of the brickwork all require a material strategy appropriate to the immediate context of the repair.*
- *Avoid the commemoration of fragmentary edges, rather seek to communicate their unification.*
- *State high level intentions that frame smaller scale judgements – for example 'false' surfaces are not acceptable'. Visual simplicity requires technical intricacy. This makes technical decisions more complex, but so they should be.*

Relevant standards and charters – a proposal for inclusion

Principle: *Internationally agreed standards set generic aims that require thorough testing before determining what happens locally.*

The conventional historical context for Conservation assumes the Renaissance in Europe as the point at which techniques and artefacts from previous eras were re-valued and made culturally significant. The recognition and theorising of this into practice generally holds that Ruskin and Viollet-le-Duc led the 19th Century contribution to conservation.

One document that stands out in this regard is Morris's Manifesto,[3] which both captured existing ideas (mainly from Ruskin, certainly not from Viollet-le-Duc), but applied social purpose through the establishment of a pro-active group – the Society for the Protection of Ancient Buildings,[4] that became a source of knowledge, practical skills and a politically sophisticated lobbying for the social importance of our built heritage. This fusion of the academic, craft and politics was far more ambitious that any of the twentieth century charters that followed, but inevitably lacks their focus in terms of attempting the definitive statement of importance that underpins a modern, bureaucratic social structure.

The definition of the importance of the 'rights' of historic built fabric centre on the Venice Charter (1964),[5] the Appleton Charter (1983),[6] the Burra Charter (1988/1999),[7] and Nara (1994).[8] These 'exhort' good practice and develop from technical origins an increasingly humanist agenda of importance, whereas the World Heritage Convention (1972)[9] is legally binding on its signatories. Interestingly this convention places authenticity as an absolute and proposes that reconstruction is only justifiable in 'exceptional circumstances', and is only possible at all with complete and detailed documentation to support it.

This strong presumption against reconstruction was emphasised in the Venice Charter and more succinctly the Burra document, and is worth repeating:

> *Article 1.8 Reconstruction means returning a place to a known earlier state and is distinguished from restoration by the introduction of new material into the fabric;*
>
> *Article 20.1 Reconstruction is appropriate only where a place is incomplete through damage or alteration, and only where there is sufficient evidence to reproduce an earlier state of the fabric. In rare cases, reconstruction may also be appropriate as part of a use or practice that retains the cultural significance of the place;*
>
> *Article 20.2 Reconstruction should be identifiable on close inspection or through additional interpretation.*

Clearly depending on perspective, the reason for reconstruction, the scale and extent of that work, and the cultural relevance such work may or may not have is actually far harder to be absolute about that such a Charter implies. The tone of dispassionate authority still leaves the actual practice of dealing with historic buildings wide open. What Burra introduces to the field is the idea that introducing new material is a definition for 'Reconstruction' rather than 'Restoration'. This academic device is clearly not written by a craftsman, who would know that a lime mortar made now to effect a repair is close, but not the same as the original, that the electrical wiring, toilets, soundproofing, level access for disabled visitors, lighting and earthquake resistance to save lives is nothing if not "new material". Understanding the Charters is more of a history lesson in evolving attitudes to conservation in our recent history than a useful guide for architects on how to intervene in old and significant buildings. For this, the Morris manifesto, with its combination of intellectual, practical and social imperatives is far more relevant.

In 2001, an initiative by English Heritage[10] called 'Informed Conservation'[11] was published. This piece of work introduced the idea of 'Statements of Significance' as a tool by which existing knowledge of a place is gathered, understood and shared in order to underpin any proposal for future change. This 'Statement' allowed relevant authorities to understand what the proposal was doing for the historic building, what compromises were being made, and the basis for the architectural judgements that were being put forward. This approach was strongly influenced, in the authors view, by Morris. If one accepts that a building in use will receive more maintenance and care than an empty one, and if one accepts that buildings are social artefacts that rely on use for their significance, then having a robust and intelligent system for managing change is essential. What is astonishing is that this English Heritage document came out as late as 2001, and until that point the means by which historic buildings were understood and altered depended for the most part on the opinions of the individuals concerned in the process.

'Informed Conservation' proposed the term CoBRA[12] – 'Conservation Based Research and Analysis' to describe: "the research, analysis, survey and investigation necessary to understand the significance of a building and its landscape, and thus inform decisions about repair, alteration, use and management".

It proposed that any proposed scheme clarify the significance of the fabric that would be affected, the potential impact of the work, the information needed before any work is undertaken (paint analysis, archaeology etc.), and to define any effective mitigation that could be used to achieve what was required in a manner less disruptive. The winning project for the Palacio Pereira embedded this thinking within the scheme – this report will allude to the 'statement of significance' model.

Structural works – establishing priorities

Principle: *The Palacio Pereira is a reasonably efficient and effective seismic design (or it would not be here now), so any remedial work needs to respect the design integrity of the original and introduce new materials ONLY after careful evaluation of both the theoretical performance, but also the practical interface of new and old. Based upon visual inspection only, the following itemised observations are made about the structure, and will be expanded upon in the final issue of the Stage A report:*

A full scaffold to all external areas of the building envelope is recommended for installation as soon as possible. The wall and roof overlay must be detailed to prevent water ingress and built at a height to permit all the required future construction activity without alteration, so the scaffold needs only to be erected once for the duration of the project.

1   *Fractures in the original compressive structure will require either a fully integrated repair to reinstate compressive unity, or the careful integration of tensile elements to bridge gaps within the structure. The fusion of compressive and tensile elements is problematic and must be the subject of specific analysis. Structural renovation to wall fractures-the mass of the walls is clearly adequate for resilience regarding seismic activity, but water ingress is a huge issue, hence item 1. The reinstatement of structural connections between the façade and the bracing cross walls with secure ties is of primary importance, as current detachment allows the façades in some areas to operate as freestanding walls, with only their inherent thickness keeping them vertical. The structural bonding of these perpendicular elements should happen promptly and is not dependent upon the construction or the new proposal.*

2   *The 'helifix'[13] system, developed in North America, used in conjunction with engineered resins is one potential technology, the craft alternative is to rebuild the brickwork bond at these points – either route will require structural and compositional tests on the mortar bond between the bricks and the bricks themselves to determine how these, or any other tying mechanism will work. It is assumed that these tests are being undertaken.*

3   *The author has not built in seismic regions, but clearly the thinner top parapet provides an edge to the masonry that will receive optimum oscillation with the*

Figure 2.4
Fractures: Palacio Pereira crossing as found.
Source: Picture by the authors, 2013

least bonding or dead weight in the event of seismic activity. A ring beam at parapet level will be required to bind the envelope together, particularly at the corner. The parapet is also the source of extreme hazard if elements of it are dislodged and fall into the public realm below. As with all buildings built with a plastic material like lime, the introduction of non-plastic elements within the structural matrix can instigate differential movement when the structure goes into shock. This movement can instigate failure as well as prevent it if the new material cannot move sympathetically with the old. The use of concrete within lime-based masonry needs very careful consideration, and the author is keen to engage in a discussion about the conflict between modern codes and historic practicality.

4   *Ensure pipe work and services routes are identified in relation to renewed below ground system and give regard to the impact on the historic building walls. Note: existing iron pipework that is buried within walls needs appraisal regarding its removal. Rust expansion will cause future cracking where the iron is fully bedded and is subject to moisture and ongoing oxidisation. The damage done through corrosion if the iron is left in place needs to be weighed against the damage done by the physical removal of the pipe work. If pipe work is to be left in place, the most effective long-term strategy is to ensure that water within the structure is kept away, slowing metal decay. A full rainwater drainage scheme for the glazed roofs needs to be established early in the design process to ensure the integration of discharge pipework in a non-destructive manner, and to anticipate future maintenance issue that 'design out' the risk of blockage and future overflow damage to the monument.*

5   *The atrium crossing roof is both structure and decoration, it is suggested that the existing iron roof elements be fully recorded in situ and taken down for the removal of corrosion and treating ready for reinstatement. The bearing points for these elements appear fragile and the removal would allow for the scale of masonry repairs to be determined. Additionally, the iron is likely to be corroding at the masonry interface, damaging both brickwork and metal alike.*

Ornamentation – restoration and context

Principle: *What remains will remain. This overarching concept requires qualification.*

1   *The survival of plaster surface decoration is not distributed equally through the building, creating varying levels of ornamentation, which disaggregates the spaces.*

2   *Significant areas of the primary crossing space within the 'great gallery' are relatively crude modern plaster approximations of the original decor. The previously restored crossing is a valid document on restoration practice at the time, it has crude approximations to the original, and its own flawed beauty as it struggles to present a coherent antique language without the required intellectual or intuitive sensitivity required. The result has almost surreal incompletion on close inspection, and far from being replaced, should be incorporated at it stands as one of the many layers of the building.*

3   *Some areas are extremely fragile and are being washed away by inadequate water protection.*

4   *If extensive replacement of missing elements is undertaken, how are the new areas handled in terms of junctions with the weather worn existing. If the new*

plasterwork is 'worn' artificially to blend in then the original fabric is hard to read, going against the principle of legibility. If the new is sharply crafted, the junction with the old is crude and develops a dissonance that reinforces the impression that the old is 'defective' rather than revered.

5   A strategy which promotes and provides craft skills opportunities for a young apprentice workforce should be considered. If craft is an ongoing practice, then new generations of craftspeople are required to gain the experience of older practitioners. The SPAB place emphasis on learning craft through craft fellow-ships,[14] and something formalised as part of the Contractor's responsibilities during the construction.

6   Buildings are social histories, the Palace is a building conceived to express an elite social position, but in its present state the visitor is as aware of the bricks and the labourers who laid them as much as the patron who commissioned the fine decoration. The responsibility of a social document is to ensure that the hand of the labourer as well as the hand of the client should be legible and understood equally. The building language is conceived in Europe, its body comes from the clay and labour of South America.

Intervention Grade 1a: exterior façade

SURFACES AND FABRIC

The external façades are relatively intact; paint sampling is likely to show that the undeniable ochre colour is likely to be original. The renewal of detached or broken render and repainting will achieve a new building. The elaborate ornamentation is relatively complete and provides a clear basis for complete renewal. Such a strategy however makes the idea of retaining the age of the building and its history inside dis-jointed and ambiguous. The paint quality in relation to the legibility of the surface and its repair is of crucial importance, just as important as the interior. Solid period colour appears harsh to modern eyes, and although the high pollution levels in Santiago will soon add a modern grey veil to the building, neighbouring buildings that have been 'repainted' in period colours (using modern paint) appear crude and synthetic. Mod-ern paint systems must not be used, their ability to retain water, to fail to move under thermal expansion, and the plasticised sheen they exhibit are entirely unsuitable for a lime-based historic building.

The ability for lime-based paints to be applied in washes of transparent colour allows the depth of colour to be cumulative, meaning that the shadow of repairs that can ani-mate and speak about the life of the façade can remain more or less obvious, depending upon the number of paint layers applied. This allows the architects to make a judgement on site, achieving the right result experientially not theoretically. Establishing 'complete-ness' at a distance can be supplemented by a readability of repair and surface quality at close range, thereby delivering coherence as well as legible fragmentation.

Stucco on brick is a common means of achieving classically inspired architecture in Europe and translated well to the Chilean context where the appropriate materi-als were also available. The variety of types of stucco are defined in England by the material and application technique, with 'common stucco' prepared with hydraulic lime, sand and horse or ox hair. Rough surface treatments were achieved through the addition of chalk. Stucco renders come in three basic types: a lime/sand mix sometimes

Figure 2.5
Façade
restoration
detail: Palacio
Pereira façade
cleaning in
progress.

Source: Picture by
the authors, 2017

reinforced with animal hair; a hydraulic mix containing either hydraulic lime and sand, or fat lime with a pozzolanic additive and sand; with various forms of mastic. A different mortar mix may well be incompatible with what exist on the building, so testing is required (a pure or fat lime is prepared by slaking quicklime (calcium oxide) made from a pure limestone or chalk. This material requires prolonged curing time, and a faster set can be achieved by using either a hydraulic lime or by using pozzolanic additives such as fired earth dust). Sand should be sourced from the original location if possible, as the grain size, hardness and sharpness would ideally match between new and existing stucco.

Lime plasters are applied in two or three coats, ideally to uniform thicknesses with keyed surfaces between them, allowing chemical and mechanical bonds. Applying the material, it should be as dry as possible, reducing shrinkage and cracking. Before the application of each coat the surface should be sprayed with clean water, helping to prevent moisture from being sucked out of each layer too quickly. Each coat of a 'fat' lime stucco needs to dry for between 7 and 21 days, depending on mix, climate, weather and temperature before subsequent coats. A hydraulic lime mix requires a duration between coats of only 2–3 days. The plaster must be protected during the work and after application to prevent rapid or over drying. In hot weather damp hessian will be needed to hang just in front of the surface.

The application of repair sections will require the cutting out of defective areas of original that cannot be saved. Cracking greater than 2 mm wide in a lime-based stucco should be carefully cut out to form a slight undercut, and carefully flushed with clean water to remove dust and loose debris before being filled with compatible mortar. Finer aggregate/sand can be used in order to achieve more effective crack penetration. Some forms of primer can be used to assist in bonding new to old work, but this depends on local availability and site testing before they can be recommended. Where render is to be applied to brickwork, the mortar joints should be raked out to 12–15 mm to provide a key.

The surface of a lime-based stucco may become friable or flaky, but can be consolidated with repeated applications of limewash, the surface excess of which should be sponged off with clean water to prevent any lime 'bloom'. The new stucco will bond to the masonry without the addition of mesh because of the surface in the masonry. It is not advisable to use metal lath on historic masonry in sound condition, as it can speed up deterioration of the repairs. Fixing the mesh causes damage to the masonry, moisture penetration can cause non-stainless steel mesh to corrode. Introducing patches of rigid stucco in a generally traditionally bended façade will simply create movement cracks between new and old material.

The existing render, or stucco is largely intact and is therefore of high quality. The Analysis of the existing stucco provides vital information about its chemistry and composition and the proportions of its mix. This will ensure that the new replacement stucco will duplicate the performance of the original as closely as possible in terms of strength, composition, and texture. The following analysis it will become clear whether the elements of the mix are still available, most sand used in modern construction in the UK is manufactured, because historically river sand, the original material is difficult or impossible to obtain. As such the appearance of the stucco is inevitably different. If original sources of the historic stucco can be identified and used, the effectiveness of the repair will be increased.

Modern synthetic paints that form impermeable surfaces are often applied directly onto historic limewashed stucco, retaining water behind the Paint skin causing deterioration. The Palacio appears to have avoided modern paint application through neglect-this needs to be established quickly, if the original paint formulation is in place, it requires detailed analysis and replication.

OPENINGS AND RE-ORGANISATION

Decorative window ironwork should receive careful manual wire brushing to remove surface corrosion and dirt; when cleaned, de-grease with a proprietary cleaner and

*Figure 2.6
Window
grille: Palacio
Pereira exterior
ironwork as
found.*

*Source: Picture by
the authors, 2013*

*prepare in accordance with the manufacturer's direction for the final paint finish.
Power tools should NOT be used to brush off the ironwork. The blackened metal
has a visual interest but is generations of acidic filth that once removed will reveal a
pitted surface that will have its own textural interest. The colouration of the ironwork
is part of the wider debate about the façade, which all parties will be contributing to.
The original colour should be available to sample and document, its automatic re-use
should be debated carefully, the metalwork has been a dirty black for more years than
it had its original colour, so which is authentic?*

One important element of the façade worth noting is the main entrance doors, the fine mahogany-like timber is almost complete and matching the missing elements will be relatively simple. It is suggested that a full surface restoration to these doors, creating a jewel would be a very public signal that the building is a celebration of the original craftsman as well as the passage of time.

Intervention Grade 1b: great gallery

SURFACES AND FABRIC

It is likely that the plaster decorations are assembled from standard or commissioned precast elements moulded on a bench then fixed to the walls using a plaster mortar or, in the case of heavy elements, mechanical fixings. The selection of precast elements is then framed in linear plaster borders and cornicework that was run in-situ. The in-situ work is effectively the part of the decoration that provides visual direction, sight lines both vertically and horizontally, with the fine detail of the moulded elements giving moments for the eye to rest and appreciate chiaroscuro.

Inspection of the decorative treatments within the Palacio are instructive about how the skin of the building was made. The use of moulds for producing an industrial scale of elements became common in the UK from the late 18th century. Fixed solid forms were used as casting beds for a form of decoration that inevitably demanded thicker, reinforced sections rather than the previous 16th- and 17th-century in-situ mouldings, which were often a hybrid of plaster and timber profiles. Earlier mouldings tended to be linear in nature, as the profile was run using a metal profile tool and layers of setting plaster. The advent of moulds, and in the mid-19th century gelatine forms, allowed for low relief three-dimensional decoration to be applied extensively without the need for a sculptor's hand.

Modern decorative plasterwork produced for the Palacio, as evidenced in the great gallery is by mass production of cast standardised details. These elements can have delicacy, but through the process of weathering in the great gallery the plaster has even more surface interest, the uniformity of repeated elements broken down by water to achieve a constantly varied surface with no two areas alike. This variety within repetition is precious.

It is very important to note the recent 'restoration' of the gallery crossing, and to understand the implications of a full detailed restoration. Although the work undertaken less than 20 years previously in the crossing was only an approximation of the detailing, it is actually carefully executed, and gives a harsh lesson in the consequences of making the old new again. The patina of age has given the precast elements even greater intricacy of detail than they had when new, so restoring their surfaces to new is in effect flattening and simplifying rather than enriching.

The current condition of the sight lines are often eroded edges that cast ruined shadows across the surfaces. To consolidate the existing fragile mouldings, and to create a more complete impression but without renewing the entire language of the relief, it is proposed to look at significant edges in relation to highlight and shadow lines. Where a decorative element makes a significant contribution to highlight and shadow, it requires physical consolidation to bring back a uniformity of line along its length, ideally running around an entire space. Surface elements that are worn or missing are less important and give a modulated texture across a wall (or ceiling) which, providing these elements are securely fixed, could be left as found and simply consolidated.

It is proposed that the areas of restoration are restricted to the in-situ linear elements, and that the chiaroscuro moulded elements are retained as existing.

The fixing technique for consolidating the existing mouldings or attaching the salvaged pieces may range from micro-drilling and inserting stainless steel pins with resin, to traditional plaster bonding depending upon the integrity of the surface to which the piece is to be stuck. Suitable micro drilling should also be trialled early in the process. The linear sight lines should be repaired in the same manner and with the same material as originally executed, on site with shaped profiles and craft.

It should be noted that the surfaces of wear are not simply visual. The acoustic of the space is profoundly affected by the nature of its enclosing surfaces. As seen in the gallery crossing, when new, hard plaster re-faces the space the chiaroscuro becomes harsh, but so too does the acoustic reflections. The original gallery had the hard gypsum plaster mouldings, a marble floor and glass roof – the reverberation time would have been measurable in many seconds. Counteracting this was its use pattern – a formal space in a socially elite house governed by strict behavioural etiquette – noise attenuation was through manners rather than absorbent surfaces. With the gallery's new role as a modern social space, a full restoration of gypsum walls, marble flooring and glass would leave the space unsuitable for open and lively public occupancy.

To determine the extent or rebuilding of cornice and sight lines, particularly the top-lit atrium crossing, it is suggested to model a typical section of the wall, a complete digital 3D description of an existing condition-wear, surface texture, missing elements and present elements faithfully modelled. This can be used to simulate actual sun paths and shadow lines, the model rotated to understand the light effect on four compass directions, with incremental additions to the model from existing, through minor repairs, to the point where the additional plaster removes the sense of the original. This point is potentially dangerous because humans are seduced by perfection, and usually regret it afterwards. If the surface of the existing beautiful decay is well rendered, it should be apparent at which point repair becomes too dominant.

This modelling option is an alternative to physical intervention and is a piece of research that should provide a working methodology that the authorities can then benefit from in other projects. Computer generated models are potentially powerful tools for conservation, but currently narrowly employed for the envisioning the new. The author suggests the development of a methodology and benchmark standard in the use of sophisticated 3D modelling for historic buildings could form part of a researchers work, in addition to the making of the model itself. If this were funded from central budget, the benefit would be wider than this project.

In addition to modelling, some sample consolidation should be undertaken on some of the elements that have been placed into storage. This may require as little as painting with a limewash to consolidate a friable surface, or it may need a stronger dilute gypsum plaster resurfacing. This form of trial, testing the surface of the plaster as well as compatibility with plaster and existing paint chemistry should be a priority.

The matte quality of surface, the ability for the plaster to bond with the paint, and the historic appropriateness of this form of colouration makes limewash a first choice for decoration. In terms of the colour, the matte whiteness of the corroding plasterwork is beautiful, and the renderings and drawings which won the competition should be the basis for the decorative scheme. Lighting requires considered integration, harsh directional light will overly emphasise the difference between original plaster and any repairs, whereas a softer reflected lighting scheme will blur the differences and make the overall impression and the detailed inspection yield different levels of information. Sunlight provides the shadow line tracking through the space; artificial light should provide subtle modulation.

Decisions about the flooring of the great gallery can be informed by the presence of some limited material fragments-marble tiles around the edges of the space still remain, and some clear photographic evidence of the original design. The expectation could therefore be for a full reinstatement. The World Heritage Convention makes a

Figure 2.8
Paint: Palacio
Pereira layers of
finish as found.

Source: Picture by
the authors, 2013

clear provision for this form of reinstatement with irrefutable proof of appearance
and an overriding cultural need for reinstatement based on cultural identity. Both
could be claimed in this instance, although both are far from absolutely provable. The
competition winning scheme presented a different vision for the territory of the great
gallery, responding to its shift from private family-based promenade to public realm.
The intensity of occupation and the demands of internal climate control (perceptual as
well as measurable), makes new demands on the space. The placement of trees significantly impacts on the ability of this interior space to register as 'outside', particularly
in relation to the weathered plaster decoration that speak about external façades and

natural processes of decay. In this 'external' context the reinstatement of the internal chequerboard marble becomes an antagonistic idea, and introduces a harsh acoustic to the newly constituted, busy public space.

The trees presented in the competition could, like the atrium of an office tower, sit stranded in large containers. The trees could, however, respond to the existing condition of a visible earth, and emphasise the powerful external environment of the gallery by being planted visibly within the ground. There are no fundamental reasons why technical root containment can't effectively harness the trees and prevent harm to the foundations, but in terms of appearance this is a radical position. Placing paved movement routes through the forest is a requirement, these doubling as services routes allowing for electrical and data management that minimises impacts on the walls.

OPENINGS AND RE-ORGANISATION

Principle: *Within the project existing openings are utilised, former openings are reopened where possible according to the buildings requirements, and new openings are minimised.*

The winning design provides for minimal interventions in the existing masonry fabric.

Locations are non-sensitive except within vestibule, where existing decoration was renewed in 1983/4. Here the existing arched mouldings will remain to frame the new opening, which is therefore integrated within the existing scale and rhythm of the decorative order.

All existing doors are recorded and locations known, most existing doors remain on site, in situ or in storage. A standard conservation position on original joinery is as follows:

To reinstate the joinery, to re-glazing and re-fit in the original location. Ironmongery such as hinges may be serviceable and if so would be re-used, if worn and compromising practical use then replaced with material and size to match. Glass should match the thickness of remaining fragments, secured with pins and (probably) linseed putty to match original. Where the timber rebate is worn, providing an inadequate depth for the new glass, the rebate should be made deep enough to provide suitable bedding. The use of power tools will require extreme care to avoid damage, hand tools are recommended.

Timber joints should be checked for serviceability – where joints are weak or loose, the existing adhesive requires analysis and matching, with the use of timber dowels of a matching species and moisture content and like for like adhesive to pin joints securely. Missing sections or elements should be carefully cut in to lose as little original timber as possible but achieve a robust repair. Grain direction must be respected where piecing in, non-ferrous 'lost head' pins (preferably copper or brass) should be used to secure while adhesive dries, driven flush with care not to over punch and disfigure the surface.

The surface of all joinery is coated in polluted debris and should be carefully cleaned with minimal abrasion to achieve a surface suitable for redecoration. Paint sampling should be taken prior to this operation as lead may be present in the paint, and suitable health precautions should therefore be taken. On no account should chemical stripping agents be used.

This standard conservation-based approach provokes two issues – firstly the technical suitability of the original doors to regulate smoke and fire spread, and secondly the question of how these doors are presented aesthetically. The fire strategy for the

*Figure 2.9
Door joinery:
Palacio Pereira
door joinery
with shutters as
found.*

*Source: Picture by
the authors, 2013*

building needs to clarify the performance requirements of each door in relation to
escape routes/times and distances, then reflect on the actual restoration specification.

The use of adhesive intumescent edging tape and fire rated glass can achieve 30
minutes fire and smoke integrity on historic doors, but the performance specification
is needed before the materials are proposed.

The presentation of doors, the most touched part of any building, establishes a
unique relationship between the fabric and the user. Wider experiential judgements
need to be made to determine how the patina of age is handled with regard to doors
and windows beyond their function. 150 years of the hand creates a legacy of use
which ceases when the age is stripped off, however if walls retain their scars too, the

Figure 2.10
Fragment:
Palacio Pereira
cornice fragment
as found.

Source: Picture by
the authors, 2013

necessary sense of renewal is avoided and ruin becomes the evidence of a breakage rather than a continuity with the past.

The need for repair on all the joinery is assumed. The extent of repair, how it is detailed, how the glass is held and the handle framed could be the moment where contemporary detailing and modern material craft becomes combined with the original to speak about ruin and renewal simultaneously. Morris is clear that we should build of our own time, we repair sympathetically the old, and we maintain sensitive use as the lifeline for the historic building. There is a strategy for intervention here which is more subtle than 'leave it as it is' or 'make it like new'.

Intervention Grade 2: interior

SURFACES AND FABRIC

The presence of ornamentation in most of the rooms is part of the visual thread that links the spaces. In a situation which is the opposite of the great gallery, some rooms contain only fragments of a cornice or string course, but this is enough from which to experientially 'rebuild' the whole. Are the few rooms which contain the vast majority of their plasterwork fully reinstated, gilt included, leaving the more ruined spaces to receive alternative strategies, or are all the rooms subject to the same treatment –and if so, what is that treatment?

If the regulating lines established by the fragments that remain are reinstated, either in relief or as incised lines (in the manner of Sir John Soane), the small fragment is contextualised and becomes the visual origin of the new lines, enhancing its importance to the room. This strategy avoids subsuming the existing fragments within a 'reconstruction' and allows the new work in all rooms, regardless of the percentage of surviving plaster, to be read in a manner "which in no way deceives".[15]

The scale of the derelict rooms without the moderating lines of the missing decoration are in some cases magnificent, with the cafe/bridge space of the new scheme showing how impressive such opportunism can be. Some spaces however suffer from this lack of subtle scale that the ornamentation gives, and particularly where plastered walls are being re-introduced, this scale aspect should be dealt with through decoration. To avoid speculative mouldings, adding new or 'borrowing' from other rooms, the incised language of Soane, adopted in some spaces of the Neues Museum successfully, would offer a strong alternative to pastiche or speculative reconstruction, whilst regaining a unity of expression.

The build-up of paint on plaster and the filling in of three-dimensional detail is a problem within the new Biblioteca in particular – its detail being the most intact. The types of paint that may be present ranges from oil-bound distemper, size-bound distemper to modern oil and emulsion paint. The accumulation appears surprisingly small, neglect in painting providing unwitting service to the monument.

Chemical stripping of paint introduces a chemical cocktail that can without great care prove destructive. A number of careful test areas are required and time to monitor results before being required on site for large areas. Most chemical strippers are caustic or alkaline and can prove highly damaging to paint and plaster alike. Water based products contain salts which can react to the gypsum, which absorbs the solution allowing the damage to penetrate deeper into the surface.

The mechanical removal of the paint involves gently scraping using small tools and brushes, however with so little paint layers to be found, this destructive process is not recommended, leaving the original layerings in situ as part of the accumulated fabric of use. Paints for redecoration should be Flat oils or traditional distempers, however if modern paint finishes are currently in place there will be a problem with the bond between traditional and new chemistry, so selective tests will be required.

OPENINGS AND RE-ORGANISATION

The core technical issue is the necessity for closure between room for sound and fire reasons. There are existing openings, for which the doors are stored for careful reinstatement, but how new openings, or openings without original doors are handled becomes a key issue. As secondary concern is the treatment of the reclaimed doors themselves, their integrity structurally, visually, and in terms of fire resistance.

With so many original doors available there is adequate proof to justify remaking facsimiles for missing doors within original openings. The issue then is the appearance. If the existing doors are refinished to appear almost new, then the addition of copies becomes a seamless exercise in deception, allowing the visitor to have a coherent impression of a completeness that currently does not exist. If the age and patina of the original doors is retained, and minimal repair to give structural serviceability only, then the replica doors will appear like new versions of the old. This presents a unifying appearance. This appears viable in terms of dealing with original openings, but does this strategy extend to all new openings – and openings within the new building also? Clearly the decision about how new and old is articulated needs to be made, how far the language of the new is located within the existing building defines or blurs the narrative. The author puts forward the following position for development:

1   *All original doors are reinstated with careful repair, reinstatement of glass and detail to make the joinery complete, but to retain the evidence of age and use.*
2   *Doors that are missing within the context of the repaired originals should be made as replicas in order to complete the space in which they sit in terms of rhythm, order and detail.*
3   *New openings require doors detailed in a modern manner to clarify the new intervention within the wall. This may introduce two languages within the original rooms, but this is part of the overlay of history and speaks about a new configuration. Romanesque cathedrals received gothic doorways – it is the quality and care with which such new interventions are made that create value or detract from the monument. If this latter strategy is adopted, the question arises about how a modern detail is inserted, how it is articulated, and how physically it sits within the wall fabric.*

The current situation of façade window and door linings awaiting the reinstatement of original doors is inspiring. There is a beauty in seeing the timber lining establishing the shape required for joinery, covering over and giving precision to the crude brick opening built to a variable accuracy of dimension. The space between brick opening and timber opening is only visible due to the storage of the doors and frames. The remaining lining and the gap describes the fundamental issue of tolerance in building, of the limitations of each material in terms of accuracy on site, and how ever finer levels of precision are applied as the materials demonstrate ever finer inherent properties of surface and workability. The distance between the site accuracy achievable during the masonry construction, and the accuracy that technology and building standard achieve now can be demonstrated through the design of new linings to brick openings. The articulation of the gap allows for the definition of a door or window that responds to current degrees of accuracy without modifying the existing brickwork unsympathetically, A form of compression connection that minimises the use of drilling and pressure fixings that can split the soft masonry can be developed.

New thresholds required for new openings also require careful detailing. Existing openings have a logical format – acting as a smooth continuity of surfaces, with changes of direction of parquet elements, borders etc. If the same language of threshold is used for new doorways, then the assumption for the visitor is that the doorway is part of the continuity of the original plan. In addition to modern door joinery, it is suggested that the treatment of the floor is used as a way of reinforcing the new overlay of movement through the old fabric, perhaps brick to understand the act of making the opening, or the modern vertical lining wrapping the wall opening of four sides not only three.

The new floors can either return the original timber structure or introduce a new material. Re-using the existing bearing points for replacement timber is the logical and responsible approach, as a flexible floor plate may be more effective in a seismic situation – a stiffer floor plate may induce lateral stresses in an earthquake. The span to depth needs to be checked for the new loadings, if the joists need greater depth then the levels will shift, and there may be unintended consequences for the proportions and decorative fragments that remain. Services distribution will most likely utilise the new floors, but the large spans will make services penetrations through the joists problematic. The direction of the joists may therefore have some influence on the positioning of the risers to take advantage of the longitudinal spaces between joists. Fire is dealt with through plaster ceilings – returning lime plaster promotes traditional crafts however it is expensive (in the UK) and time consuming (everywhere), and may contravene safety requirements in a seismic situation. Cable access needs careful detailing within the floor finishes, and the need for access could add a layer of detail to a new floor language rather than simply try to hide floor access requirements within an imitation traditional parquet or board floor.

If a new floor is required for additional fire, seismic or loading reasons, the means of connecting into the masonry is challenging. Any reduction in the masonry thickness to provide modern bearing requirements are inadvisable, so a method of creating this bearing whilst maintaining the existing flexibility within the lime-based wall structure is needed.

As with the wall treatment, the distinction between the new building language and that of the original is problematised by the amount of 'new' that goes into the 'old'. The distinction between old and new can be easily over simplified and become trite. More subtle is to determine a single coherent material such as timber that can be detailed according to requirement and let those details speak of the underlying structural principles at work. Timber fixed to concrete screed has different joint sizes, element sizes and fixing methods than nailing the same wood species to a joisted floor. Allow the presence of nails, joints and the scale of pieces communicate the nature of the intervention within the building.

Intervention Grade 3: courtyard

SURFACES AND FABRIC

Understanding the physical limits of the building's survival is essential in navigating the courtyard. From the centre of the courtyard, the inner colonnade brings the space into one coherent whole. When seen within the cloister, the Biblioteca walls should make clear that this spatial structure is the mediation between new and original.

The courtyard has a sequence of elements that frame the open space. Each element constitutes a layer that makes a visual contribution to the progression through the building. The glazed layer is a thermal boundary that prioritises the view, but equally acts to visually reflect the doubled columns of the 'cloister' and aurally reflect the sound of the building back onto its source. Within the courtyard the presence of an enclosing glass screen in shadow within the column screen will mirror the outer columns and allow the inner layer to recede. The strategy for inhabiting the garden – the activities that are encourages and the sound it creates will be amplified by the glass – its planting will moderate this acoustic and the temperature.

Internally the glass completes a cloister that is bounded by a range of surfaces. In close proximity to the column screen is the original Palacio walling that encloses the new Biblioteca. An absence of existing decoration and the strong presence of weathering is a register of the external weather to which it has been exposed. This ability to read the exposure is important to the history of the building up to 2013, with the enclosure of these weathered walls in the cloister facing the new courtyard part of this historic continuity. As such the weathering make intuitive sense when in such close proximity to the glazed garden.

The surface quality of the brickwork is powdered, having lost the face to weather action with the loss of the internal gypsum-based plaster without the protection of external stucco. The exposure of this brick to internal climate will arrest the weathering, however the ability for the bricks not to give off dust within the space needs to be monitored once the building enclosure is complete. Proprietary sealants can adversely affect the colour and quality of the surface, and tests should be undertaken to judge the effectiveness of this approach. Liquid silicone treatments such as products supplied by the company 'Lithofin' are inert and colourless, but depending on the surface of the bricks once cleaned, this may not prove appropriate.

As with exposed brick surfaces within the internal rooms (Grade 2), brick dust can provide inconvenience, however lime mortar dust is highly alkaline and can be an irritant for skin, eyes and lungs. The exposure of the walls facing the new courtyard has meant more exposure than most internal wall faces, so remedial works here are particularly important. Repointing the bricks will provide stability to the mortar, and through weathering the joints are generally powdery and recessed from the brick faces. It is proposed to rake out the existing mortar to a depth of 15–20 mm, to prepare a stiff pointing mortar to a mix as close in composition as possible to the original. Following thorough flushing out of the joints, and while the bricks are wet repointing should deliver a lime joint which is flush to the brick faces. After a period of consolidation the face of the pointing should be 'bagged' with a coarse natural hessian to soften any trowel marks and ease the mortar into the irregular bricks. Re-pointed areas of wall will require constantly damp hessian draped just in front of the walls to create humidity next to the wall and prevent rapid drying out. If this occurs the pointing will crack and will come loose over time. It is vital that the workforce is skilled in the procedures of lime-based work. The timescales for material preparation, materials storage, material application and consolidation/setting are profoundly different from cement-based work.

OPENINGS AND RE-ORGANISATION

The retained walls were conceived as needing to bear no additional load. The structure of the new building either cantilevers new floors to almost touch the brickwork, or additional columns will stand in front of the old walls to pick up the floor edges. If the new colonnade is in situ concrete, then the additional columns will require a similar construction technique to ensure the colour and detailed surface of the concrete is consistent.

Shuttering requires working space, so the proximity of the additional columns to the original brick walls required careful judgement. Adequate protection will be needed for the soft walls, particularly as the angled columns will require complex support.

If the new courtyard structure is precast, the connection of elements introduces a further set of details into the language and provides hinge points within the structure. Intuitively the author would opt for in-situ as the repetition of the structural elements would benefit from the small-scale surface variation that give interest to the eye whilst providing a regular uniformity to the space-much as a precedent carved stone cloister. However, as the decorative language of the historic building was an assembly of pre-cast decorative elements, it would be possible to claim the use of precast concrete as a logical extension of the original.

The floor edge meeting the original façade will require a seismic spacing to avoid deflection impacts. This tolerance may will be needed within the integral concrete structure, so provides an additional detail that can contribute to the subtle language if differentiation between the new and the original. Buildings such as the Sackler Gallery (Foster and Partners) at the Royal Academy in London use glass to emphasise the modern floor meeting the historic façade. This language is brittle, in the authors view, and introducing a third element into the meeting of two materials/moments in time complicates what should be a simple and profound moment of the design.

There is debate about the extent to which the inner façade is retained is important in establishing the balance of new and original, and in the status of the courtyard as a condenser of time. It is the author's view that the existing walls currently acting as a corridor, in the future containing the Sala de Reuniones, be retained to enhance the interplay between new and historic. Although this section of the Palacio has been discussed as an 'addition' to the original, the term 'addition' is not a pejorative term and the fact that the original was added to within a lifetime is surely an important fragment of history that the new proposal should encompass.

Intervention Grade 4: new building

SURFACES AND FABRIC

The key interfaces of the new and original fabric have been outlined in previous sections. One core aspect of the new building is that it has no 'elevation' other than the roof. This statement presupposes that the courtyard is a 'room' rather than an external envelope.

The roof is a highly visible elevation given the height of adjacent buildings. While the winning design hides its presence from street level and courtyard, its presence, and its relation to the restoration of the historic roof is important. The setback given by the presence of the cruciform gallery allows a tension between them. The overt modernity of the current form will likely develop, the present asymmetrical treatment of the corners of the new roof are an intuitive response to the inherent lack of form that modern waterproofing systems have. The traditional roof was largely determined by economic timber truss spans and the operational pitch of hand laid tiles. New methods of roofing lack the determinism of traditional limitations so the form needs to be imposed. One governing factor needs to be the sky shape created by this asymmetrical roof edge when viewed up through the cruciform gallery glass. The inflections of the roof will tend to make the glass roof appear to act like a distorting prism, we expect the shape of the

*sky to be as regular as the classical building implies, but find the view bringing us back
to the modern Santiago skyline. This is a real experiential asset and should be taken
further in the design development stage.*

*There is a great opportunity to develop a modern language for doors and windows
within the courtyard room which learns actively from the existing but avoids imitation.
The copy serves to unhelpfully blur how the building communicates its heritage of
use, but wilful and de-contextualised designs distract attention and break up the users
experience of the building such that an unhelpful blur also occurs but for the opposite
reason. The greatest issue in designing for UK monuments is fire and security. Neither
have any regard for the context they are in, and consequently in complying with their
practical and legal obligations often render good ideas useless. The author has little
knowledge of how Chilean regulation and security requirements will impact upon
the definition of openings, only that they will. Making such integration an immediate
design issue will give time for positive iteration.*

*On a positive note, the existing doors show a good balance between glass and solid,
and between fineness and weight of section that establishes a sound precedent. In setting strong and consistent horizons of view, there is enough structure within the doors
to allow for security and fire technologies to be incorporated without compromising
their quality. When ultra-fine sections are offered as 'invisible' solutions for integrating
modern design into historic buildings such designs usually fail visually, technically and
when in use.*

Grade 5: demolition

Principle: *Care, skill and supervision.*

*Demolition of or within any historic building requires the clear definition of the
line up to which material is to be removed. The marking of this line must be made
with care for what is to remain, and clarity about why what is to be removed can be
removed. This is the 'what' of demolition. The 'how' also requires care – on the part
of the worker, and relies on their skill to execute the line. Supervision is the necessity
to ensure the care of 'skill' and the care in the definition of 'the line' are aligned.*

*Method Statements are the UK mechanism for workers demonstrating their under-
standing of their practice. In stating the workers responsibilities to undertake a specific
set of operations, and to identify risks associated with those operations, the contractors
Method Statement is a document that should demonstrate an engagement with the
work, and not simply as a paper requirement produced by people in an office. This is
particularly important in demolition works to historic sites, as once original fabric is
removed from the building in error, the concept of repair shifts into the counter concept of 'restoration'. Method Statements are only useful if the workers involved are
party to their implementation. If their management draft such statements and are not
effective in enforcing the process they describe and the architect requires, then 'care'
leaves 'skill'. The workers need to understand the purpose of the line to which they
work, and to realise that they are active participants in the change, not simply autom-
ata programmed to respond to direction. This aspect of craft is highly important and
requires the work programme on an historic monument to be more than a bureaucratic*

exercise. Architect and worker are level. Both participate in the craft of positive change for the building. Without positive engagement, or if management replaces respect, the project will become compromised.

The area assigned for demolition at the Palacio is clearly demarcated, within which is tabula rasa. Two areas are of concern to the author. The first is the corridor - discussed in the previous section in relation to the mixed identity of the courtyard perimeter, it appears to have been designated as dispensable but it is unclear precisely why. There are financial implications in the retention of this section of the building, and while it appears to be of mixed value, it is on close inspection materially related to the original with precast plaster decorative casings to columns on the ground floor. The competition drawings retain these fragments, with secondary modern columns relieving floor loadings. This juxtaposition is valuable and should be fully reviewed before demolition is undertaken.

The second is in the courtyard itself. Within the dust is clearly seen the semi circular remnant of the former Palacios' courtyard structure. Below the dust is the foundation of the remainder of the building. If the Palacio is a monument, why is this part not? Clearly there needs to be a clearance to make way for the new structure, but the play between new and old has to be quite finely judged. Where the new is inserted into the old, the language of the building becomes sophisticated. In the courtyard there is the old (the foundation line) within the new. The author suggests that the ground of the court-yard 'room' retain the remains of the missing building, as it is just visible. This creates a palimpsest like the Roman City wall within the City of London, a subtle wayfinder.

CONCLUSION

The conservation framework established for the competition entry made a series of philosophical assertions that gave priority to Morris's proposition that the historic building is a human document, and the protection and celebration of the traces of its use is equivalent to the protection and celebration of the people who contribute to its ongoing usefulness. Morris once said "give me love and work, nothing else". These simple and essential aspects of humanity sidestep the academic detachment that often informs the conservation work undertaken on our heritage.

The author considers scholarly technical work essential to craft, but that knowledge and skill must be harnessed through an essential respect for the traces of human occupation. The technical rebuilding advocated by Viollet-le-Duc prioritises craft over judgement, but it is the judgement about what remains and what is valuable that this conservation strategy document seeks to address.

(Report A presented to the 'Cosejo de Monumentos Nationales – Ministerio de Educacion' in Santiago, Chile. Author: Alan Chandler in collaboration with Cecilia Puga, Alberto Moletto, Paula Velasco)

2.3 After the strategy, the tactics

Detailed correspondence (excerpts)

The following edited selection of correspondences are between Alan Chandler, Cecilia Puga and the project team and are included to offer examples of exchanges among experts and include progressive adjustment based on spatial and regulatory requirements and discussions on details and materials which speak about an attentive approach to the building. After the email exchange, edited extracts from meetings follow. All emails from Chile were digitally translated from the original Spanish, a facility that enabled the conversations to happen. The symbolic and physical value of its constituent parts was consistently measured against representative ambitions, availability and calibre of local craftsmanship and notions of integrity, identity and fragility.

Date: Wed 05/10/2016
Object: RE: Cielos salones
From: Cecilia Puga

Dear Alan, Fernando and Luis.

1. Original ceilings

The IFO (Hector Andreu, who may know Fernando because I understand that was in charge of the Cathedral) supports the retention and restoration of the site ceiling whenever authorize to make 6 holes through which can pass the scaffolding structure as shown in figure I send.

A complicated issue raised with respect to the ceilings is that the beams to which they are attached have surface xilófagos and they penetrate into the heads of the beams that are in the masonry. This means they have to remove the timber, clean, treat, etc. and then relocate them in their original position. This manipulation can compromise existing ceilings. If there are procedures that we should know about this, it would be very good that we made them know as soon as possible. Regarding the scaffolding structure that pierces the heavens, the idea is to allow work up disarming (deconstructing as said Luis) the masonry wall without danger to workers and make structural reinforcements that requires envigado; create a platform for the restoration of the ceiling and that works, movements, etc. vibration do not affect the original.

I'd love to have your opinion. Tomorrow we have to say yes or no to this proposal.

Personally I think the lesser evil: the ceilings remain in situ and are not cut, while the work can be performed safely for workers. It remains to determine which are the areas where drilling would generate less damage, what kind of safeguards must be taken to make them and how then proceed to retape, including the consolidation of quincha (or stem elongation).

2. Finished floor level 2nd level

In this respect there was total rejection to cut the doors by the MOP (Ministry of Culture) at the policy level. However, it does not seem so complicated lower drilling in masonry, with straight and precise cuts to lower working beams and remaining the same but lower. In contractual terms, this is not an extraordinary (since the construction must meet established levels in the project), and instead cut doors and yes it is a very expensive one. This is the solution and plotted them forward here so they know what is being proposed.

Also on this we would like to have your opinion.

Tomorrow we have the meeting with the construction and these issues will be raised.

Luis, if you have any recommendations to us regarding scaffolding and drilling in the ceilings, the patching of wooden beams, the eventual movement of beams to which is attached the quincha holding the ornamentation of the heavens, the recess of the bricklaying and other issues that are watching and that we do not, I beg you to let us know as soon as you can.

Love to you both,
Cecilia

Date: Wed 05/10/2016 13:10
Object: RE: Cielos salones
From: Alan Chandler

Dear Cecilia,

I have translated from Spanish online, and attach at the bottom of this email what I respond to, as there may be some differences in what I read and what you have written

Original ceilings

By Xilofagos I understand beetle infestation. If the decay is only surface then injecting them in situ allows the plaster ceiling to be retained. The whole can be supported and the decayed bearing ends can be cut out and new, matching timber pieced in with steel stiffening plates if required. This requires good carpentry skills, which is a way to promote craft in the execution of the project. I can source some examples – I had to deal with a diagonal beam in a building from 1790 where the 300 × 300 mm beam had rotted down to 150 x 150 mm caused by a leaking bath, we removed a metre of the beam, inserted a 2000 mm x 12 mm steel plate vertically and bolted matching timber over the steel to reconnect it to the masonry. With smaller section sizes a simple side plate bolted through is fine as it will not be visible. If the beam is cut on a diagonal then the end can be extracted from the wall without disturbing the rest of the horizontal beam and ceiling. Local damage to plaster is inevitable, but the whole is preserved – this is the conservation way.

Cutting small holes in the floor/ceiling for scaffolding seems to be a sensible way to ensure safety but minimise damage.

FFL 2: Correct me if I have read this wrongly, but I think we are discussing which element has to be compromised when the new floor goes in-as the doorways are relating to a floor which is not at a uniform level there is the question about either shifting the openings up/down to suit the new floor level, or cutting the actual timber doors so they swing in the same door openings but don't hit the new floor level and get stuck – I hope that is the right interpretation.

As I said before the new floor is a new technical intervention that has its own logic, and is in a way uncompromising. I would follow the example of the Doges Palace on St Mark's Square, where settlement over centuries required terrazzo layers to be added to the grand floors, they got thicker, the doorways had their doors cut to continue to open. This is a story told to me by a Professor of

Conservation at IUAV, and quite beautiful as it sees the timber door as the soft element which can accommodate the needs of those who use it within a more fixed and hard structural shell.

I would not personally prioritise changing the structure to suit the door, the changes to the proportion of the door are a consequence of the technical floor being added, the door is a documentation of that intervention which would otherwise not be noticed. This change can be drawn and recorded as part of a possibly interactive archive that children and adults could experience so they can see how the new interventions were made, and that aspect of recording and teaching fulfils the requirement to conserve (knowledge), even when we make alterations.

I hope that is relevant . . .

Best,
Alan Chandler

Date: Wed 05/10/2016 14:07
Object: RE: Cielos salones
From: Alberto Moletto

Many thanks Alan for your answer, your translation is quite accurate.

We also agree with what you suggest but we must deal with contracts and bureaucracy regarding the doors but make much more sense.

Best
Alberto Moletto

Date: Wed 05/10/2016 18:21
Object: Re: Cielos salones
From: Alan Chandler

Where there is a fixed timber panel above the door this could be the area of adjustment, however that still requires dismantling the head (top) of the frame, removing without breaking the panels and cutting-my fear is to create more harm than is saved, whereas removing a door panel from its hinges, cutting the lower edge and replacing is a standard practice and relatively pain-free for the door.

For me the use of spray has health concerns, injection under pressure to remove the pests from the timber is a better option as it enters into the timber not simply soaking into the surface. This depends on the systems you have available locally of course. Whatever the system, retaining the timbers in place is critical. As Morris would say, it is both correct ethically and financially-do as much as is necessary but no more.

Alan

Date: Thu 12/01/2017 20:33
Object: Re: Pintura Puertas
From: Alan Chandler

Hello friends,

The wood was clearly painted originally, and I recall the original brief requiring the restoration of 'all original splendour' to the project? Unpainted wood was unacceptable at the time of construction – in England in the 17th and 18th century where wood was to be seen it was actually painted on with fake wood grain – because everyone knew that the timber needed protection with paint. Often the fake grain was oak even though the timber was pine, architecture has always been pretentious! Exposed wood on architectural joinery was not acceptable throughout the 19th century – it is a 21st century option here.

For me the honesty of the timber comes in the fine detail of noticing the joints of the timber or careful repairs under the paintwork – whereas from a distance there is an impression of completeness and rhythm of the panels and shadow from the mouldings. Exposed timber creates visual distraction, with repairs glaringly obvious. There may be some instances where the age of a door that has its paint worn away would be important to retain-if George Orwell or Bernardo O'Higgins walked regularly through the door its worn paint or exposed timber grain speaks about that historic moment and that persons presence – but throughout this building it is important to balance the marks of age and the necessity for it to operate as a backdrop to busy people's lives.

Happy to reconsider if I mis-read Google and you all want timber exposed – but I rather like paint that is chemically right for the history but that speaks about now.

Alan

Date: Thu 12/01/2017 20:33
Object: Re: Pintura Puertas
From: Cecilia Puga

We all agree with you Alan, without any ambiguity. Thank you!

Date: Fri 13/01/2017 22:26
Object: Re: Pintura Puertas
From: Alan Chandler

Colleagues,

I rely on Google, but the translation was surprisingly good this time – these points of Luis are all very astute and clear.

My strategic starting point for this project was William Morris – the defining idea at the start of the movement to conserve rather than 'restore' was characterised by Morris's phrase 'anti-scrape'. This approach to the historic fabric of places starts with respect for what is there-in this case it is the build up of paint layers that tells us of the life of the building. We are adding to this document, not ripping all the pages out of the book and leaving an empty cover!

We should carefully prepare the surfaces for new paint, formulated in the same way as the original (pigments/casein etc) to bond to the existing paint surfaces, and add our new layer. The colour can echo one of the layers that are found-it could be contemporary colour that adds a new layer to the document, but correct materials applied with skill is key. That would be Morris's view . . .

Saludos,
Alan

Date: Sat 18/02/2017 16:19
Object: Re: Varios temas (bien largo. paciencia . . .)
From: Alan Chandler

   Dear all,

Fernando returned us to a very useful point about perception – we are in the same place we were responding to the original brief to 'return all splendour' to the Palacio. Seeking a definition of what 'splendour' means is such an interesting question – for the public they see a palace but will not find Disney – how far they look into detail is perhaps the answer to this – the inattentive glance sees wholeness, the more one looks the more layers one sees that constitute it.

Best.
Alan

Date: Mon 27/02/2017 20:41
Object: Re: PP Restauración: Respuesta preguntas Reunión de Obra 150217
From: Alan Chandler

   Dear Cecilia,

The EETT I am assuming from the context is the conservation plan. In the UK the Conservation Plan is seen as an evolving document that is reviewed as new evidence and information is made available. Hector's response in 4, at least via google translate seems to see the Conservation plan as a specification, but how can it be when the building gives up the truth so slowly, and at inconvenient times.
   Safety (fire and stability) are the only technical issues that regularly override heritage concerns. I would say that the inserted frames fall into that category.
   The treatment of the original painted surfaces is fascinating from a theoretical perspective. The erasure of the additional layers is both conserving and destroying – revealing and erasing the years between 1873 and now. Of course these added layers and weather effects will not restore the same as was originally applied, but a damaged version of it. As such what are we left with, a window not onto the past but onto the specification and act of restoration. This is a tense moment. The Neues Museum falls into this twilight zone of authenticity and fabrication-that is not to say that it is not without merit-one can say that this is the right contemporary response-it is the fusion of the historic with now, with the craft of the original and the craft of the means of restoration. There is so much that is broken on the building that the collection or original and repair will inevitably make the Palacio into a collage-and for me this is the exciting part. What is unfortunate for the authorities is that they don't have the German

Figure 2.11
Arched moulding
detail: Palacio
Pereira complete
moulding
reinstatement –
regulating lines.

Source: Picture by
the authors, 2018

Government's budget for Neues, because like the marble treatment it is better to work on the whole like a large canvas oil painting – adjusting the elements continuously together to achieve a whole out of the parts. That will cost too much in time and finance. I am happy to help via google to navigate this complicated situation and hope at least some of what I can contribute may be of use.

The building is fortunate to have you supporting it!

Best,
Alan

Date: Wed 01/03/2017 10:59
Object: RE: Respuestas de Consorcio a las observaciones entregadas por Luis Cercos
From: Alan Chandler

Thank you Cecilia for this document – some thoughts I have on the text:

> *Respuesta a "COMENTARIO GENERAL DE LO OBSERVADO":*
>
> *It seems you have the right workers for the task – I find that with the passing of time the lime-based plasters change their chemistry to the point where they make problems when applying new material – even if it is matched – so that the performance of the two are different – moisture retention, flexibility etc, I am hoping that the aspect of movement will not prove to be an issue – here we get cracking between old and new – with earthquakes that may be more problematic. If I was a sceptical member of the authorities I would like some more detail with perhaps reference to a case study where this patchwork of old and new plaster was made and how it performed over 1 and 5 years – but perhaps that was talked about and simply not reported on in this text. Lime is an amazing material but I have found that because it is a fairly crude technology that its performance is variable. Added to the old material changing its properties over time, one gets quite a cocktail of performance issues. That said I have no doubts about the skills of the team, and I am sure this is being taken into account.*
>
> *The mould question is interesting – the original moulds did not have the advantage of silicone, so the geometry of the shapes and undercuts was dictated by the mould-making limitations. Clearly using this system makes sense, I have done it myself and have no concerns, but in terms of the details, the surface definition available with silicone means we will be picking up the textures from the old ornamentation that it never had originally. Do they copy the old texture to make new ornaments, or refinish the surface to make it smooth as it was originally with simpler mould making, so that it is 'new'. That then introduces a question about copying for authenticity or copying to make a copy. There is not a right answer, just yet another question at a ridiculous level of detail so apologies, perhaps I am being too focussed here!*

Reinforcement is a very good point – safety is vital and no one wants any detachment of the new work. The ability to recast the moulds as original means solid plaster I presume. In using modern mould making some weight of plaster can be saved by hollowing or inserting voids, but at the expense of 'authenticity'. If the ornament is authentically solid then an inauthentic fixing method will be needed to ensure it cannot fall. Which is cheaper or more reliable? Which is more authentic? In the end it needs to be safe. I note the last sentence "to be installed by the client" – a careful passing over of liability. I think this question needs to be made very clear so that all parties can agree on a way forward to ensure that no single individual is left exposed should a fall happen – that would be unfair as it is a team project.

Alan Chandler

*Figure 2.12
Restored
plaster to the
vaulted crossing
ceiling with
contemporary
frameless
rooflight.*

*Source: Picture by
the authors, 2018*

Date: Fri 19/01/2018 16:37
Object: RE: ficha hidrofugante/antigraffiti
From: Alan Chandler

Dear all,

It seems from the scientific research I can find that the fluorinated copolymer technology is superior in external performance over non-fluorinated products (reduced yellowing, longer performance life etc.) however the papers I can find are all tested on natural stone rather than roman cement/stucco/pigmented artificial surfaces. There may be research I have not found on the use of this material on stucco, but as time is clearly against us there is no opportunity to undertake any long-term testing before building completion. However we can turn this around – rather than having the research before the Palacio completes, perhaps the Palacio can become the research.

As the issue of graffiti on historic buildings is significant, I would suggest that it is worth engaging polymer scientists from a University in Santiago to monitor the Palacio so that its use here can inform how future restoration projects can be protected. If graffiti needs to be cleaned again the effect of cleaning on the surface could be monitored and evaluated by the scientists so that a body of evidence on the effectiveness of fluorinated copolymers can inform future façade restoration practice. I am undertaking cleaning trials on the terracotta decoration to St Pancras Church in London with Historic England to inform their publication of best practice advice as well as to inform our future restoration of the building. This kind of long-term technical partnership with heritage bodies is very valuable.

Best,
Alan Chandler

In October 2018 two visits to the project in Santiago led to a number of conversations as the works progressed to conclusion. The notes are transcribed in the following, and illustrate how heritage projects continually reveal issues at a detailed level that require reflection on the core ideas in order to give consistency to the result. In particular the level of reinstatement of plaster details in the significant spaces of the Palacio in relation both to how perfect the new work becomes in relation to the condition of the existing, and how extensive that new work should be – compositionally the balance between 'first glance' coherence and detailed differentiation between new and old is a judgement call often best made on site – challenging in a contemporary contractual environment. However, reflection on site as the work progresses is not de facto cause for cost additions; sometimes omitting a process saves time and labour and allows the building to speak more clearly.

Site report 08.10.18 with Paula Velasco and Alberto Moletto

THE SCALES OF REPLACEMENT/REINSTATEMENT

Scale 1 – Architectural – at a spatial scale that defines the context of the whole volume in terms of rhythm and structure – pilaster, capital and brackets allude to supporting architectural load, their absence creates visual instability detrimental to the appreciation of the space.

Scale 2 – Regulating lines (ref. Le Corbusier) continuity of the whole – particularly horizontal, the modelling of shadows through sympathetic modelling of absence – extruded profiles rather than moulded detail. Hard shadow edges need careful shaping to avoid distracting the eye from softer, less distinct original detail. The application of scored 'block' limes to the repaired areas of plasterwork will connect the new to old and establish a regulating measure to the walls whilst retaining a legibility of old and new plasterwork.

Scale 3 – Detail – aesthetic loss remains lost – the finest grain of detail allows for close attention to the fragility of the surfaces.

*Figure 2.13
Graffiti: Palacio
Pereira façade
graffiti after
cleaning.*

*Source: Picture by
the authors, 2018*

COLOUR LAZURE

Minimise the marks of cleaning and consequent repair – the colour wash test retains close surface variety whilst giving a distant impression of consolidation. There is an issue with the dense and uniform colour of large areas of new plaster, particularly the apricot – perhaps a thin whitewash would break up the uniformity and is worth testing. Internally some areas of existing plaster is grey with occasional iron oxide staining – the consolidation layer could be tinted to shift the new white plaster down in tone so that the contrast is reduced – applying an even, un-mottled wash to the new work rather than attempting to lighten the old is an 'honest' in that the old reads old, the new reads new. In hindsight a slightly grey repair plaster would be used so that the contrast is automatically moderated.

Comment on the clarity of the concrete work in relation to the lime repaired masonry and basalt flooring (related to historic Santiago streets). Note first floor connections through – a wider than anticipated gap between concrete frame and brick rear façade giving unexpected views of the cornice, partly missing plasterwork its structure of projecting masonry and wrought iron support work providing a rare close-up understanding of the construction. A glazed connection here would offer an architectural gift.

The planked timber ceilings that replace the lost plasterwork reinstate the volume and shape of space without artifice – the gaps between the boards offering a texture that provides surface rhythm without mouldings. The Morris ceilings deliver a striking remembrancer for the contribution Morris made to the thinking of the project.

Site report 12.10.18 with Cecilia Puga

Review of the three scales – agreement on the brackets, on the replacement of ornament on the capitals.

Courtyard – the junction of the new concrete structure and the existing: External fragments above door openings and plaster fragments on the two historic walls facing the new courtyard to be left as existing – the severe weathering and aged surfaces speak about the exterior and should not be subject to the fine restoration of the internal spaces. The contrast to the new concrete structure is therefore more pronounced and agreed that this is a very positive move.

Crusero – crossing: Tinting of the consolidation material for the new white plasterwork – already purchased – commencement next week can begin with the original plasterwork so that the programme is not affected by the test process – suitable pigments to be sources and a set of panels prepared to test the relation of new and old in a variety of lighting situations – all agree that one solution will fit everywhere.

Agreed that the base of each roundel where the portrait is missing should not be at the same depth as the rear wall – this emphasises the ring as an object rather than the entire disc as an applied portrait. In reducing the inner edge of the ring to 4mm the identity of the roundel is reinstated. Change agreed with contractor.

Note heavy water staining on the roof of the crossing – 30% dilution of a white wash used to knock back the darkest stains. This is potentially controversial, however as the entire ceiling is original it is not about artifice and confusing new with old, rather its status is that of a repair that prevents the damage from dominating the quality of the whole.

Retain the patina in the cornice work – cease cleaning and retain with only light brushing – predominantly white but the paint remnants have a beauty that the adjacent room with a single coating of gloss olive green does not possess. The question of authenticity is critical – the actual or the reinstatement of the lost? With the competition text stressing the actual, the layers of history and the questioning of the restoration of splendour, the retention of the paint layers within this room is both a recognition of the aesthetic value of 'as found', but also ensuring that the strategy is manifest in the detail. Corner where the entire depth of the frieze is missing to be re-run as a profile without ornamentation as elsewhere – painted white as ceiling and walls. This

*Figure 2.14
Moulding detail
regulating lines:
Palacio Pereira
architrave
reinstatement –
regulating lines.*

*Source: Picture by
the authors, 2018*

*records the damage to the corner of the room and connects the new wall and coved
ceiling surfaces. The coving to the ceiling in pine is having the egg and dart mouldings
re-fixed in short sections having been numbered and removed – re-fixing uses inset
screws to ensure fixity during earthquake situations. The flat plastered sections have
been renewed allowing for secure fixing to structure above.*

*Note olive room with an identical ceiling design as above is scheduled to have the
ceiling removed to secure it as the slab has already been poured above – a problem in
scheduling as the laths could have been secured from above without damage to the
interior surface. Secure from below using appropriate length stainless steel screws with
mesh and washers to ensure the whole is held by the timber structure above in event
of earthquake – repair over the screws that are to be inset within the plaster. This
space is currently having the oil-based olive-green gloss paint removed – approximately
50% complete – no layering of paint is visible below the green, agree to continue to
be stripped to plaster with the colouration of the plaster simply consolidated. Note
importance of sustaining the question of a narrative within the building – having two
treatments in two adjoining rooms is not an issue but an exposition of the actions taken
to reconstitute the building.*

*Support the decision for the painting of the 1st floor room with coloured, decorated
plaster fragments to match the background colour to the new surfaces fragments,
necessary to ground the old and avoid the sensation that the old is simply detached
and floating on the new surface. Plaster infill to screw fixings required for security to
be retouched as with the Royal College of General practitioners (a contemporaneous
project in London by the author) – new plaster is painted, so too is the screw repairs.*

*Fragments of basalt cobbles found in the entrance for horses, matching basalt cob-
bles sourced for the area but originals retained in situ – almost unnoticeable colour*

Figures 2.15 and 2.16 Stripping cornice and olive cornice: Palacio Pereira cornice stripped back to clean plaster finish and final condition.

difference but the surface is distinct and adds a quality and narrative to the floor. A similar set of fragments of Carrara-like marble was found in the main entrance – the relationship to the new marble that is being used will be checked but providing the two marbles have a form of harmony the pieces will be used in original locations. This narrative extends the principles applied to the wall decoration to the floors, and is a positive outcome.

The value of documents

The importance of documentation within all projects goes without saying; however, in the Palacio and other similar significant heritage projects reflection and exchange are critical. Unlike the precision of 'new-build' the goal cannot be pre-defined in the same way. The variables are, despite all the documentation possible, going to require reference back to a strategic set of principles in order to address their challenge. If those principles are loose or lack definition, such reflections become haphazard and risk incoherence at best, and at worst simply accommodate poor work.

In the case of Palacio Pereira, the project was pre-loaded with a weight of expectation, as one of the two heritage projects chosen to commemorate the Bicentenary of the Chilean Republic, and as a vehicle for the Chilean Government to restructure the national approach to conservation, the Palacio became in itself a document to read and interpret, charged with both emotional and intellectual ambitions. The initial philosophy needed to be unambiguous, yet robust enough to provide an ongoing set of values that allowed for a consistency of response to the kinds of issues that such a complex and important project generates. The use of the documents within the chapter aims to show how that set of philosophical tools are used, and the variety of situations to which they are applied.

Critical to the project has been the formal acceptance of the philosophy by politicians and authorities. Some inevitable exceptions aside, consistency in decision making was supported by having a usable intellectual benchmark. The reports, the competition panels and selected email exchanges reproduced in this case study clarify how the reflections evolved towards action. In this sense, the approach to materiality of the professionals involved is engaged with the institutional effort to articulate the value of philosophy in conservation practice.

Significantly for the team, the documentation passed between two countries and two languages. The author was invited to collaborate as restoration expert from the UK, with the intention to bring a different perspective on 'restoration' to the Chilean context. This was not an intellectual confrontation, rather it became almost immediately an articulation of a common architectural sensitivity that the work of Morris found sympathy with. Indeed, any recommendations to look to the UK for legislative and procedural ideas was in no way meant to underplay the quality or depth of knowledge available in Chile, but was rather an occasion to pick up from the cultural debate on the historic built fabric that characterised the UK in the last two centuries. With notions borrowed from William Morris especially, the necessity of considering the social importance of the built fabric was supported and underpinned.

Other notions as the 'Statements of Significance' proposed by English Heritage in 2001 and the *Conservation Based Research and Analysis* proposed by *Informed Conservation* (Clark, 2001) were referenced as useful tools. They suggest mechanisms to gather, understand and share existing knowledge of a place to underpin any proposal for future change; and to clarify the significance of the fabric that would be affected, the potential impact of the work, the information needed before any work is undertaken.

Also, the Smithson's notion of 'as found' was proposed in order to demonstrate that Morris's attitude to the existing, the ordinary or as he put it 'humble' (Morris, 1877), was valuable and relevant to architectural practice considered 'modernist'. Morris's ideas are not 19th-century revisionism, but in their social underpinning provide contemporary practice with a position beyond historical style. They suggest a respectful approach to the existing, trying to read the building as a layering of information and minimising the impact of disruptive restoration. The aesthetic and philosophical value of this practice underpinned the teamwork on the Palacio to ensure that the 'as found' was evident both in the structure and in the details, with many elements consolidated rather than substituted. Reading the traces of history became paramount to ensure a respectful project merging old and new and to render the Palacio as an evolving document capable of review as new evidence and information is made available. Paraphrasing president Sebastián Piñera, the palace became an occasion for the society to pick up from its own history, and a mission to build the future from the memory of its traces.

Lessons learned

Through the Palacio Pereira we have raised awareness of underpinning ideas of conservation their differences and the physical consequences that they lead to, and offered an explanation of the role that various international charters play in the way heritage is officially interpreted, giving a context for how questions of heritage value are handled. From the beginnings of the conservation strategy, the project opened up a debate on the value of physical heritage for the community – the Palacio Pereira as a symbol of national identity since President Piñera's government took the unprecedented step of intervening in the fate of the derelict building; intentionally weakened, it appeared, in order to hasten earthquake damage and redevelop the site profitably. This decision to intervene in order to acknowledge heritage value gave the building a highly representative power, and gave the competition winning team a significant weight of responsibility to deliver. Born for elitist consumption, the Palacio is now for all the citizens, a collective resource hosting the Department for Heritage, Museums and Libraries, a public gallery, public courtyards, library and cafes.

Piñera's right wing government was replaced by a socialist one prior to the project commencing on site; yet, to the team's surprise the project maintained the confidence of the left and was supported across the political divide. It is ironic that prior to completion on site the Palacio sees Piñera back in office, able to formally open the project his government started seven years earlier.

There are wider questions around how the Palacio will be interpreted, not by professionals, critics and journalists, but by the people of Santiago. The public facilities – library, cafes and public courtyard as well as workplaces for the employees of the government – will establish an ongoing contact with their users who will make up their own minds as to what the recovery of the building means to them. Are the strategic decisions made about the whole and about every detail of repair likely to be understood? Are the absences of the building's fabric going to communicate the building's transitional history from an elitist environment through dereliction to a public monument – or appear simply to lack 'completion', the visibility of age deemed a mistake and evidence of 'cost and corner cutting'? Public perception is critical, as we will explore in

Figure 2.17
Raw brick
and roofing:
Palacio Pereira
completed
anteroom.

Source: Picture by
the authors, 2018

later chapters, but that perception is not neutral. It is conditioned by an image-based environment that idealises, preconditions expectation and exploits anticipation. The task of those who learn from Morris is to articulate not why the instinct for a perfect past is wrong, but that being able to read the human engagement with the past through the buildings and places that surround us is better.

Perhaps people can only appreciate history and social narrative when it is not camouflaged in an image of completeness and timelessness delivered by 'restoration'. The quality of the new, and how it develops and responds to the original is therefore critical. Within the Palacio the debt to Morris was repaid by the reinstatement of a missing

Figure 2.18
Palacio Pereira
'Morris' ceiling
design by Cecilia
Puga based on
Morris' 'Brother
Rabbit'.

Source: Picture by
the authors, 2018

plaster ceiling with a rescaled Morris and Co. pattern, the scale of the textile print equivalent to the ornate plasterwork in adjoining rooms, but in bold graphic red print. This transformation of the past without imitation as a form of narrative construction avoids confusing restoration and conservation and allows the new to be clearly understood whilst being a part of the whole.

Throughout the corresponding documents presented in this chapter, a consistent approach to material and technical choices evidences the value of strategically defined conservation principles. We would argue further that the approach that Morris and Ruskin articulated extends beyond repair and recovery, but through its social agenda actively informs the design of new work. The recovery of lost plasterwork within the Palacio prompted Cecilia and her team to develop the use of timber planking rather than lime plaster to complete three coved ceilings, adopting a huge scale Morris textile pattern 'Brother Rabbit' to replace the lost ornate coffered mouldings with an equally rich visual pattern.

Examples of narrative conservation such as the Palacio are necessary to provide alternatives to the 'restoration' imaginary; it is only with these alternatives that people can see that there are choices in how history is reclaimed, understood and used.

Notes

1 For more information visit: www.youtube.com/watch?v=C8ZIMIcKkc0
2 The panels can be found at the page: www.patrimoniocultural.gob.cl/portal/Contenido/Noticias/6832:Arquitecta-Cecilia-Puga-gano-concurso-para-restaurar-el-Palacio-Pereira
3 Manifesto for the founding of the Society for the Protection of Ancient Buildings, 1877.
4 Society for the Protection of Ancient Buildings (SPAB) – a voluntary membership group dedicated to the repair and re-use of vulnerable historic building, opposed to 'restoration', conjectural or otherwise, which deprives the building of its history of craft and use.
5 Concordat establishing principle of ICOMOS, defining a code of professional standards that gives an international framework for the preservation and restoration of ancient buildings.
6 Esp. "avoidance of conjecture, distinguishability of new work, use of traditional materials and techniques, maintenance of patina, reversibility and respect for the integrity of the structure" (Venice Charter, May 1964).
7 "as much as necessary, as little as possible" (ICOMOS Stained Glass 1993: 12, Chapter 3 Korn, U. D. Notes on the protection and restoration of Medieval and Renaissance stained Glass).
8 Authenticity: linked explicitly to "form and design, materials and substance, traditions and techniques, location and setting, spirit and feeling" (Larsen and Marstein, 1994: 132–133, quoting ICOMOS Conservation of Historic Timber Structures).
9 UNESCO defining 'World Heritage Sites' – UNESCO 1988: Operational Guidelines for the Implementation of the World Heritage Convention pp. 79–86 – http://whc.unesco.org/statutorydoc
10 English Heritage: The historic Buildings and Monuments Commission for England, established in 1983, reporting directly to the British Government.
11 'Informed Conservation', K. Clarke, London, 2001.
12 'Informed Conservation', p. 22.
13 Helifix: www.helifix.com
14 SPAB: www.spab.org.uk/education-training/
15 William Morris: SPAB Manifesto, 1877.

Bibliography

Books, journals

Benjamin, W. (1940) *On the Concept of History*. Translation by E. Jephcott. Reprint, Cambridge, MA and London, England: The Belknap Press of Harvard University Press.
Clark, K. (2001) *Informed Conservation: Understanding Historic Buildings and Their Landscapes for Conservation*, London: English Heritage.
DIBAM noticias (2012). [Online] Available at: www.dibam.cl/Vistas_Publicas/publicNoticias/noticiasPublicDetalle.aspx?idNoticia=42498 (Accessed: March 2013).
Government of Chile (2012) Competition brief 'Recuperación patrimonial, El Palacio Pereira Será Sede de la Dibam y el CMN'. [Online] Available at: https://www.patrimoniocultural.gob.cl/614/w3-article-33727.html?_noredirect=1
Kracauer, S. (1963) *Das Ornament der Masse, Essays*, Frankfurt am Main: Suhrkamp.

Larsen, K.E. and Marstein, N. (1994) *Conservation of historic timber structures. An ecological approach*, ICOMOS. [Online] Available at: https://ra.brage.unit.no/ra-xmlui/bitstream/handle/11250/2373604/Conservation_of_Historic_Timber_Structures.pdf?sequence=1

Marx, K. and Engels, F. (1848) *Manifesto of the Communist Party*. [Online] Available at: Marxists Internet Archive (marxists.org), 1987.

Morris, W. (1877) *The Society for the Protection of Ancient Buildings Manifesto*. [Online] Available at: www.marxists.org/archive/morris/works/1877/spabman.htm for more information visit: www.spab.org.uk/about-us/spab-manifesto (Accessed: 30 March 2019).

Mumford, L. (1961) *The City in History*, San Diego: Harcourt, Brace & World.

Pastorelli, G. (2012) 'Ganadores anunciados del Palacio Pereira y Eje Bulnes', *Plataforma Arquitectura* (CL), 4 December. [Online] Available at: www.plataformaarquitectura.cl/cl/02-213738/ganadores-anunciados-del-palacio-pereira-y-eje-bulnes (Accessed: 30 March 2019).

Pye, D. (1968) *The Nature and Art of Workmanship*, Cambridge: Cambridge University Press.

Simmel, G. (1903) *The Metropolis and Mental Life*. Translated by K. Wolff. Reprint, in *The Sociology of Georg Simmel*, New York: Free Press, 1950.

Spengler, O. (1918) *Il Tramonto dell'Occidente. Lineamenti di una morfologia della Storia mondiale*. Translated by J. Evola. Collana La buona società n.16, Milano: Longanesi, 1957.

Charters and documents

Appleton Charter (ICOMOS). [Online] Available at: www.icomos.org/charters/appleton.pdf

Burra Charter (ICOMOS). [Online] Available at: http://icomosubih.ba/pdf/medjunarodni_dokumenti/1999%20Povelja%20iz%20Burre%20o%20mjestima%20od%20kulturnog%20znacenja.pdf

Competition brief 'Recuperación patrimonial, El Palacio Pereira Será Sede de la Dibam y el CMN'. [Online] Available at: https://www.patrimoniocultural.gob.cl/614/w3-article-33727.html?_noredirect=1

Competition Panels 'El arte de la negociación', presented to the 'Cosejo de Monumentos Nationales – Ministerio de Educacion' in Santiago, Chile. Team: Cecilia Puga, Alberto Moletto, Paula Velasco, Alan Chandler. [Online] Available at: www.patrimoniocultural.gob.cl/portal/Contenido/Noticias/6832:Arquitecta-Cecilia-Puga-gano-concurso-para-restaurar-el-Palacio-Pereira (Accessed: 30 March 2019).

Conservation of Historic Timber Structures (ICOMOS) Available at: https://www.icomos.org/images/DOCUMENTS/Charters/wood_e.pdf

Nara Document on Authenticity (ICOMOS). [Online] Available at: www.icomos.org/charters/nara-e.pdf

Report a Presented to the 'Cosejo de Monumentos Nationales – Ministerio de Educacion' in Santiago, Chile. Author: Alan Chandler in Collaboration with Cecilia Puga, Alberto Moletto, Paula Velasco.

Steering Committee Meeting, Santiago, March 2013.

Venice Charter (ICOMOS). [Online] Available at: www.icomos.org/charters/venice_e.pdf

The World Heritage Convention (UNESCO). [Online] Available at: http://whc.unesco.org/uploads/activities/documents/activity-562-4.pdf

Websites

Helifix. [Online] Available at: www.helifix.com

Morris, W. (1877) *Letter to the Athenaeum*, 4 March. [Online] Available at: www.marxists.org/archive/morris/works/1877/tewkesby.htm (Accessed: 12 March 2019).

National Planning Policy Framework. [Online] Available at: https://assets.publishing.service.gov.uk/government/uploads/system/uploads/attachment_data/file/779764/NPPF_Feb_2019_web.pdf

SPAB Craft fellowship. [Online] Available at: www.spab.org.uk/education-training/

Online dictionaries and definitions:

Dictionary.com, "craftsmanship", https://www.dictionary.com/browse/craftsmanship (accessed June 1, 2019).

Merriam-Webster Dictionary, "patina", https://www.merriam-webster.com/dictionary/patina (accessed June 1, 2019).

Oxford Dictionaries, "adaptation", https://www.lexico.com/en/definition/adaptation (accessed June 1, 2019).

Oxford Dictionaries, "authentic", https://www.lexico.com/en/definition/authentic (accessed June 1, 2019).

Oxford Dictionaries, "demolition", https://www.lexico.com/en/definition/demolition (accessed June 1, 2019).

Oxford Dictionaries, "intervention", https://www.lexico.com/en/definition/intervention (accessed June 1, 2019).

Oxford Dictionaries, "significance", https://www.lexico.com/en/definition/significance (accessed June 1, 2019).

Oxford Dictionaries, "splendour", https://www.lexico.com/en/definition/splendour (accessed June 1, 2019).

Chapter 3

Place

Material and the urban imaginary

Approach

Significant regeneration projects in recent history show a strengthening of the relationship between real estate dynamics and the inclusion of cultural references. In Chapter 3 we take note of two urban case studies separated by two decades and the neoliberalisation of the UK economy, which reveal how the texture of regeneration has changed – both in the way it is framed politically and how its delivery mechanisms have been finessed: Covent Garden and Battersea Power Station developments.

Their stories are characterised by narratives building on the legitimising presence of history. If we assume that heritage is 'made' and not inherited (Graham and Howard 2008), and that memory "works by reinvesting places with new accretion of significance" (Kearns and Philo, 1993), we understand the pivotal importance in observing cultural narratives. They reveal how the process of selection has been made, and who is the final beneficiary of a certain interpretation of heritage. Moreover, they show how the urban project should be considered not only as a final outcome, but also as a resource to the same policies that generated it. As stated by Hobsbawm and Ranger (1983: 16):

> we should look at those mechanisms that, deliberately or unconsciously, collaborate in their production. On the one side the marketing strategies that make them readable, the rules that guide planning, and the languages used to convey and distribute an idea of city. On the other side the mechanisms that make these strategies possible, and therefore the market, with its enabling power and its branding attitude.

What is at stake is not only the concept of past and the power of history, but also our ability to imagine alternative futures.

The redevelopment of Covent Garden in the 1970s was driven by a London-wide plan for regeneration that attempted to eradicate key infrastructure deficiencies around the vegetable and flower market through the provision of tourist- and business-led facilities on a scale missing from the 'London offer' at that time. The project began as a comprehensive redevelopment that through cultural resistance was transformed into a heritage-led urban consolidation. Operational forces of real estate that underpinned the original strategy were required to make a significant shift that incorporated rather than swept aside historic urban fabric, the resulting revaluing of built heritage achieving the original population displacement and capital investment potential – but without being obvious.

The project of Battersea Power Station, on the other hand, disclosed the pivotal role of narrative in the shaping and promotion of urban change. Far from being a banal sequence of failed projects, the history of Battersea Power Station (BPS) proves how the regeneration of the built environment needs to be observed alongside the regeneration of political, economic and social ambitions that support it. Every time, a renewed context created the opportunities and then dismantled them. Its functions evolved, different subjects took part in the discussion, national and international interests were involved. Every time, someone was heard saying "This time it is going to happen" (Watts, 2016), and was punctually neglected. The role of history, culture and heritage entered the narrative in different ways, being in turn the reason for the preservation of the building, the reference for marketing strategies, or for feeding a romanticised approach to the project.

The outcomes in both instances, although sharing strategic goals, differ in the way media was managed to serve key stakeholder needs. Covent Garden's local community, through direct action and the use of available communication channels of newspapers, television and posters, created interest so substantial that the physical restructuring of their community was abandoned. We will focus on the timeline of events through the campaign but bring new questions around the relationship between community heritage and the built heritage that the community inhabits. The two are ostensibly the same, but subsequent events through the 1980s and 1990s show this not to be the case.

In the same timeline, community opposition by the BPS Community Group (BPSCG) battled against the economic interests behind the Battersea development, and questioned the use of the iconic building to spur private interests. What will be traced back to the present is the meaning that heritage and legacy occupy in the marketing strategies of this project and how they evolved in time. The way modes of communication changed by employing the symbolic building inside promotional narratives, together with the vastness of the project and its pivotal role in the regeneration of London and its Opportunity Areas make Battersea an exemplary case like no other. Here, heritage grew as one of the rising forms of asset in the deregulated landscape of housing investments. The marketing strategies are clearly influenced by a globalised mode of communication; there's a declared need to render the uniqueness of the places by including elements that can make them recognisable. However, this search of identity is increasingly linked to branding: cultural difference is one of the values that supports distinctiveness and becomes more and more important as the built environment grows generic and simplified. The inclusion of heritage becomes a metaphor, easy to read and to understand because it promotes a synthetic version of the reality.

The Covent Garden and Battersea projects talk about how the concept of heritage, intended as a narrative, evolved since the 1980s. They recognise the phenomenon of heritage valorization and compel us to think about what imaginaries lay beyond the concept of history. They also ask us to acknowledge the valorization of heritage as a complex process: the patrimonialisation of these objects, commonly referred to as professional practices of urban conservation, is necessarily linked to the other forms of valorization, coming from public and private subjects. The local community, the administration and the private developers all contribute to the shaping of meaning. Along with the official narrative, parallel descriptions can exist and other stories can input to the significance of heritage. The predominance of the visual narrative, in this sense, is useful in order to understand how the promotion of a patrimonial object is always shaped by someone for someone else and what constitutes the layered codes that deposit onto an image. This invites us to reflect on how the relevance of heritage is built, and for whom.

GLOSSARY

Community: *noun – a group of people living in the same place or having a particular characteristic in common.*

The condition of sharing or having certain attitudes and interests in common. (Ecology) A group of interdependent plants or animals growing or living together in natural conditions or occupying a specified habitat (Oxford Dictionaries, online).

A physical proximity, similar characteristics or shared attitudes, 'community' like 'material' has tangible as well as intangible significance. Care required to ensure both aspects of these keywords are understood and accounted for – in particular how the interdependency is manifest in shared attitudes and the spatial consequences of those attitudes.

Collage: *noun – to glue from the French 'Coller': the fixing of disparate physical elements together on a common plane, the juxtaposition creating associative meaning through difference between elements.*

A collage as a piece of art, defined in 1912 by Picasso and Braque, affirms and questions significance through the re-contextualisation of multiple meanings the viewer attaches to each element. Collage is a process of assembling found fragments, each of which can retain its acquired meaning but also contribute to a complex arrangement that communicates a new narrative. Collage therefore requires active 'reading' or reflection to decode potentially multiple or even contradictory messages. Collage as a practice also applies to the incremental addition of structures and building elements over time and it as old as architecture.

> "A *church of the 11th century might be added or altered in the 12th, 13th, 14th, 15th, 16th, or even the 17th or 18th centuries; but every change, whatever history it destroyed, left history in the gap, and was alive with the spirit of the deeds done midst its fashioning.*" (William Morris: 1877).

Curtilage: *noun – origin: Middle English from Anglo-Norman French, variant of Old French 'courtillage', from 'courtil' (small court), from 'cort' (court). An area of land attached to a house and forming one enclosure with it.*

The intimate setting around historic buildings affects the financial landscape as much as the visual or cultural landscape and the judgement regarding preservation, adaptation or demolition remains variable. The growth of 'Permitted Development' under successive market-focused governments weakens the notion of curtilage.

   In the UK local planning authorities decide on the extent of the curtilage of a listed building. A clear framework centrally considered against benchmarks is the alternative, however if development rights around a listed building are removed, then that determination requires robust justification. All listed buildings require clear fields of context to be defined around them, supported by a simple matrix of values reflecting the purpose and historic relationships the ensemble of buildings sustain.

Halcyon(ism): *adjective – origin: Middle English 'alceon', from Latin 'halcyon', from Greek 'alky n', 'halky n'(Merriam-Webster Dictionary, online). Alluding to a period of time in the past that was idyllically happy and peaceful – the desire for a conflict-free and unarguable state of reaffirmation (Oxford Dictionaries, online).*

Montage: *noun – from the French 'monter' (to mount, to put up).*

Montage is a process of assembling temporal fragments where the fragments are made, not found, holding meaning collectively in an arrangement creating a seamless, singular experience, often immersive to communicate a distinct message. In cinema, montage is the process or technique of editing together different pictorial sources into a single, coherent composition. This critical cinematic process was articulated by Sergei Eisenstein (1989–1948) as a form of dialectic – structuring how image sequences create tension and confirmation to provoke emotional responses with the viewer – for Eisenstein montage was essentially ideological. Montage overtook collage as the 20th century's preeminent assembly practice, Montage's cinematic and time-based determinism grew appropriate for the computer generated representation.

Nostalgia: *noun – a sentimental longing or wistful affection for the past, typically for a period or place with happy memories. Origin late 18th century: modern Latin translating German 'Heimweh' (homesickness), from Greek 'nostos' + 'algos' (to return home + pain) (Oxford Dictionaries, online). Note reaffirmation of a better time or place indicating profound unhappiness with the contemporary – a negative with the appearance of the positive.*

Repair: *noun – replacement in order to effect ongoing performance and purpose, usually in response to a particular event or material failure.*

Repair was advocated by Morris as the means to prolong active use and sustain historic buildings.

Renovation: *noun – the interface between an old building with new construction in order to attain new requirements for physical or operational performance.*

This operation should require a high degree of historic fabric expertise, ability in user and stakeholder engagement to co-create an effective and achievable brief that balances the needs of the users with the long term heritage interests of the building, and design ability to realise a contemporary intervention that adds positively to the fabric of the building. This is the most complex process in heritage work.

Tangible: *adjective and noun – origin: late 16th century, from French 'tangible', or from late Latin 'tangibili' (perceptible by touch; clear and definite; real) (Oxford Dictionaries, online).*

Tangible heritage is a term describing apparent physical historic fabric.

Intangible: *adjective – origin: early 17th century, from French, or from medieval Latin 'intangibilis', from 'in' (not) + late Latin 'tangibilis' (tangible). Unable to be touched; not having physical presence (Oxford Dictionaries, online).*

Intangible heritage is a term used to describe historical association not necessarily evidenced in the materiality of a place. Among the others, it can include notions linked to culture, memory, traditions, legacy, authenticity, locality.

Value: *noun and verb – origin: Old French, feminine past participle of 'valoir' (to be worth), from Latin 'valere'. Importance, worth, or usefulness of something, the material or monetary worth of something; principles or standards of behaviour; important or beneficial (Oxford Dictionaries, online).*

Important, beneficial, useful and monetised, the concatenation of social value with financial value is a critical flaw within the word that is interchangeable between something commonly shared and used or privately owned and traded. This double bind has consequences for the language of heritage and its production.

3.1 Covent Garden

Covent Garden sustained a relationship between dense collective work and dense, collective built fabric. A market garden for the Abbey of Westminster, the presence of a vegetable market existed from the 14th century until the late 20th. The consistent history of the place is one of redevelopment and displacement – Henry VIII co-opted the convent and through his largess the Earl of Bedford built an impressive home on the 47 acres known as Covent Garden. The fourth earl instigated the largest urban redevelopment project in London since Roman times when, in 1630 he commissioned Inigo Jones to draw up a comprehensive Italianate piazza with exclusive housing, requiring the creation of a new parish and church positioned in relation to the piazza as the temple was positioned in a Roman forum. The existing cottages of the poor were removed. The fire of 1666 destroyed many of London's markets and Covent Garden, having escaped the fire, expanded to fill the void, becoming a chartered market in 1670. The market commenced a socio-economic shift as the wealthy moved to newer areas of development, leaving space in a reverse gentrification of the 100 acres the area had become to artists, writers and performers alongside the market and small tradespeople.

By 1740 significant commercial activity characterised the area, a brewery covered 4 acres, an iron foundry filled an entire city block and printworks joined the highly mixed economy that the Bedford estate actively facilitated. In the 1830s Fowler's neo-classical market buildings filled the piazza and still stand. The positive statistics of activity came at a social cost, however, as the dense urban fabric in which the urban working poor lived was squalid – Lord Shaftesbury brought his philanthropic 'Society for Improving the Conditions of the Working Classes' to Covent Garden in 1854, when a thousand people lived in thirteen ten-roomed houses with no sanitation. The intensity of the place was documented by Dickens (1857) – "a place of past and present mystery, romance, abundance, want, beauty, ugliness, fair country gardens, and foul street gutters; all confused together."[1]

> Cultural memory is the collective understandings of the past as they are held by a people in any given social and historical context. . . . Ideas of cultural memory are therefore laden with politics and power relationships as statements about the past become meaningful through becoming embedded within the cultural and material context of a particular time.
>
> (Harvey, 2008: 21)

As a physical environment the tightly arranged historic street pattern and predominantly 19th-century buildings sustained an intense set of occupations including printworks and a brewery in addition to the expanding vegetable and flower market. Redevelopment in the 19th century was sporadic; raised rentals arising from new buildings quickly falling foul of subletting as the community maintained its presence, although demolitions that cut highways such as Charing Cross Road through the dense urban territory (which displaced four thousand people alone) were already demonstrating the priorities of the authorities who increasingly saw urban density as a problem to be solved through infrastructure – movement as a paradigm for efficiency allied to health combining to underpin a modernity that generated intensity but expended huge reserves of capital and energy in cutting through it or undermining it. From

Haussmann's Paris to Robert Moses's Bronx freeways, the city fabric of human interactions and small-scale entrepreneurialism was considered an issue to be mastered rather than the body politic of 'capital' itself. Covent Garden acutely illustrates this difference between social capital and a capitalised society.

By the 1960s the market had filled much of the large-scale industrial space of ironworks and brewery. The exponential growth had led the Bedford family to look at state adoption of the market; the unwillingness of the authorities to do this led the Beecham Estate to take it from their hands. The war damage led to a significant decline in population, dropping from 1901's census of nine thousand to only four thousand in 1960. Lower residential numbers did not mean lower working numbers however; in the 1960s the area supported thirty thousand workers in seventeen hundred businesses with five thousand in the market alone, seventeen theatres, two national newspapers, two opera houses, four hospitals and six churches. Poverty remained, with a lack of sanitation and overcrowding lasting into the 1970s.[2]

The Greater London Council (GLC) finally took control of the market in 1961, purchased at a cost of £300,000 per acre of its 14-acre site. Its removal to a peripheral site released not only congestion, but the site and the ambitions of the infrastructure led redevelopment of the site, with a four-lane highway through the centre of the site being the driver for change. The 'Covent Garden Area Draft Plan' was issued in 1968; within it text and image combine to articulate the GLC's attitude to the place under redevelopment, much of it being the curtilage to numerous listed buildings:

> Apart from few well known buildings of importance such as the Royal Opera House, the Theatre Royal, Drury lane, and St Paul's Church, the Covent Garden area may not at first sight appear to contain much of architectural merit.[3]
> (GLC, 1968: 20)

The Plan acknowledged the family businesses, the "special flavour" of the area, detailing "a surprisingly large number of buildings of real merit and interest" and "a long and distinctive history still subtly expressed in its present character", however also noted that preservation was within the context of "planning objectives for the area". The only record of the area within the Draft Plan, entitled rather uncompromisingly *Covent Garden's Moving*,[4] is a double spread of a collage of photographic fragments that cut away the ground and show a sparse number of people, emphasising the need for redevelopment and the unimportant ground on which the buildings sit.

The acknowledgement of what was about to be removed was tragic in the real sense of the word, as land values rose to £1 million per acre in anticipation of capital return, the impact on the residents through rent rise evidenced in the erosion of daily life – the thirteen greengrocers in Neal Street in 1960 fell to four in 1970. With landlords stalling building repairs in the lead up to wholesale demolition, people's environments decayed around them.

After the relocation of the flower market, the working-class quarter of Covent Garden was subject to a Greater London Council *Comprehensive Development Plan*, placing an international conference centre onto Inigo Jones's piazza, hotels by the corporate architect Seifert and Partners and seven and a half thousand parking spaces (when the total car ownership within Covent Garden was three hundred cars). Some of the heritage buildings were retained in the plan, but the area was divided into commercial strips and a park, cut through with new roads and pedestrianised retail.

*Figure 3.1
Covent Garden's
Moving – GLC
draft plan, 1968.*

*Source: Courtesy
Covent Garden
Community
Association*

COVENT GARDEN'S MOVING

COVENT GARDEN AREA DRAFT PLAN
CONSORTIUM OF
GREATER LONDON COUNCIL
CITY OF WESTMINSTER
LONDON BOROUGH OF CAMDEN

The redevelopment proposed the following:

- Five historic theatres would be destroyed, and many more compromised.
- A new office and walkway complex would dominate the south side, with a conference centre and high-rise tourist hotel on the east side and an extended Royal Opera House along much of the north side.
- The central market halls would be rehabilitated with shops and restaurants, under a plastic roof.

THE MARKET BUILDING

ST PAULS & THE PIAZZA

ROYAL OPERA HOUSE & BOW STREET

GREAT QUEEN STREET

BROAD COURT

Figure 3.2 and 3.3
'Character Study' from 'Covent Garden's Moving' Draft Plan, 1968.
Source: Courtesy London Metropolitan Archive

Figure 3.3 (Continued)

- The glass and ironwork floral halls and the Jubilee market hall demolished.
- Cambridge Circus replaced by a 'major new landmark' with a sports centre, an 'elevated public transport corridor' and residential units on the upper floors.
- Most of Seven Dials across to Holborn would be rebuilt as offices and new housing blocks.
- A 4-acre park would eliminate half the buildings from King Street up to Shelton Street, destroying the Woodyard Brewery and half of Long Acre.
- More than 7,500 parking spaces would be created in the area; yet the local population then owned fewer than 300 cars.

The planning authorities conducted a communication strategy using the tactics of disempowerment, described by Gordon Gardiner MP as "the most exciting comprehensive development scheme since the Great Fire of 1666" (Bransford, 2012).[5] The sensitivity deficit was intrinsic to the belief that redevelopment benefits were strategic for the city, allied to an attitude towards the 'old city' that saw it as a dormant opportunity for financialisation. The definition of key heritage emblems to populate the 'new city' betrayed a curious echo of le Corbusier's Plan Voisin for Paris in 1925, where the central arrondissement was erased save a handful of key monuments that sporadically populated an urban park for the modern metropolis surrounding it. The requirement for compulsory purchase required a public enquiry, and this legal oversight mechanism forced a more 'conservation'-based approach to the redevelopment which revised the Plan in 1971, shrinking the demolition area by approximately half, dropping a portion of the ring road and facilitating only five thousand car parking spaces.

The announcement of the plan created community action and financial reaction in equal measure. With newspaper headlines such as "London theatres at risk" and "Revolt in the cities", Covent Garden soon became a national issue. Over the next few months *The Times* and *The Guardian* devoted entire pages to the subject. In parallel, by 1971 the land was now worth £2 million an acre. What is of interest to the discussion of cultural value is identified accurately by the cultural magazine *Timeout* in an edition on 14th May 1971 "All those tourists the GLC expected to fill the new hotels and the developers want to see shopping in the new boutiques didn't come for Covent Carnaby at all, they came looking for England. Soon they won't find it anywhere".[6] *Timeout* understood the fundamental disjuncture between cultural value created by individuals, social collectives and circumstance, and the subsequent exploitation of the capital value that development of such cultural expression.

It is estimated that seven hundred residents, – about a quarter of the permanent population – were moved out of Covent Garden between 1971 and 1972, by which time the land was changing hands at £5 million per acre, still without the redevelopment being ratified by government, but with the entire expectation that it would be.

> Individual freedom is to be sacrificed to a public good that is in the minds only of the planners – and possibly the developers. The plan aims to make the developers the privileged heirs to a domain in which individuals have long enjoyed freedom.
>
> (Robin Middleton in Bransford, 2012)

The objectors to this modernisation focussed on the community, their rights and the undemocratic processes used, it was claimed, to achieve the land consolidation

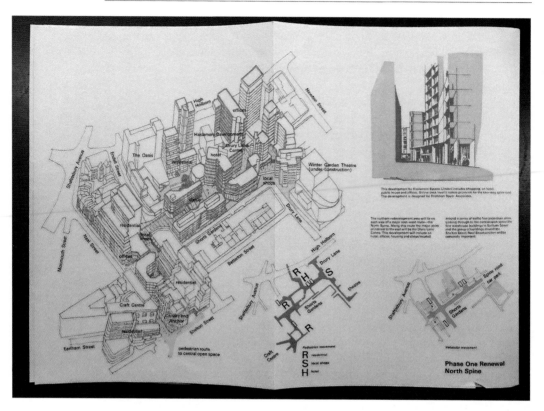

Figure 3.4
Covent Garden – the next step – Revised Plan for the Proposed comprehensive development Area, May 1971: Phase One Renewal North Spine. The creator and copyright holder could not be established according to Westminster City, Camden and Metropolitan Archives.
Source: *Courtesy Covent Garden Community Association*

necessary for redevelopment, with vandalism and arson allegedly employed by the GLC to hasten the emptying of properties. The arguments countering the redevelopment were utterly valid, but conceding ground to highly publicised community action only a few years after the student-led riots in Paris in 1969 would set a dangerous precedent. The mechanism that the (then) secretary of state, Geoffrey Rippon, used in January 1973 to concede a very political volte-face was to list two hundred and fifty buildings located sporadically throughout the area and require detailed public consultation on the redevelopment – effectively halting the process but without overturning the machinery of the state. Buildings that were simply built to be socially useful and never as 'heritage' became heritage and therefore a means of conserving the communities that built them and occupied them. With the buildings in poor condition, the community led a series of initiatives to demonstrate that localised repair was a viable alternative to localised redevelopment through the Covent Garden Forum – culminating in the community's alternative development plan *Keep the Elephants out of the Garden*, which was largely adopted in the new *Area Plan* in 1978. Consistent pressure from the community over the provision of social housing in the area culminated in the

GLC losing a judicial review in 1981, which established for the first time the rights of community groups, not only landowners, to take legal action over land disputes.

History is (not) what it used to be

"The sickening hideousness of London, the metropolis of the nation, which has worked out the sum of commercialism most completely, seems to me a mark of disgrace branded on our wire-drawn refinement to show that it is based on the worst kind of theft – legal stealing from the poor".

(Morris, 1888)

"I just not leave the truth unstated, that it is again no question of expediency or feeling whether we shall preserve the buildings of the past or not. We have no right whatsoever to touch them. They are not ours, they belong partly to those who built them, and partly to all the generations of mankind who are to follow us".

(Ruskin, 1889: 197)

Heritage and the historic built fabric can be critical in framing social relations and, in the case of Covent Garden, play a political role in the lives of ordinary people. So were Ruskin and Morris right? Can the relationship between local people and historic buildings provide a vehicle for resistance to capitalisation and refocus on the key question of who inherits what when considering the space of the city?

However, when articulating preservation over restoration, Ruskin was speaking about buildings of monumental importance – the Gothic and the Byzantine, the palazzi of Venice or the ruins of Rome. With the subsequent articulation of conservation through successive interpretations, this difference between the historic everyday and the monument has become blurred. When Morris extolled the virtue of historic change over time, with "history left in the gaps"[7] (Morris, 1877) between historic accretion and addition, was he talking about the same buildings as Ruskin? Or was he rather discussing a more prosaic version of historic buildings related to the everyday? The resistance shown to comprehensive redevelopment in Covent Garden was an attempt to secure the effective everyday rather than preserve the monumental. Frequently we understand heritage as built fabric. The community actions evidence an alternative reading of heritage, where the built fabric has value as an indivisible part of everyday life. Significance is not the fact that a building has a history, but that is has a present which is part of a continuity of use which has intrinsic social value and sustains social capital. This definition of heritage creates problems, however, when viewed through a conservation expert's lens. If the greatest significance an old building has is that is sustains the everyday, then there is nothing to interpret. There is nothing to restore because it is what it is. Later in the book we will explore the ramifications of heritage 'as found', but the role and importance of the everyday requires further evaluation.

There is a distinct critical narrative around the political role of the everyday that has its clearest expression in the writings of Henri Lefebvre, and is usually interpreted as a valorization of the everyday as a form of nostalgia blended with an act of resistance –

As Henri Lefebvre emphasized, the concept of everyday life is politically ambivalent – organised passivity of mass consumer society and the historical

KEEP THE ELEPHANTS
OUT OF THE GARDEN
covent garden community association 836 3355

Figure 3.5
Keep the Elephants Out of the Garden', cover, 1978.
Source: Courtesy Covent Garden Community Association

resource for emancipation from that passivity are located in a world before the dominance of consumerism and the bureaucratic state.

(Sands, 2013)

The interesting aspect of Covent Garden is that, as we see in the earlier quotation from the Pall Mall Gazette in 1888, this is not a new phenomenon, and consequently each generation's 'everyday' is constantly shifting to defend and develop its place in the city. The cities historicisation in the late 20th century is in itself an historically derived phenomena, an extension of the commodification process that extends beyond the stimulation of desire for the new into a realm where the old can itself be reinvented as new, re-valued and re-experienced. That hard evidence around historical significance is lacking is, according to David Lowenthal, unimportant to the public, "who are mostly credulous, undemanding, accustomed to heritage mystique, and often laud the distortions, omissions, and fabrications central to heritage reconstruction" (Lowenthal, 2011: 249). Risk in using the everyday as a political rallying cry is the risk in fictionalising an area as a distinct historical trajectory – naming it separates it and defines both collectivity and segregation that historically never existed. Covent Garden and the world observed by Dickens' *Little Dorrit* had overlapping everydays, not a singular identity of a singular group. History is an interesting phenomenon in this regard – while it is being made in the moment it is a complex interplay between actors and places; once studies and 'written' it becomes a partial fabrication subject to subjectivity, available evidence and hearsay. History is subject to the degradation of evidence over time; voices, memories, documentation and buildings all weather at different rates and blur the clarity of the moment as it passes. For the protestors of Covent Garden, the experience of continuity of occupation was the most immediate priority and the buildings formed part of that continuity.

The historical fabric was in effect a *de facto* 'commons', its role being to resist enclosure. The historic fabric was not a proxy for a social body, not used as a monument to be defended but simply the place in which the social body resided. This lack of sentimentality about the buildings is perhaps explained by the consistency of poverty in the area. There was no nostalgia for poverty as a past collective experience with which to identify and unify; it was a living, fragile actuality that simply resented being evicted through bureaucratic opportunism. This strategic use of heritage as a tactical asset was, for a short time at least, able to generate a number of locally led interventions that could be, somewhat romantically, characterised as the end of wholesale redevelopment of existing urban settings and forcing a shift to brownfield sites such as Canary Wharf or the London Docklands to realise the vociferous demands of efficient land capitalisation. Only after the resistance was successful did the consequences of designating the area as 'historically significant' become visible.

The financialisation process proved itself to be highly flexible. In reality, overturning the Covent Garden redevelopment agenda simply altered the redevelopment agenda, rather than replacing it with an alternative. "The true and tragic irony of the original GLC plan was that the people of Covent Garden, the living, breathing Covent Garden, would be destroyed by the crowds scrambling to be part of that culture themselves" (Bransford, 2012). The original 1968 assessment of the area as having a 'special flavour' became the tool to revalue land.

> There was a time in the 80s and 90s when it was absolute heaven – small, local, crafty shops with real community feeling. Artists, originality, greasy

cafes, Covent Garden General Store, the pen shop where Charles Dickens bought his nibs! And going in there you just really get the sense that these were the floorboards Charles Dickens walked on. . . . Then came the commercial rape when Starbucks, Costa, and mediocrity squeezed out the greasy cafes and swamped us with their crap, so uniform and corporate. The M&S on Long Acre replaced the General Store and the floorboards of the pen shop are now shiny and clean.

(Jo Weir in *ibidem*)

Figures 3.6 and 3.7
Covent Garden in the 1970s, from 'Covent Garden, the next step. The Revised Plan for the proposed Comprehensive Development Area' and Covent Garden today.
Source: *Courtesy London Metropolitan Archive and picture by the authors, 2019*

That the Covent Garden Community Association didn't play the 'heritage card' in their initial confrontations with the GLC is not because the fabric of Covent Garden wasn't valued. On the contrary, Jo Weir's comments show exactly how significant the relationship between buildings and people was. Weir articulates very clearly that it is the unfolding continuity of action that is important, one that absorbs changing activities and faces because there is a relational value that evolves within its environment. Rape is a powerful word that she uses when referring to the new owners of a café lease – how significant is the proprietor of the café? The building and the coffee are the same, surely? If buildings are heritage then there is a preservation at work that secures the significance of the place – or not? Clearly not. As Covent Garden's evolution demonstrates, when the tactics for maintaining a local social fabric is broken by corporate rental agreements and

Figure 3.7 (Continued)

the importation of capitalised and globally standardised goods and an underpaid work-force that cannot afford to live anywhere near central London, the disconnect between people and the buildings that occupy and define a place has profound implications.

The disconnect between buildings and actions began as soon as the GLC redevelopment plan was abandoned. The GLC Architects Department shifted attention from replanning to restoring. Fowler's Central Market Building was 'conserved' between 1975–80 as a retail venue to accommodate a pub, shopping and restaurants; the project was a model of 'scholarly' restoration and adaptation. In order to meet the demands of fire regulations, and in parallel to amplify lettable floorspace, the southern glazed hall was excavated at basement level to create a sunken floor of shops. The large 'gas' lanterns were electrified and crowned with pineapples provided 'heritage hints' to the building's former use, whilst providing a scholarly reference to the status of the pineapple in Georgian high society, it being a highly prized indicator of wealth, influence and taste on the part of the gentry who were able to procure such hard-to-obtain fruits from the colonies. That the pineapple has the associations with privileged colonial exploitation might have, on reflection, made its emblematic use inappropriate; however the sign has a limited

Figures 3.8 and 3.9
Covent Garden arcade in the 1970s, from 'Covent Garden, the next step. The Revised Plan for the proposed Comprehensive Development Area' and Covent Garden arcade today.

Source: courtesy London Metropolitan Archive and picture by the authors, 2019

number of significance levels and, as Lowenthal already noted, most people wouldn't get it anyway. Pineapple – used to be a fruit market – heritage communication done.

Capital has the legacy of emptying meaning whilst exploiting meaning. The natural tactic for contemporary capital requires the neutralisation of heritage as an impediment to development. The simplest method for doing this is the adoption of its language, the language of reassurance. The increasing retention of post-industrial fragments within hard-nosed urban regeneration schemes such as Kings Cross, or any number of factory loft conversions in the major former industrial cities or docks of Britain attest to this strategy. The politically pessimistic look dejected at the way heritage buildings become heritage 'assets', how major redevelopments since Covent Garden are now called 'regeneration', and projects such as Kings Cross shift landmarks and features such as gas holders, railway lines, cobblestones and connectivity, remove working class people and their jobs, privatise public space and make heritage the centrepiece of otherwise mediocre commercial space.

The tactical definition of built heritage as both sign and signifier became the mechanism by which the employment of five thousand people as a collective, socially interactive enterprise in the market and the ability to buy groceries from a local shop are replaced with contractually tenuous retail and service sector employment. The continuity between the market costermonger and the shop assistant is that neither were paid adequately for their work, but the difference is the presence of a working community that sustained the daily life of the costermonger and the lack of it now.

Figure 3.9 (Continued)

Figure 3.10

Covent Garden today.

Source: Picture by the authors, 2019

So is the adoption of history a bad thing? When does 'creative reuse' for public benefit slip into the exploitation of historically derived culture for profit? Is culture really anything more than a financial transaction? This leading question is revisited through the following narrative as its implications are huge and the answers it provides are nuanced. What is the difference between contemporary heritage preservation and the one discussed by Morris? Rather than attempt to answer directly, partly because the answer is far from definitive, we would suggest that conservation has the capacity to shift power from corporate level to local level, which is intrinsically interesting, and offers a tantalising alternative mode of operation from conventional architecture which exists to fulfil the brief of individuals, not the collective, often those holding corporate power.

> At one level, heritage today is about "the promotion of a consensus version of history by state-sanctioned cultural institutions and elites to regulate cultural and social tensions in the present. On the other hand, heritage may also be a resource that is used to challenge and redefine received values and identities by a range of subaltern groups.
>
> (Smith, 2006: 4)

3.2 Battersea Power Station

Battersea Power Station (BPS) is part the Vauxhall, Battersea Power station and Nine Elms opportunity area (VNEB OA),[8] 195 hectares of land including former industrial and transport spaces which have been in disuse until recently. It includes the site of the new Covent Garden, when it was moved entirely across the river to Nine Elms in 1974, when the city centre was no longer able to absorb the complex disorder associated with the place. Just on the other side of Nine Elms Lane lays the plot of Battersea Power Station. The area was subject to a number of tentative projects of regeneration since the 1980s when the power station shut down. Every time the area of interest modified slightly, expanding from the first projects inside the single building of the power station to wider schemes involving its surrounding. Surely, both visionary plans and lucrative projects alternated, up to a point when distinguishing the two was impossible. Some of them lasted longer, under developers who more than others held to the scheme; others were the result of competitions, open bids, or tenders forming a more ephemeral and heterogeneous group of proposals.[9] For some, BPS could be a new home for Westminster or the European Parliament, it could host flats for the elderly, an industrial museum, a church, a mosque, a sport centre, a leisure centre (1980); a shopping centre, a conference hall, a refuse burning plan (1984), a business design centre (1990); it could be transformed into a floating art piece as imagined by Cedric Price (1984) or a religious theme park as for the proposal of the Holy Trinity Church in Brompton (1996); a Noddyland Theme Park by the Trocadero company at Leicester Square (1996); a "self-contained fantasy centre" in a joint venture between Michael Jackson and a Saudi Arabian Prince (1997); or a new home for Chelsea Football Club and stadium as the ambitious idea of owner Roman Abramovich (2012). Planning approval was granted in turn to different projects (1982, 1986, 1997, 2000, 2005, 2010) and every time overseen by the Borough of Wandsworth, whose laissez-faire attitude had often been cited as allowing this number of failures to happen.

In time, the area of interest around the iconic building expanded, including the borough of Lambeth. With the expansion of the city, these boroughs occupied a convenient semi-central position and plenty of available land, which had been increasing its value in time due to the failure of the projects on site accompanied by a number of planning permissions with active legal status. While the city lifestyle rose in attractiveness, connections to neighbouring areas with historical prestige, such as Chelsea, started to be promoted. Wandsworth and Lambeth were desirable areas where yields could be guaranteed despite the aggressiveness of the housing market. Battersea Power Station became an iconic point of reference for the area, while the presence of institutional buildings such as the US embassy contributed to building the prestige of the location. It is interesting to observe how the regeneration projects that were proposed, time after time, evolved around the narratives associated with the power station. It is argued that the expanding allusion to heritage scaled up with time, becoming a matter of global proportions. Heritage grew as a symbol of authenticity and originality, eventually supporting the economic value of the interventions through culture. The result is

> a luxury real estate for wealthy investors to put their money into, high-spec
> apartments that save the needs of investors' portfolios rather than home

Figure 3.11
Battersea Power Station building site from the adjacent neighbourhood.
Source: Picture by the authors, 2016

seekers, vanity projects that in their architectural inadequacy, damage the fabric and integrity of the power station itself.

(Watts, 2016: 231)

The observation of communication strategies and promotional images helps to understand the simplification of meaning associated with urban transformation and the process of value creation that employs heritage as a creator of meaning.

However, it is not our intention here to recall all the events that led to the project as we know it today, or to describe how each phase dealt with regeneration. The book by Paul Watt, *Up in Smoke: the failed projects of Battersea Power Station* effectively traces back the main events for the design and development of the power station since its early days and analyses in detail the evolution of the project during the Broome years (1984–1993), the Parkview years (1993–2006) and the Treasury years (2006–2010).

Rather it is interesting to operate a selected focus on heritage and to highlight the initiatives that contributed to the process of heritage valorization that built the significance of the power station with specific reference to notions of history and culture. These include planning proposals focussing on national culture, design inspirations recalling the element of English vernacular architecture, the adoption of marketing narratives rooted in popular culture, the recognition of the attractive power of heritage in terms of investment, and the will to tap into global rhetoric of national representation.

Surely, since the very start, the project for Battersea Power Station was tightly bound to context-related concerns and had to address a number of issues. One of them was the pleasantness of the design: with a generating capacity of 360,000 kW, it was the first building of that dimension to be created in London. It was expected to provide electricity for the whole city and become a symbol of English industrial intelligence.

When in 1930 the London Power Company (LPC) announced the project, it needed to prove the quality of the design and to do so it insisted on efficiency, clean emissions, and "distinctive elevation" (*ivi*). This last point was to be cared for by Sir Giles Gilbert Scott. Scott was popular for the design of the K2 kiosk, the famous red phone box. Quite interestingly, his design for the kiosk featured elements of traditional British architecture: the domed top was inspired by Sir John Soane's mausoleum and its application to a modern object, otherwise alien to the streets of the city or town, had the effect to make it reassuring (*ivi*: 51). The same strategy was applied to Battersea, where references to the past were collected, mixed and pasted together with the aim to make the object both innovative and recognisable, massive and detailed, traditionalist and modernist. The final solution was characterised by a prevailing art deco style, but the chimneys are neoclassical fluted columns. Again, they bridge a double aspiration: if their aspect is reassuringly familiar, their size points out to a different epoch – to skyscrapers rather than temples. The building was completed in 1935. The *Daily Mail* defined it as the "flaming altar of a modern temple of power" (*ivi*: 57) and in 1937 it appeared on the cover of *Wonders of World Engineering*. As early as 1939, a poll conducted by the *Architect's Journal* voted it as the second most popular modern building in Britain (*ivi*: 61). The fourth chimney went up only in 1955, and at the time it was providing power to a fifth of London. However, the diversification of national electricity generation started to make the building rapidly obsolete and Battersea started powering down, until the very last operating chimney was shut in 1983. Before the area was sold to John Broome in the same year, some proposals were put forward.

A first proposition by Mark Leslie aimed to create a technology theme park inspired to the funfair that stood on Battersea Park between 1951 and 1974. However, the idea was soon replaced by a new proposal when Broome, a funfair operator father to the Alton Towers, was brought in. The Texan firm (LARC) he appointed presented the consortium with a scheme based on their interpretation of British history.

> They decided that Britain's best contribution to the world was the British Empire, so they designed a whole theme park . . . on the theme of the Empire. They'd never heard about Industrial Revolution, they thought America had invented everything. Except that were struggling to find anything to celebrate the Empire that wasn't contentious. They could have a cracking theme park on the horrors of Empire, slavery, massacres, sodomy – but the bankers would have hated it.
>
> (Leslie *ivi*: 124–125)

Indeed, dealing with history was complicated. Some decades later, culture was put at the centre of the theme park, this time referring more softly to general cliché belonging to the five continents. Surely, the inspiration offered by local culture – as for the Leslie's scheme, and national culture – as for the LARC proposal, was central to the approach of Battersea area. In the following years, the scheme grew less bounded to notions of memory and history: John Broome imported the idea of theme park and fit it inside the power station. The drawings of the time are generic, although some allusion to Tudor architecture can be spotted inside the watercolours. In general, very scarce relationships with the context were established, to the point that the advertising materials avoided showing the power station itself. Interiors and exteriors simply excluded it, maybe due to the fact that Broome's team was finding difficulties in stitching the Alton Tower model inside an oversized location for which there were no existing regulations. Nevertheless, other references to historic buildings were used to promote the site. The Battersea Powerhouse bulletin issued in September 1985 and 1988 include a wireline 3d of the power station with St. Paul's in it, announcing: "The Battersea could engulf St. Paul's!" (Watts, 2016). This will be one of the most repeated parables in the story of BPS marketing. "You could fit Trafalgar Square and St Paul's Cathedral inside, that's how big it is", Hwang would tell to *The Guardian* in 2005. And still today, the LIVE magazine, one of the most circulated real estate brochures with an international attitude declares: "St. Paul's cathedral could fit inside the main boiler house of the Power Station". The power station brochure (no date: 14), on the other hand, does not fail to recall the connection that links the power station with the red phone box: "Two design icons, one designer. The world-renowned London telephone box was one of architect Sir Giles Gilbert Scott's most memorable creations. The other was Battersea Power Station".

Figure 3.12
The once majestic view of Battersea Power station from Victoria Bridge.
Source: Picture by the authors, 2018

During the Parkview and Treasury years the reference to notions of history and cultured lowered all the more. The focus back then was on big projects and mixed-use redevelopments. Luxury hotels started to be imagined for the site, along with residences, high-end facilities and even a permanent location for the Cirque du Soleil. Projects from these years involved architectural firms and designers as John Outram Associates (JOA), Grimshaw Architects, Cecil Balmond and Raphael Viñoly.

In 2010 planning approval was granted to the revised scheme signed by Raphael Viñoly, and is the one that we know today. Overall, "the development was 57% residential, and of the remaining 43%, 1.2 m square feet were retail and restaurants, 1.7 m square feet were offices and the rest was hotel, leisure and community space" (Watts, 2016: 213). High density is promoted in the VNEB OA report as a way to "create a sense of place", a "place of growth with a distinctive heart", a "location with a strong sense of place and identity" but also an opportunity to upgrade the existing public realm, and provide strategic open space and new facilities. Well-known architectural firms were then called to deliver portions of it: Ian Simpson Architects are responsible for the apartments, offices and shops called Circus West on the railway-side; Norman Foster and Frank Gehry are inputting the scheme with some mixed-use buildings called Battersea Roof Gardens and Prospect Place; BIG is designing the Malaysian square at the end of Electric Boulevard; and Wilkinson Eyre is taking care of £1 billion refurbishment of the power station, with the rooftop gardens being designed by landscaper Andy Sturgeon. The power station itself will be turned into a shopping centre, with three floors of retail (as envisaged by David Roche 30 years before), a floor of leisure, a 2000-capacity arena and offices to be partially occupied by the MAC creative quarter. Cafés, bars and restaurant will be placed around the corners of the turbine hall and two additional glassed volumes with 245 apartments will be built on the roof between the chimneys and above the boiler house. Some of these apartments were sold off-plan for almost £4 million, and one studio flat was sold in 2014 for £1.5 million, which is how much David Roche paid the entire building and the land in 1984 (*ivi*: 217). The possibilities to invest in the area are eased by the fact that VNEB OA gained the status of Enterprise Zone in 2012. Financial facilitations as the incremental tax financing (TIF) and Community Infrastructure Levy (CIL) propose "new power that would allow councils to borrow against their predicted future increase in business rates over a 25-year period. The borrowing could then be used to fund development projects" (Out-Law, 2012). These tools are seen as of great importance for the future of redevelopments in the absence of new money by way of government grants. However, they also facilitate private capitals and financial interests to concentrate on specific areas, which then need to respond with proportionate returns to the risks undertook by market players. The New Covent Garden Market area, for example, will be reduced to make space to real estate development. The New Covent Garden Site announces: "new Covent Garden market, which currently operates on three sites totalling 57 acres, will be consolidated onto a single 37-acre site freeing up 20 acres of land for development". The shift towards real estate investments as a way to tackle the housing crisis is something that opened many debates on affordability. It is curious to notice how the present scheme for Battersea power station recalls another one that was put forward for the CEGB competition in 1983. The plan proposed a mix of luxury flats, retail, a hotel and a marina. At that time, in the hyper capitalistic 1984, the luxury flats that now dominate regeneration were considered socially unacceptable, and the scheme was rejected as being "substantially outside the brief" because it was giving nothing back to the community.

Figure 3.13
'The market that feeds London': hoarding around the new Covent Garden site set for
regeneration.
Source: Picture by the authors, 2017

Obviously, the political aims and economic needs which supported the project over the last 40 years changed considerably: developers grew more attentive to advertise and produce inclusive spaces, and Battersea Power Station ended up being a central location rich in potentiality. When in 1980 nobody was thought to love living close to an old industrial ruin, now the race for old buildings as valuable pieces of design has turned the attitude upside down. The economies supporting this trend act at both global and local level and the political discourse, more than anything else, reveals the centrality of this kind of operations.

The representation that we can see in the commercial brochures are the result of a long process that layered spatial visions and new means of representation and that fabricated the significance of well-recognisable symbols, as the chimneys of the power station. In this sense, the computer generated images (CGIs) that we know today, portraying the power station from the quay along the river, embed the evolution of CGIs since the 1980s, the pictorial feelings of the scenes from the Broome years, the elevate point of view from the Parkview years, lowered and counting on city context. One of them, by Wilkinson Eyre, shows the power station in the sunset, with lenient lights glimmering on the glassed façades. The tones and the colours are soft, sweetening the appearance of the giant building that is partially covered with reassuring and luxuriant trees. The perspective and the clouds in the sky recall another famous image, well planted in the mind of the viewer. And it's here that the lesson coming from embedding references of cultural significance is most evident. The image that is recalled is the cover of the album *Animals* by Pink Floyd, where the power station is portrayed with a similar angle, circled by clouds and dominating the urban context. However, the CGI by Wilkinson Eyre alleviates the anxious aspect given by the contrasting tones and dark shadows of the cover (in line with the contents of the album) and replaces them with a more pacified version of the landscape, suggesting harmonious and communal feelings.

Another symbol linked to the same album is used with ease inside the commercial brochure. This is the silhouette of Algie the pig, hanged between the two chimneys in 1977 thanks to an intuition of Roger Waters, who lived in Battersea at that time. The use of the pig and the constative tone of the album can't help but recall George Orwell's moral fable *Animal Farm* (1943), where the author was denouncing the corrupted political, moral and social landscape of the time. But Algie, in a way, did more than just become a symbol for the album and a prophetic act of contestation. It was considered fun by the people, without all its implicit political meanings, and contributed to shaping the imaginary of the power station, connecting to popular culture in a potent way. The advertisements in the brochure of the redevelopment exploit this symbol by detaching its cultural meaning from the political one and transforming the pig into a pop icon that nothing has to do with contestation. "Be at the heart of a pop cultural icon", says the *Office to Let* brochure of Battersea Power Station.

Although manufactured, the sense of continuity is a key element in the process of value creation through cultural rhetoric, because the connection with the past helps to give a sense of stability. This is central to proving the worth of big regeneration projects which, in fact, alter the surrounding extensively. However, continuity is mainly a matter of representation and has little to do with the reckoning of a layered process coming from the past. Rather, it establishes a connection with history through selected images chosen specifically to exclude any problematic legacy. In the last century, references to tradition have been widely used to instil values and behaviours whose implicit continuity with the past was expressly crafted.

When the project of the 'Crystal Palace' was firstly put forward in 1988, it reinterpreted Victorian high technology in a modern way, building on the palace's pioneering role on progressive engineering. At the time, Thatcher was eager to emulate former glories; it was clear the opportunity to restore political capital by offering continuity with the past. Similarly, Battersea Power Station, once the symbol of British industrial innovation, is about to host the Apple general quarter. The old polluting image of the building that created so many controversies in the first years of its functioning is replaced by a much brighter inaugural proposal: a "new spectacular campus" hosting 1,400 employees will make the productivity on the site active again. What is produced, this time, is clean energy. The white apple, icon of the Mac industry, becomes the symbol of a renewed way to think about innovation. Advertisements talk about a 'creative industry pole' bringing benefits for all: works on site and valuable manufacturing for the masses. The allusion to continuity is clear, as is its improving nature: the new 'producer' of electronic devices will settle on the same old site that generated energy for the city. Obviously, this is a simplification. The history related to industrial production of Battersea Power Station is far more complex than this. Most of all, what is excluded from the narrative is that the old factory offered works to local inhabitants, who were housed nearby as show the pictures of the epoch. Now, the Mac workers – as many others – will be more likely 'imported' from elsewhere, either commuting to work, or finding home close to the site thanks to a better salary. Work places for locals in these redevelopments are often relegated to service-related, low-paid roles. Other selections informing a sense of continuity involve specific parts of the power station. The iconic chimneys, dismantled and rebuilt 'as they were', acquire the grade of symbol of the symbol – proof of preservation and character. Once again, the preservation of the material and immaterial legacy of a site operates through cautious choices. Manufacturing the continuity with the past aims to generate emotional and symbolic recognition, and stability can be easily recalled because present choices seem rooted in the past.

As the highest symbol of the building's past industrial activity, they are among the features that developers cared about the most. That was not only a matter of heritage preservation, but a matter of image preservation that in turn meant preserving originality and securing the investment. Also, the chimneys in time became the symbol of the building and depositary of the affection that the larger public had for it. Wandsworth council leader Ravi Govindia said: "These giant chimneys are recognised the world over. The site's owners have understood their significance from day one and have gone to great lengths to restore them to their former glory. And delivered on their promises" (Prynn, 2017). The production of surplus value pairs with the credit to originality and the will to preserve historic architecture.

Heritage building

The relevance of heritage was built thanks to a number of inputs. These include both a process of patrimonialisation of the object and a tension linked to the market, interested to raise the value of the historic building. Its representations, therefore, are the result of layered efforts, some of which linked to the profession and to official recognition, others to the economic process. Both tap into the cultural significance of the building and exploit the affection it accumulated in time. This very special relationship between urban conservation and capital accumulation recalls Summerson's work *Georgian London* (1945), where the author analyses the genesis and development of Georgian London, highlighting how architecture was conditioned by social, economic and financial circumstances and discussing the value of permanence. In the case of the power station, the efforts to render it significant at the city and national scale evolved to the point where it became an international object of value. The change of scale, now tapping into global mechanisms of power, reveals how the construction of the narratives around the 'patrimonial object' shifted towards international interests. The proof being that the Malaysian SP Setia Company purchased the site in 2012 for around £400 billion, and now operates the scheme sharing the holdings with Sime Darby Property and EPF in the Battersea Project Holding Company, the joint venture which is the holding company for the project, while Battersea Power Station Development Company (BPSDC) is the main managing actor. "The Malaysian shareholders purchased the site in September 2012 and have since made significant progress including the successful completion of the first phase of the development which is now home to over 1,000 residents and a collection of independent retailers and restaurateurs," a BPSDC spokesperson said (Greenfield, 2018). Once again, the project became the vehicle of a political statement: it is "the symbol of the Malaysian's ability to play on the international stage" says Rob Tinknell, a Treasury Holding man now working for SP Setia (Greenfield, 2018). More recently, in January 2018, it was announced that the Malaysian sovereign wealth fund Permodalan Nasional Berhad (PNB), alongside Employees Provident Fund of Malaysia, intended to buy the Grade II listed building for £1.6 billion, making Battersea Power Station one of the Britain's largest-ever property deals (*ivi*). After the deal was announced, a BPSDC spokesman said: "The Battersea Power Station building would provide both investors with a unique investment opportunity to own an iconic development in the heart of London" (*ivi*). BPSDC will continue managing the site in this way creating a "solid platform that will ensure the protection, active management and control of the historically important building" (*ivi*).

A few months later, in June 2018 an article in *The Guardian* revealed that the deal was under threat after the frontrunner of Malaysian coalition Anwar Ibrahim, leading the recently elected Pakatan Harapan, said that the purchase would be investigated as part of the "dubious" investments secured by the previous coalition (Ramesh, 2018). But let's go back for a moment. On the 14th October 1980 the Secretary of State for Environment announced that BPS was to be given Grade II* listed building status. English Heritage explained that

> It was added to the National Heritage list in England in recognition of its powerful scale, celebrated silhouette, and that, as a power station it was the first to rationalize large-scale distribution of power. The building is a master-piece of industrial design. It is one of London's most prominent landmarks and one of a few with genuine claim to the title 'iconic'.
>
> (Watts, 2016: 100)

That looked unusual because, as it normally happened, discussion about listed buildings would circulate a while before they were prized. This time it happened all of a sudden although two campaign groups, the Thirties Society and the SAVE Britain's Heritage, had already been pushing for Battersea's protection (*ivi*: 102). At the same time, Battersea's listed status was seen as the clog to potential exploitation. Parkview's Michael Robert said

> I told them that they could do as much preservation as they wanted, but if you can't make the power station into a goose that lays a golden egg, it's only a question of time before it comes down. What we wanted was something for tomorrow and all they cared about was something for yesterday.
>
> (*ivi*: 167)

However, when Wandsworth calculated for a moment the possibility to knock it down to unlock development, it knew it would be a tough mission, going against both English Heritage and public opinion at the same time and so immediately discarded the option. The newspapers of the time recognised the building's significance not only in the eyes of experts but also to the population. An article from *The Times* explained that Battersea had "a place in the affection of many who care nothing about architecture", and it was a "supreme embodiment of thirties ideas about cathedrals and industries" (*ivi*: 103).

Through time, not only its historical status was regarded and protected, but was also exploited to inform heritage-based projects as the one by Terry Farrell, who proposed to transform BPS in a managed ruin. This proposal came towards the end of BPS's

Figure 3.14
'Icon Seeks Icon': hoarding on the Battersea power station working site.
Source: Picture by the authors, 2016

story, when many developers tried and failed, and when the contestation over the utility to keep the artefact were reaching a tipping point. His idea was that, if the power station needed to be the centre of the scheme, you could appreciate it much better by subtracting elements than filling the scheme with other volumes. The project – a giant park with few elements in it – was influenced by La Villette in Paris and the Emscher Park in the Ruhr, both incorporating industrial relics in the landscape. Another inspiration was Benjamin Franklin's Museum in Philadelphia, which is a steel frame structure of the house on its original site (*ivi*: 205). According to Farrell, this "would create a memory of the building that is truer to its history than what will actually happen" (*ibidem*). Besides the speculation on its historic value, the building became increasingly charged in cultural meaning. Since the inflated pig by Pink Floyd informed the minds of Londoners as a first imaginative postcard, a number of artistic productions followed suit to exploit the site. The film industry, in particular, often used Battersea as a filming location. Productions include Alfred Hitchcock's *Sabotage* (1936), *High Treason* (1951), *The Quatermass Experiment* by Hammer (1955), *Smashing Time* (1967), *Doctor Who* episode "The Dalek Invasion of Earth" (1964*), Children of Men* by Alfonso Cuarón (2006), *Superman III* by Richard Lester (1980), *The Meaning of Life* by Monty Python (1983), *Nineteen Eighty Four* by Michael Radford (1984), *Richard III* by Richard Locraine (1995), *The Dark Knight* by Christopher Nolan (2008) where Batman was unfurling his cape in the main turbine hall, *RocknRolla* by

Guy Richie (2008), *The Imaginarium of Doctor Parnassus* by Terry Gilliam (2009), and *The King's Speech* by Tom Hooper (2010) with scenes shot in the control room. Additionally, it was the location for BBC2 launch in 1964, it featured in the romp *Help!* from the Beatles (1965), it provided the backdrop for a number of launches (for Nike and *The Simpsons*), parties, concerts and challenges such as the annual Sport Vision's *London Freeze* event.

In 2017, the main Battersea Power Station redevelopment brochure dedicates two sections out of four to advertise the significance of Battersea Power Station through time. The sections are tiles HISTORY, CULTURE, PLACE and DESIGN. The first two can be read as a sort of legitimising prelude to the last two and aim to support a 'thought through' approach to design. The section called "HISTORY" starts with stating: "The very site which provided power for two generations now empowers yet another. It once created the energy that enabled people to live, work and entertain in the city, supplying a fifth of London's demand. Now, it will provide the venue for them to do the same". Other slogans follow: "A symbol of an age of industry, ingenuity and progress", "Power to drive London forward". To prove the role of history, a number of pictures portraying the silhouette, the workers, the architect and the interiors are paired with small texts reconstructing its story. When after 1980 BPS was granted the status of Grade II listed building, SAVE was worried to preserve as much as possible the buildings, including "features of interest in terms of industrial archaeology" such as coal crane and jetty, the huge cranes and gantries in the turbine hall (Watts, 2016: 106). What can be spotted on the billboards of the building site of the power station at the time of writing is exactly the same proposal. Cranes would be recovered; the industrial past will be a witness of the progress. But not only. The current project as presented is surrounded by an aura of eternality, as if it had always been there. This is typical advertisement style for many regeneration projects happening in London. They go as far as naming that "the heart of The Power Station, its turbine hall, had giant walls of polished terracotta and was likened to a Greek temple devoted to energy". Activating an imaginary linked to past glories is part of a strategy that aims to render the building an icon. "Icon seeks icons", screamed a giant banner around the construction site in 2016, and while we are cajoled by the fact that this could be addressed to us, other images show the rising importance of the site in relation to Chelsea. Traditionally one of the richest boroughs in town, Chelsea is now associated with the rising borough of Battersea. The geographical proximity is not only a good reason to reflect and rival the neighbour's richness, but also to compete on the symbolic value of the place. Battersea can welcome the new riches and equip them with one of the most loved monuments available.

The section called "CULTURE – A powerful Urban Canvas" pays tribute to the extremely rich series of events which contributed to the shaping of Battersea Power Station as a popular location. "Ever since opening, the iconic backdrop of Battersea Power Station has formed a versatile cultural canvas. From Pink Floyd to Batman, fashion catwalks to art from the Serpentine Gallery, the venue was, is, and always will be a focus for music, film, fashion and art". And again "For the 31 years since its closure, the unmistakable silhouette of Battersea Power Station has lured the cream of global culture into its mighty and powerful frame". Based on this CV, other slogans are put forward: "A venue for everything and everyone", "A new venue for a new era of performing arts", "A source of much inspiration" and promises are made explicit: "The recent cultural history of Battersea power station will be embodied in the new development and the biggest impact will be made with the turbine project space".

We should notice, at this point, that English culture is the only one involved in the project. It is sure that the Malaysian presence had been a big impact on the financial feasibility of the scheme up to now, and also on the architectonic outputs, showing how the two matters are intimately related. Malaysian Square, the main open space at the end of Electric Boulevard, is named after the investor's origin. But the tribute to culture involves architecture besides than naming. BIG's initial scheme, a sort of two level canyon, was 'inspired by Malaysian landscape and geology' (Watts, 2016: 211). This reveals how much the global financial exchange brings along with it transnational tributes to culture, and especially the culture of those sponsoring the redevelopment. It is not the exchange of favours that happened in the form of typical goods and objects of marvel between reigns, and it is not an exchange of expertise that instructs architecture. That is a tribute designed by a European company for its employer, an interpretation of a distant land through shapes – which disguise the geographical inspiration behind an all-too-obvious computer-generated landscape. Quite ironically, a very common means of visualization, the globally abused CGI, becomes the vehicle to inform and communicate place specificity. This is a key aspect to consider when looking at contemporary projects, all exploiting the exactness of virtual representation to describe generic landscapes.

Lessons learned

The dystopian movie *The Children of Men* by Alfonso Cuarón (2006) offers a good example of how preservation becomes a symbol of power, at the condition that there's someone able to recognise the privilege. In the movie, the protagonist Theo visits a friend inside Battersea Power Station, a building that mixes state functions with private collections. Artistic treasures and cultural objects are preserved inside here: Michelangelo's David, Picasso's Guernica hung behind the large dining table, and Algie, the Pink Floyd's pig flying between the chimneys, while the same power station is preserved as a heritage artefact (Fisher, 2009). The two men, clearly belonging to an élite, distance from a world fated to end: because of some catastrophe that caused mass sterility, humankind will disappear. When Theo asks his friend: "A hundred years from now there won't be one sad fuck to look at any of this. What keeps you going?", the other one answers: "You know what it is, Theo? I just don't think about it". He knows, "no cultural object retains its power when there are no eyes to see it" (*ivi*: 4). Without recognition, without a future, the past will disappear and will lose its significance. What does this mean? On the one hand, every past reference is reduced to an eternal present: opportunities are here and now, and references to history are used to validate the present due to their recognised authority. On the other hand, this produces a culture which is excessively nostalgic and unable to truly generate any novelty but just re-composed pre-packaged meanings.

The observation of Battersea Power Station story proves how the notions of culture and memory are increasingly used as redevelopment drivers to support operations which are financial in nature. We need to remember, however, that heritage is a very selective process, and that it refers to the ways chosen objects from the past are rearranged in new narratives (Harvey, 2008). Cultural, history, memory, traditions, are nonchalantly mixed under the overarching rhetoric of heritage, even if we know that they are very different things. What makes the reference to the past so intriguing is the contrast between the constant changes and innovations that characterise the present world and the attempt to attribute some eternal character to it (Hobsbawm and Ranger,

1983). This is because history lends a sense of everlasting legitimation and therefore the past is appropriated in order to construct the future as required. Overarching projects involving heritage carefully select a series of values able to build on this promise. Lowenthal (1985), identifies the principles that make past meaningful in four groups. Firstly, the past underpins the idea of continuity, progress and development. Secondly, the iconic status acquired by artefacts or landscapes helps to connect the present with the past alluding to evolution. Thirdly, the past provides a sense of termination: what happened in there has ended and we can continue our trajectory towards the future. Lastly, the past provides a "point of validation, a legitimation for the present in which actions and policies are justified by continuing references to" narratives of the past (Graham and Howard, 2008: 6). By extension, we can imagine the same traits to be applicable to heritage. Picking up from these reflections we could observe how legitimation was built by creating a sense of continuity with the past and offering a sense of stability. Another technique exploited to build the sense of legitimation is the fostering of recognisable elements at global and local levels. The global dimension is deemed to attract national and international attention, well-off and up-market investors, while the local one is deemed to involve inhabitants on the appreciation of on-site qualities and to nurture a sense of belonging. Examples at the global scale include the promotion of projects through the advertisement of 'unique qualities' liked to an historic English legacy. What can be noticed, overall, is that notions of heritage, memory and identity are often used to build and promote a number of redevelopment projects: pictures of monuments, parks, recognisable architectural and design features, are frequently included in the brochures and accompanied by key historical facts. "A cultural Icon", "A British Icon", "A design Icon", "Your home in a Global Icon" is the sequence of titles that appears in the LIVE brochure of Battersea Power Station. This strategy addresses a more general growth in aesthetic reflexivity (Kearns and Philo, 1993) that brought important consequences in the appreciation of the notion of authenticity. More and more, authenticity counts on visual taste and atmospheric appreciation, generic references and well-known symbols that can be easily circulated and understood, as the red phone boxes, the dome of St. Paul, and some images from the archives of the area. Their inclusion means instant recognition by external buyers, and therefore involvement. At the same time, the rhetoric linked to heritage involves the local scale. Newham Council's website titles one of its pages "Heritage and Place-making. By exploring and discovery what's on your doorstep, and rediscovering the past, we can gain a new appreciation of our localities by connecting people and place" (Newham Council). This reveals how heritage is also central to the inner promotion of the area and counts on local approbation beyond national attention.

The projects showed how a number of factors helped to build the significance of the place, the iconic status of a building or the affection of the population towards it. The value of the project was informed by layered processes that combined solid and more ephemeral proves of legacy until becoming not architectonically and culturally significant. But what is cultural significance? This is not simply a question of the composition of lime, it comes before the sourcing of the correct bricks or establishing the ingredients of original paint. Cultural significance is as relevant to the urban working class as it is to the discovery of Roman antiquities and forces us to become aware of how we prioritise one set of cultural values over another. Here value quickly becomes both social and financial, and the interplay between these two antagonistic understandings of value is at the heart of the heritage debate. Once the 'value' of a culture is officially established through expert recognition, conservation then engages historical and physical analysis to elaborate the evidence of cultural value, preserve that evidence, sometimes restore it, adapt it and as is frequently the case, make it into a financial as well as a cultural asset.

The Burra Charter[10] attempted to rebalance the archaeological or materialist bias of heritage definition through a focus on the cultural value of heritage and monuments; however, social meaning is far harder to define than the historically correct combination of lime and sand or method for evaluating a decayed piece of wood, so the tendency is still for heritage to be managed through science and image rather than socio-political criteria. Society is factional: what one street means to one group of people, another group may think the opposite. A single building in a bucolic setting presents fewer issues of contested social connection than a district in a metropolitan city centre, which is why perhaps the immediate image of a heritage building may be a castle rather than a street market or a tenement building. Our inherent attitudes to heritage require forensic examination because the overlooking of cultural heritage is part of the mechanism for supporting, even justifying, physical redevelopment. The issue with image and science in combination is precisely the appearance of social neutrality, making them very user-friendly tools for authorities in power. The strategic financial advantages to undervaluing working class neighbourhoods while lauding palaces were clearly recognised by John Ruskin as early as the 1830s, who in writing for J.C. Loudon's *Architecture Magazine* developed an argument for valuing ordinary vernacular buildings such as cottages and farmhouses for the contribution they made to the identity and legacy of a place (Burman, 2018: 34). The social value of local practice fundamentally informed Morris and Webb in their definition of conservation and dovetailed directly into Morris's developing socialism.

A capitalist society operates on the stimulation of consumption, with an unrestricted understanding of heritage becoming a potential impediment to such economic drivers. Heritage is a culturally loaded aspect of society; it has importance and creates identity. This is a threat therefore to economic opportunism and the need to utilise power structures to aid the accumulation of surplus capital. What was of interest in the narrative of Covent Garden was the role the historic buildings initially didn't play in the contest between the community and the planning authorities of the Greater London Council. Their role was developed within an unfolding narrative of redevelopment, social resistance and political expediency that saw, for a short historical moment, social heritage becoming fused with built heritage. Ultimately the balance was not to be sustainable and heritage was eventually used to support the regeneration and soften the political resistance.

The projects for Battersea Power Station absorbed the lessons, and heritage was eventually used as a pacifying element supporting both local character and national prestige. Here, the narrative linked to real estate promotion engulfed the complex process of patrimonialisation that layered in time. If up to a certain moment the different voices that contributed to the relevance of the object intertwined, after 2010 the process started to bend rapidly and to become something else. Something that surpassed the city and national ambition of representation to become a heritage product, distinctive of English taste and design, iconic of a lifestyle, and ultimately a safe investment.

However, recognising that heritage is a highly political process gives also the opportunity to reconsider the narrative that supports it. We should take into consideration the flexible nature of the rhetoric that generates around heritage and the possibility to be adopted by different subjects to support private or collective interests. On the one hand, heritage promotes

> consensus vision of history by state-sanctioned cultural institutions and élites to regulate cultural and social tensions in the present. On the other hand, heritage may also be a resource that is used to challenge and redefine received values and identities by a range of subaltern groups.
>
> (Smith, 2006: 4)

In the book *Tokyo Vernacular*, Jordan Sands (2013) explains how the rapid modernisation of the city paired with the will to preserve and promote heritage. In particular, the rediscovery of the past focuses on small and interstitial places that embody the vernacular language of the city and "seek what could be claimed as common property outside the spaces of corporate capitalism and the state" (*ivi*: 11). The neighbourhood scale and the space of daily appropriation become opportunities of adoption, and the antidote to a more cynical commodification of heritage by the market. These observations include the notion of change; they welcome mutability and recognise diversity.

It is urgent, therefore, to explore the language of heritage in order to understand how the concepts associated with it can be used in a productive way by different actors. Their malleability, despite being often exploited by ruling powers, can also be appropriated by other subjects. Language is not neutral, as we know. Language codifies cultural and political intentions and informs our understanding of place. The fabrication of visual languages associated to regeneration projects, as much as the fabrication of the built environment, always entails the making of shared meanings. We should distinguish the role of representation *per se* and narratives as tools able to shape urban understanding beyond marketing. When freed of distortion, urban imaginaries have a positive value and are essential to nurture the political dimension beyond technical and negotiating matters (Olmo, 2018: 22). Positive imaginaries help to inform an idea of city counting on knowledge, diversity and specificity as opposed to a city counting on the spectacularisation of procedures, the rapidity of change and the primacy of scientific answer to complexity.

It seems necessary to open up the tactics of development that adopt the inheritance of others for the purposes of real estate development and optimising investment return. By understanding the tools of 'regeneration', communities can advocate better and professionals can become aware of the processes that their work either challenges or enables. Also, by recognising the different voices that contribute to the shaping of spatial significance, it would be possible to start inclusive processes that interlace the inputs of private and public subjects.

Notes

1 From Charles Dickens (1857) *Little Dorrit*. Reprinted edition (1996), Wordsworth Editions Ltd, Ware.
2 Covent Garden Community Association (CGCA) Website. Available at: www.coventgarden.org.uk
3 Covent Garden's Moving, Draft Plan, GLC p. 20.
4 More information on the plan: www.sevendials.com/resources/CG_is_Moving_1968_GLC.pdf

5 Covent Garden Memories (2012) 'The Development Battle' by Bransford, A. Available at: www.coventgardenmemories.org.uk/page_id__37.aspx

6 Time Out Magazine (1971) 'Rhubarb to the Covent Garden Plan', Editorial comment, 14 May, pp. 8–13.

7 Cfr. H. Lefebvre (1997) 'The Everyday and Everydayness' in Harris, S. and Burke, D. (eds.), *Architecture of the Everyday*, New York: Princeton Architectural Press, pp. 32–37.

8 Mayor of London (2009) *VNEB OAPF Non-Technical Summary*. Available at: www.london.gov.uk/file/5318/download?token=UWb49MVo

9 Cfr. Montanari (2015) and Olmo (2018).

10 We are particularly interested in the focus of the Burra Charter and the importance of cultural significance in the definition of heritage and what it means. For more information visit: https://australia.icomos.org/publications/burra-charter-practice-notes/

Bibliography

Books, journals and newspapers

Bransford, A. (2012) 'The Development Battle', *Covent Garden Memories*. [Online] Available at: www.coventgardenmemories.org.uk/page_id__37.aspx (Accessed: 13 May 2019).

Burman, P. (2018) 'Prophet of Preservation', *SPAB Magazine*, Winter.

City of Westminster (1968) *Covent Garden's Moving, Draft Plan*, London: Paperback. [Online] Available at: www.sevendials.com/resources/CG_is_Moving_1968_GLC.pdf (Accessed: 12 March 2019).

Dickens, C. (1857) *Little Dorrit*. Reprinted edition (1990), Ware, England: Wordsworth Editions Ltd.

Fisher, M. (2009) *Capitalism Realism: Is There No Alternative?*, Winchester, UK and Washington, USA: Zero Books.

Graham, B.J. and Howards, P. (eds.) (2008) *The Ashgate Research Companion to Heritage and Identity*, Franham: Ashgate Publishing.

Greenfield, O. (2018) 'Battersea Power Station to Be Sold for £1.6bn', *The Guardian*. [Online] Available at: www.theguardian.com/business/2018/jan/18/battersea-power-station-to-be-sold-for-16bn (Accessed: 15 December 2018).

Harvey, D.C. (2008) 'The History of Heritage', in Graham, B.J. and Howards, P. (eds.), *The Ashgate Research Companion to Heritage and Identity*, Franham: Ashgate Publishing, pp. 19–36.

Hobsbawm, E.J. and Ranger, T. (1983) *The Invention of Tradition*. Reprinted edition, Cambridge: Cambridge University Press, 1992.

Kearns, G. and Philo, C. (eds.) (1993) *Selling Places: The City as Cultural Capital, Past and Present*, Oxford: Pergamon Press.

Lefebvre, H. (1997) 'The Everyday and Everydayness', in Harris, S. and Burke, D. (eds.), *Architecture of the Everyday*, New York: Princeton Architectural Press, pp. 32–37.

Lowenthal, D. (1985) *The Past Is a Foreign Country*, Cambridge: Cambridge University Press.

Lowenthal, D. (2011) *The Heritage Crusade and the Spoils of History*. Reprinted edition, Cambridge: Cambridge University Press.

Montanari, T. (2015) *Privati del patrimonio*, Torino: Giulio Einaudi Editore.

Morris, W. (1877) *The Society for the Protection of Ancient Buildings Manifesto*. [Online] Available at: www.marxists.org/archive/morris/works/1877/spabman.htm For more information visit: www.spab.org.uk/about-us/spab-manifesto (Accessed: 30 March 2019).

Morris, W. (1888) 'Ugly London', *Pall Mall Gazette*, 4 September, pp. 1–2. Sourced from: The William Morris Internet Archives. [Online] Available at: www.marxists.org/archive/morris/works/1888/ugly.htm (Accessed: 15 May 2019).

Olmo, C. (2018) *Città e democrazia. Per una critica delle parole e delle cose*, Milano: Donzelli.

Orwell, G. (1943) *Animal Farm*, London: Penguin Books.

Prynn, J. (2017) 'World-Famous Chimneys of Battersea Power Station Are Fully Restored', *The Standard*. [Online] Available at: www.standard.co.uk/news/london/worldfamous-chimneys-of-battersea-power-station-are-fully-restored-a3557386.html (Accessed: 28 May 2018).

Ramesh, R. (2018) 'Malaysia to Investigate Battersea Power Station Property Deal', *The Guardian*. [Online] Available at: www.theguardian.com/business/2018/jun/11/malaysia-to-investigate-battersea-power-station-property-deal-anwar-ibrahim (Accessed: 3 November 2018).

Ruskin, J. (1849) *Seven Lamps*. Reprinted 6th edition (1889), London: Paul Mellon Centre for Studies in British Art.

Sands, J. (2013) *Tokyo Vernacular*, Berkeley: University of California Press.

Smith, L. (2006) *Uses of Heritage*, London: Routledge.

Summerson, J. (1945) *Georgian London*. Reprinted edition, Paul Mellon Center for Studies, 2003.

Time Out Magazine (1971) 'Rhubarb to the Covent Garden Plan', Commentary 14 May, pp. 8–13.

Watts, P. (2016) *Up in Smoke: The Failed Projects of Battersea Power Station*, London: Paradise Road.

Websites

Covent Garden Community Association (CGCA) Website. [Online] Available at: www.coventgarden.org.uk

Mayor of London (2009) *VNEB OAPF Non-Technical Summary*. [Online] Available at: www.london.gov.uk/file/5318/download?token=UWb49MVo

New Covent Garden Sites. [Online] Available at: www.newcoventgardensites.com/the-masterplan/

Newham Council 'Heritage and Placemaking'. [Online] Available at: http://newhamndp.org.uk/projects-services/heritage-placemaking/

Out-Law (2012) 'Nine Elms Enterprise Zone to Be Set Up to Finance Northern Line Extension'. [Online] Available at: www.out-law.com/en/articles/2012/february/nine-elms-enterprise-zone-to-be-set-up-to-finance-northern-line-extension-/ (Accessed: 24 May 2017).

SPAB Manifesto. [Online] Available at: www.spab.org.uk/about-us/spab-manifesto

Brochures

Battersea Power Station. [Online] Available at: https://batterseapowerstation.co.uk/pdfs/shop-brochure.pdf

Battersea Power Station LIVE. [Online] Available at: https://batterseapowerstation.co.uk/pdfs/live_brochure_feb_2017.pdf

Battersea Power Station Office to Let Battersea Power Station, Office to Let. [Online] Available at: https://batterseapowerstation.co.uk/leasing/office-brochure_email_version.pdf

Movies

Cuarón, A. (2006) *The Children of Men*, Universal Studios.

Online dictionaries and definitions:

Merriam-Webster Dictionary, "halcyon", https://www.merriam-webster.com/dictionary/halcyon (accessed June 1, 2019).

Oxford Dictionaries, "community", https://www.lexico.com/en/definition/community (accessed June 1, 2019).

Oxford Dictionaries, "curtilage", https://www.lexico.com/en/definition/curtilage (accessed June 1, 2019).

Oxford Dictionaries, "halycon", https://www.lexico.com/en/definition/halcyon (accessed June 1, 2019).

Oxford Dictionaries, "nostalgia", https://www.lexico.com/en/definition/nostalgia (accessed June 1, 2019).

Oxford Dictionaries, "tangible", https://www.lexico.com/en/definition/tangible (accessed June 1, 2019).

Oxford Dictionaries, "intangible", https://www.lexico.com/en/definition/tangible (accessed June 1, 2019).

Chapter 4

The memory of surfaces
The physical nature of visual memory and its illusion

Approach

Why is it important to recognise the scars of everyday life? What is the value of recognising the imperfections of our surroundings rather than overlooking them in order to preserve the idea of the ideal? For conservation idealist William Morris and for the philosopher John Locke this is a question of humanity. Experience is formative, creating who we are, and shaping who we will be. Locke defines the immediate, unquestioning appreciation of the visual as 'sensational thought', equated with the superficial application of untested idealism typified by a Cartesian detachment from real space. For Locke the ability to compare, contrast and investigate often conflicting ideas or phenomena created 'reflection'– a prerequisite for empirical action. 'Reflection' requires the messy business of engagement, critique, evaluation and negotiation. The surface provides the raw material for reflection – the relationship between the two is critical.

More often the role that surface plays in our comprehension of time and identity in a historic building is the defining element – the actual surface we see is in reality an extension of the original surface overlaid periodically and consistently by decoration. The traces of obscured surfaces are evident academically, and can be proven sequentiality, as we will see, but for the passer-by experiencing the space the upper surface matters – clean or dirty, bright or dull, cracked or immaculate – these states deliver sincere responses that colour our receptivity and responses to a place. Surface is the place where the most fundamental arguments around conservation take place. And however, we should remember that every surface is also linked to a more ephemeral dimension: the one of use, social relationship, events and all the doings that characterised specific times. When we modify an existing building, we need to be conscious of the fact that we are handling both material and social history, and that intervention has the power to highlight or erase part of the narrative that buildings present to us. Technical precision, therefore, should pair with accuracy – in this way knowledge, according to William Morris, can embed processes of social signification. For him, the readability of built fabric was the readability of human action, and the layering nature of buildings was a mechanism to demonstrate authenticity of memory as an unequivocal physical reality.

Taking a cue from this approach, and bringing it further, it is our intention to appreciate the surface record of accumulated work on a building as a means of understanding its value. Current narratives of heritage tend to prioritise the recovery of original features for reasons that are both ideological and economic. Ideologically, the custodianship of a building means the preservation in perpetuity as originally conceived. An exclusive connoisseurship of its 'beauty' is reserved to the ones who have the means to understand it. As Bourdieu noted in *Distinction. A Social Critique of the Judgment of Taste* (1979: 2), "one can say that the capacity to see (voir) is a function of the knowledge (savoir)". Clearly, this approach to restoration prevents a plurality of voices entering the discussion on value, and therefore distances the contribution of the citizenry as non-experts, recipients of someone else's technical and cultured choice. The second reason, economy, recovers the appearance of original architectonic features, because authenticity sells better and at a higher price. With time, capital appropriated the value of craftsmanship and now many regeneration projects advertise it as a valuable 'add-on' linked to genuineness and ancient mastering. Indeed, 'restitution' is one of the recurrent words inside the rhetoric that accompanies building recovery in our cities. The meaning of 'fabrication' (of the city, memory, identity, value) within neoliberalism recovers the idea of craftsmanship and dedicated design but at the same time cherishes a fictive idea of authenticity. We asked, therefore, how fiction could be used in a positive way, to reveal rather than to conceal, to question uniqueness rather than offer a ready-made version of originality.

The *Memory of Surfaces* installation, created throughout the East Wing of the historic Somerset House on London's river Thames, explored the appearance of the reality that encloses the everyday life of the Courtauld Institute, revealing the legacy of its inhabitation by employing the techniques of paint layer analysis (stratigraphy) in order to reconnect the surface of the present with the accumulation of colours behind them, each of which represents a previous 'present'. Some of the revealed layers in the installation were real, others fictional, reflecting an approach to a particular space. Through the analysis of William Morris's approach to ancient buildings, we reflected on the difference between 'conservation', 'protection' and 'restoration'. The attempt was made to define 'authenticity' in terms of honest readability linked to daily use. The contested surface returns in the discussion of Clandon Park, where the disastrous fire at the house in 2015 created a shell that can be left, adapted or returned to an appearance of itself. How and why surfaces are revealed or concealed is an argument often played out with conservation authorities. We rehearse and reflect on this argument here.

GLOSSARY

Bricolage: *noun – French, construction or creation from a diverse range of available things (Oxford Dictionaries, online); something constructed or created from a diverse range of things, the French equivalent of 'do it yourself'.*

Italian 'Arte povera' artists in the 1960s constructed sculptures out of rubbish in an attempt to devalue the art object and assert the value of the ordinary and everyday. Bricolage as an operation is not interested in meaning without operation, and is an intervention of expediency that is not about imposing and ideal or pre-existing narrative, but about sustaining use value. The readability of historic buildings through their visible changes over time, so important to William Morris, is actually the legacy of Bricolage. For Claude Lévi-Strauss (1962: 11) the artist is comparable with the 'Bricoleur' who "shapes the beautiful and useful out of the dump heap of human life."

Conservation: *noun – English from Latin 'conservatio' – the act of preventing something from being lost, wasted, damaged, or destroyed (Oxford Dictionaries, online).*

Also ethical in relation to the act or guarding or protecting, using "any methods that prove effective in keeping that property in as close to its original condition as possible for as long as possible" (Walston, 1978). In heritage terms and for the documents observed (charters, guidelines, conferences' proceedings) it is explicitly related to 'tangible' artefacts and materials and not intangible relations or meanings.

Fabric(ation): *noun – the physical substance of a thing or place, a woven cloth constructed from numerous opposing threads – including components, fixtures, contents, and objects.*

Fabrication is how a thing is made, including a lie. Synonyms: invention, concoction, fiction, falsification, untruth, falsehood, deception, manufacture, making, creation, construction, building, assembly.

Memory: *noun – the faculty by which the mind stores and remembers information (Oxford Dictionaries, online).*

- the power or process of reproducing or recalling what has been learned and retained especially through associative mechanisms;
- the store of things learned and retained from an organism's activity or experience as evidenced by modification of structure or behaviour or by recall and recognition;
- a capacity for showing effects as the result of past treatment or for returning to a former condition, used especially of a material (such as metal or plastic);
- the retention of information over time for the purpose of influencing future action.

Memory is a complex set of definitions, not conflicting but nuanced – it is both the recall of what has been directly learned and recall through association, which is interpretative. Memory implies a fixed relation with a something constructed or created from a diverse range of things. Latterly the neurological purpose of memory is to understand contemporary situations to link the past directly to future action.

Integrity (completeness): "Even where painstaking efforts are made to retain the authenticity of a building, it can be compromised by harm to aspects of its integrity. For example, the extensive subdivision of an old church during conversion to domestic use may damage the integrity of its design form. Integrity could also be undermined by dismantling and re-erecting a building in another location, gutting it or reducing it to merely a well conserved facade in front of a new structure" (Building Conservation). Heritage, pragmatic facadism' or 'death mask architecture'?

Preservation: *noun – origin: Late Middle English via Old French and Latin – maintaining the fabric of a place in its existing state and retarding deterioration (Australian ICOMOS).*

According to the Merriam Webster Dictionary, 'Preservation' is in the bottom 10% or word search, whereas 'Development' is in the top 1%.

Protection: *noun – from Latin 'protectio' – the action of protecting, or the state of being protected (Oxford Dictionaries, online).*

Protection was preferred as a term to conservation when William Morris Founded the Society for the Protection of Ancient Buildings (SPAB) (1877). The protection of the living practice of building and making in order to sustain historic fabric in use was essential to Morris. The readability of built fabric was the readability of human action – a mechanism of demonstrating authenticity of memory as an unequivocal physical reality rather than a notion or sentimentality that is open to manipulation.

Restoration: *noun – Restoration is the process of returning a building or ecosystem to its former state through intervention.*

"Restoration is said as the act or process of accurately depicting the form, features, and character of a property as it appeared at a particular period of time by means of the removal of features from other periods in its history and reconstruction of missing features from the restoration period". (Technical Preservation Services). A selective editing of history for the purpose of presenting a particular narrative at the expense of all other narratives that shaped the building.

Style: *noun and verb – a distinctive manner of expression, custom or behaviour.*

- a particular procedure by which something is done; a manner or way.
- a distinctive appearance, typically determined by the principles according to which something is designed.
- a particular manner or technique by which something is done, created, or performed
- a convention with respect to language.

Distinctive yet conventional, referring to both appearance and technique it applies to the material and immaterial qualities of place.

4.1 Artificial Realities: Courtauld Institute East Wing Biennial 2016/17

The author's installation at the Courtauld as part of the East Wing Biennial in 2016 drew on Morris's call for readability, for recognition of the continuity of inhabitation that our historic buildings can register, and made manifest the value of conservation research in opening up our appreciation of sympathetic (and even on occasion unsympathetic) use which contributes to a building as enclosure of the everyday. This emphasis on the everyday is an active tactic for resisting museumification – even within a museum itself. Jacques Lacan once said that truth has the structure of a fiction. The project discussed two forms of reality: 'the constructed and the revealed'. Both give a new shape to the reality we call 'everyday', revealing the legacy of inhabitation through the physical depth of the surfaces that defines the spaces of the Courtauld itself.

The Memory of Surfaces was a site-specific installation for the Courtauld Institute 2016–17 East Wing Biennial – entitled *Artificial Realities*, an art exhibition organised, curated and run entirely by the students of the Courtauld. *Artificial Realities* "seek to expose the realm between reality and falsehood" and to "provoke the viewer into evaluating his or her own unique perception" of truth (The Courtauld Institute of Art). The

*Figure 4.1
Somerset House
exterior.*

*Source: Picture by
the authors, 2019*

exhibition was held in part of Sir William Chambers' Grade I listed Somerset House built between 1779 and 1801 for the Royal Navy, then housing The Royal Academy of Arts, the Registry of Births, Marriages and Deaths and the Inland Revenue. War, art, life and tax themes characterise the story of the building – making the perfect site to explore authenticity and its opposite. The installation oscillated between the scientific reality of Helen Howard's painstaking conservation-based stratigraphy[1] and a fictionalised (re)presentation of that knowledge.

Joshua Compston, student founder of the East Wing Biennial, understood the social and artistic role of the Courtauld Building not as a fixed monument but a dynamic process of renewal and social interaction. His radical, cyclically temporary intervention challenged the artistic priorities of the Institution and the way it was shown, subverting both institutional taste and space by making 'public' galleries out of 'private' spaces. Through the co-option of these 'back' spaces, controversial, provocative artworks redefined the establishment. Compton understood that events and community engagement are knowledge mechanisms allowing both institutions and public to sample and test new ideas. The installation *The Memory of Surfaces* defined and alluded to the renewal of the Courtauld and its relevance for public and private users, showing this fine building for what is – a social structure as much as a museum piece. Through the tools of fabric conservation, the role of people in the processes of building signification is revealed and discussed, and the reduction of our historic buildings to static conservation spectacle can be confronted and refuted.

For the Courtauld, the building for art is also a building of art, as old or older than most of its artistic content, the narrative of its use overlays the original narrative of its design many times. The interpretation, conservation and investigation that any significant painting undergoes can equally be applied to the building itself: this ambiguity of art and architecture, content and container is at the centre of the installation.

A reflection on the installation was presented at a lecture at the Courtauld on the 4th February 2016, and primarily circled around the problem of authenticity, within which lies the very word 'authentic' itself. 'Authentic' is both "of undisputed origin, a genuine original' and "made or done in the traditional or original way, or in a way that faithfully resembles an original" (Oxford English Dictionary) – in other words a copy or deception. When a word defines what is real and at the same time defines a convincing fake, we find ourselves with a semantic problem with unintended consequences that require exploration. It is suggested that the inherent confusion between the genuine and the fake is embedded in much conservation practice and theories that are assembled to justify it. This confusion is not the sole domain of the lowly practitioner or critic, but infects conservation thinking from Historic England and the National Planning Policy Framework downwards. This is an accusation that underpins the following exploration.

Built history is the physical evidence of lived history. If we rewrite buildings by either arresting their development or reimagining their fabric, we need to be conscious of the fact that we are handling both material and social history, and that intervention has the power to highlight or erase part of the story, as any narrative would do. This chapter discusses authenticity and identity in order to question who benefits from the increasingly prevalent 'reinvention' of heritage.

Visiting the Courtauld East Wing for the first briefing, the density of paint on every surface of the spaces was striking, with rich rooms and humble corridors equally accreted. This paint layering is a record of inhabitation, taste and practicality and reveals a legacy of occupation. As with an oil painting, the decorated surface is the building's identity, the moment the paint leaves the brush, that paint becomes the protected surface of a Grade I listed monument. The main stair was under scaffolding, being decorated prior to the Biennial. The value of such a highly protected surface? The paint for the East Wing main stair cost £14.39 for ten litres, ordered online or available at the corner DIY store. Yet the week following its purchase, the surface it made on the curved walls of the stair demands acid-free adhesive for Marco Maggi's beautiful artwork that was also part of the Biennial.[2] A salutary note adjacent to Maggi's fine paper embellishments to the wall telling the viewer that "N.B. The micro paper used has an acid-free adhesive. It will not damage the walls or their paint".

Figure 4.2 Artificial Realities – installation by Marco Maggi.

Source: Picture by the authors, 2016

This shift in importance from a tin of cheap Dulux trade emulsion to the visual expression of a listed monument and piece of art is both profound and ironic. Cultural value and material value are not the same – and *The Memory of Surface* project aimed to disturb this uneasy relationship even further. The concept for the installation required a presentation of the ideas to the curators and key staff, in which the Courtauld itself was the primary reference – both as an historic venue and as an institution renowned for teaching painting conservators how to physically analyse historic paint layers on canvas and wall paintings. The idea was to involve the painting conservation students in the de-layering of the Courtauld East Wing. At a spatial level, the student's presence in the school is registered through the successive stratification of paint applied

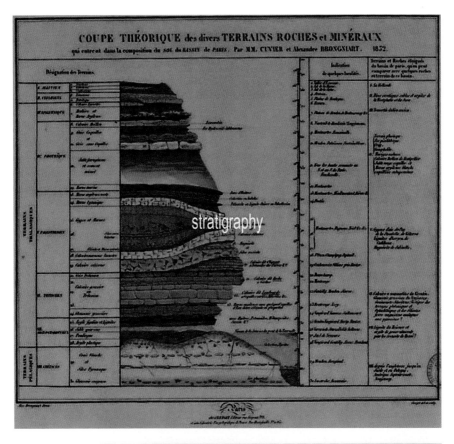

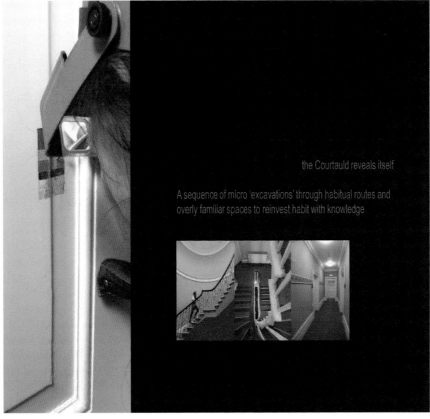

Figure 4.3a–b Author's Courtauld presentation: frames of the pitch to the East Wing Biennial curators.

Source: Picture by the authors, 2015

by them to the walls for every show, or through the planned institutional maintenance cycle. The project wanted to reverse this action, bringing to the surface the different layers that were produced for these activities and covered in time. Through intervening in discrete locations using the skills of the students themselves, the history of the present could be revealed. The installation was more than site-specific in the sense that the idea was not only determined by the location, but it was about the location, driven by the thinking of William Morris to 'read' the building as a document of human interaction with it and within it. The following eight images are taken from a presentation to the Biennial committee to gain the commission.

*Figure 4.4
Paris Arcade
stratigraphy
investigation.*

*Source: Picture by
the authors, 2015*

However, with the wall painting conservation students studying abroad and needing listed building consent to subtract tiny sections of the paint layers, the vast proportion of which were Dulux emulsion or similar, the project developed more in line with the theme – *Artificial Realities*. *The Memory of Surfaces* became intrinsic to the Biennial idea of "work arranged in thematic microcosms, dispatched across the Courtauld's unconventional setting", part of a wider group of projects reasoning on authenticity. The aim of the installations was to "disorientate a seemingly established truth" (The Courtauld Institute of Art). The ambiguity of maintenance and alteration, of the permissible and the disallowed formed the basis for the project. 'Artificial' rather than the 'originally authentic' became the mode of operation, using stratigraphy to multiply the realities we inhabit daily.

To gain a factual underpinning to a fictional installation, contact was made with Senior Scientist Dr Helen Howard from the National Gallery, who had undertaken a paint analysis of the main rooms of the Courtauld in June 1997. From this analysis, we understand that the strata of paint, both traditional and modern formulation, is keyed together over a soft plaster substrate that cannot withstand the various chemical and mechanical operations required to remove them. Nor indeed could the Courtauld afford the cost of doing so.

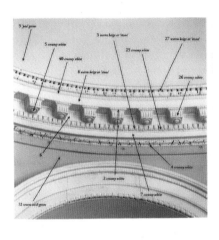

Locations for samples 2-9, 25-27, 32 and 40.
(Photograph: Photographic Department, Courtauld Institute, 1997)

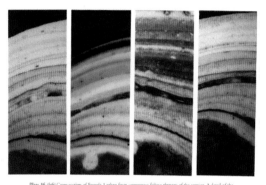

Plate 36 (*left*) Cross-section of Sample 1 taken from uppermost foliate element of the cornice. A detail of the lower portion of the sample (Plate 37, *below*) shows the yellow plaster support with the creamy white original paint layers, and a layer of dirt on the surface. Plate 36 shows the numerous phases of redecoration—mostly in white, beige or a creamy yellow colour—of total thickness (500 μm (1.5 mm). Plate 38 (*centre left*). Cross-section of Sample 1 photographed in UV light. The dirt layers which terminate each phase of decoration show up particularly clearly in UV light, as does the original paint layer which fills pores or air bubbles within the plaster substrate. Plate 39 (*centre right*). Cross-section of Sample 1 stained for oil with Sudan black B. The plaster substrate, original paint layers and the majority of the phases of repainting have an oil-based medium. Plate 40 (*right*). Cross-section of Sample 1 stained with sodium rhodizonate, which produces a pink/ purple colour in the presence of sulphate ions. The test clearly indicates that the plaster substrate contains sulphate—likely to be in the form of calcium sulphate— and that the uppermost emulsion paint also contains sulphate ions, here likely to be in the form of barium sulphate.
(Photomicrographs: Howard 1997)

Figure 4.5
Somerset House: Scientific examination of the original decoration, 1997.

Source: Reproduction courtesy © Helen Howard.

This means that the slow sedimentation of paint is turning the fine decorative mouldings into soft caricatures – in another fifty years of paint application there will be no sense of the fine decoration at all. So, stripping the paint layers would 'restore' the original fineness but the removal of paint destroys the layered legacy of history; however, the addition of paint through ongoing 'maintenance' also destroys the readable legacy of the decorative language. The term 'maintenance' requires further clarification, as it figures prominently in Morris's 'alternative' to restoration and is underpinned in the conservation charters – how then is it destructive? The word implies continuity but is in fact about insidious change. We are confronted with a sort of 'Sistine Chapel syndrome' – what we see on the ceiling is not what Michelangelo painted, but restorations of restorations, paint over paint, but we believe that it is in fact original and authentic – an illusion and delusion simultaneously. At the Courtauld the surfaces are certainly not what the architect William Chambers imagined either.

William Morris was clear founding the Society for the Protection of Ancient Buildings (SPAB) (1877) that art, crafts and buildings are all cultural documents that are centred on the working lives of their makers and users. 'Conservation' as a concept was rejected, replaced by the notion of 'protection' – the protection of the living practice of building and making in order to sustain historic fabric in use. The readability of built fabric was the readability of human action – a mechanism of demonstrating authenticity of memory as an unequivocal physical reality rather than a notion or sentimentality that is open to manipulation: hard evidence of hard work. The means by which we conserve is an active and collaborative pastime that allows the fabric we work on to re-inform and re-inspire modern hands, eyes and minds. For Morris, the word 'maintenance' became a radical political term. The use, not replacement, of historic fabric, buildings and artefacts was indicative of a critique of capitalism, and its perpetual economic growth based on material production, availability and replacement, exploiting the fetishisation of history to support economic gain. The key for Morris to make 'continuity' (intrinsic to conservation) into radicalism is to define what it is you need to maintain, and by definition what you do not. In 1877 Morris saw that the fabric of historic places and buildings are subject to the demands and influence of capital. Economic drivers require change, and heritage along with all other cultural meaning was, and still is negotiable, tradable and commodified. As a mask of reassuring continuity, heritage is frequently restructured to deliver our cultural expectations rather than evidencing the material facts of our actual shared past.

A work of art as the art of work

To counter this hollowing out of historic identity, William Morris reframed the idea of a work of art as the art of work – by re-evaluating what constitutes work as a social practice, he began to define its cultural and political value. Morris held a fundamental intellectual position that we observe as a continuity of what is called 'English Empiricism'. John Locke[3] proposed that our identity and understanding of the world is a product of our engagement with the world, rather than via any pre-existing ideal. Locke asked us to value experience, engagement and reflection over sensation, passivity and spectacle. The authenticity of that engagement and the rejection of idealised imaginaries in favour of concrete lived experience we will return to later. Morris understood the fabric of historic buildings to be the documents of past labour, records of the lives that the buildings framed and nurtured, the elaboration, damage and alterations being the visible presence of human culture. Through skill-based work the artisan created cultural value, therefore handcraft was for Morris the means of reconciling history with the present. The record of accumulated work on a building is the means of understanding its value – what we now term 'significance'. With time, capital appropriated the value of craftsmanship and now many regeneration projects advertise it as a valuable optional linked to authenticity and ancient mastering. The details of industrial

Figure 4.6
Solidarity of Labour. Walter Crane, first published in Commonweal 24th May 1890 no COPAC record.

Source: www.marxists.org/subject/art/visual_arts/satire/crane/

buildings, for example, are re-imagined into crafted elements of design, bricks and mortar talk about 'English authenticity', while the modern look of 'branded buildings' invite us to inhabit the edgy position between the past and the future.

Opposed to this model of ongoing, sympathetic working practice, Morris identified and vilified the then-widespread practice of 'Restoration' as the characterisation of history rather than its material fact. Restoration is the process of returning a building to its former state through new work. Historic England define this state as being "a known earlier state, on the basis of compelling evidence, without conjecture" (Historic England, definitions). The persistent idea of 'characterisation' is now enshrined in the British Standard for conservation practice:

> Restoration aims to achieve a high level of authenticity, replicating materials and techniques as closely as possible. Where necessary, modern works, such as replacing outdated utilities, or installing climate controls, alarm systems, and so on, are undertaken in a concealed manner where they will not compromise historic character.
>
> (Edwards, 2015: 45–46)

The appearance of history, gathered into the phrase 'historic character' is a form of idealisation that extends, amplifies, restates and ultimately subverts the evidence of

Figure 4.7
Palazzo Gritti
Morosini Badoer
with laundry.
John Ruskin
and Le Cavalier
Iller, Venice. c.
1846–52.

Source: Picture
courtesy ©
K&J Jacobson
19th Century
Photography:
http://www.
jacobsonphoto.com

lived history for the presentation of a selected, academically rectified 'history'. In Morris's time, that was exemplified by the work of French architect Eugene Viollet-le-Duc who was interested in scholarly, erudite and historically informed replacement and re-imagined augmentation of medieval buildings throughout France. For Morris, this intellectual completion of originally artisan works of art that were scarred and adapted over time was a form of vandalism. The act of 'restoring' a building or space to some

*Figure 4.8
Palazzo Gritti
Morosini Badoer,
today 'Hotel
Residenza –
Residenzad'epoca'
[Hotel
Residence,
classic/vintage
residence],
the domestic/
work use of the
'campo' replaced
with touristic/
leisure use,*

Source: Picture by
the authors, 2019

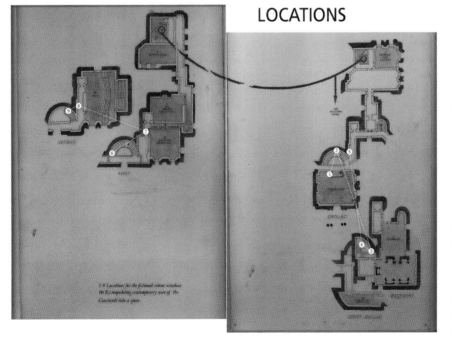

*Figure 4.9 Map
of the authors'
Biennial
installations
Memory of
Surfaces within
the East Wing,
overlaid on
a 'found'
plan hanging
anonymously
in a services
corridor within
Somerset House.*

Source: Picture by
the authors, 2016

previous ideal state goes directly against the principles of 'English Empiricism', and for Morris involved the removal of the marks of time and hand, both of which define our humanity. Morris attempted the definition of 'authenticity' in terms of honest readability linked to daily use. The touchstone for John Ruskin that actively illustrated a continuity of lived history was Venice; his drawings, surveys and daguerreotype photographs sought to evidence the authenticity of this lived history.

Clearly in the Venice example an alternative form of 'authenticity' has prevailed. Is what we inherit ours to use, or merely to show? A cultural experience too valuable to inhabit, no longer a place to hang out your washing. Ironically for Morris the mechanism for the physical protection of buildings such as Palazzo Gritti Badoer perpetuates the semantic problems of authenticity – the building remains in splendour while the inhabitants of Venice cannot afford to stay. ICOMOS, was built on the shoulders of the 1964 Venice Charter, which in turn was somewhat ironically based on a reading of Morris. The question in relation to the Courtauld became one of actively using 'English Empiricism' to re-engage its staff, student and visitor community with the fabric of the building itself, not as an ideal but as historic continuity maintained through everyday actions.

The purpose of 'revealing the Courtauld to itself' in the installation appears at first reading to prioritise the fabric of the building – conservation is by definition focussed on the object of study but we know that it implies the conservation of memory as much as of fabric. The fictional paint 'windows' relied on Helen Howard's factual analysis, but their status as a 'story' opened up another connection to Morris: "for you must remember how different that modern historical research is to the chronicling, the story-telling of times past" (Morris, 1879).

Morris was less inclined to value scientific precision, which strives for absolute values, preferring an idea of to how closely our action relates to a purpose. The work on the surfaces that surround the daily activity of the Courtauld provides a register of those very activities and of the purposes that generated them. From the information gained, we proceeded to unfold the narrative bringing together the pieces of evidence. For example, Howard's study of paint layers within the fine rooms of the Courtauld provided in precise terms the colour history of one space. Our task was then to realise Morris's 'chronicle', the translation from precision to accuracy, from fact to narrative. Colourways from the authentic colour history of the fine rooms uncovered by Howard were extrapolated into colour swatches and painted in selected locations around the building. Rather than excavating the actual history under the surface, a new fictionalised history re-imagined the layered colour history of walls, ceilings and staircases, and was written up as an illustrated catalogue of the changes that the building underwent. This site map, printed for the visitor to the Biennial was 'found' framed in a back corridor, scanned and overlaid with the locations of the colour 'windows' – original and fictive clues aimed to drawing the attention of the visitors and inhabitants to their role in the surface history of the place itself.

These historically based 'fictions' are applied colours rather than excavated reality, but then that is the purpose of the East Wing theme after all. The task of the project *The Memory of Surfaces* was not to precisely reveal, nor was it to fabricate a falsehood; instead the work sits between the two and asks impertinently whether we really know the places we inhabit.

The truth or artificiality of this conservation-inspired artwork opens up complexity: how are artists, conservation specialists or cultural commentators providing the interpretation of our historic environment? Communication is both the liberator and the gaoler of meaning. How is making a more direct and meaningful engagement of people with the fabric of their surroundings useful?

We would suggest that Morris was right to insist on work as the means of framing our engagement with our environment, with meaningful experience through work being a direct counter to experiencing history as spectacle. Through observation it became clear that some of the actual surface history of the building was visible through scars of use – chipped paint on the servant stair revealed the actual colour layers. With the layers, colours and sequences for 'wall', 'ceiling', 'architrave' and other room elements determined by Howard's findings, we added 'stair' derived from the actual layers of paint revealed through use damage found on the servant's stair itself.

The mezzanine 'wall' incorporates a scar where the paint, removed back to plaster by a carelessly removed sign on a new lift wall, revealed only a very un-historic coat of gypsum plaster added to the building when the lift was installed. These fragments of actuality were incorporated into some of the swatches, blurring what was fictionalised and what was real.

Why is it important to recognise the scars of everyday life? What is the value of recognising the imperfections of our surroundings rather than overlooking them in order to preserve the idea of the ideal? Levi Strauss's use of the term 'bricolage' helps to describe the process of additive adaptation that *The Memory of Surfaces* employs, a creative improvisation using material at hand, to conceptualise mythological thinking in direct opposition to the engineers' creative thinking which proceeds from goals to means. Mythical thought, according to Lévi-Strauss (1966), attempts to re-use available materials in order to solve new problems – a variation of Morris's 'story telling', bricolage gains value through use, it defers its own importance to the activity it supports. It resists commodification because its value is in its operation – without which

Figure 4.10 Colour specification developed from Howard's analysis.

Source: Picture and specification by the authors, 2017

category	site	phases	colour spectrum	category	site	phases	colour spectrum
DADO	1	16 phases	original: Pale grey / Cream/white x11 / Dark brown / Yellow / Pale green / Current colour	COVING	6	14 phases	original: Pea green / Dark green / White / Cream/white / Pale green / Current colour
ARCHITRAVE	2	14 phases	original: Pale grey / Grey / Cream x10 / White / Current colour	MOULDINGS	6	14 phases	original: Cream/white / Dark Beige / Cream/white x11 / Current colour
CEILING	3	16 phases	original: Pale blue-green / Dark green / Cream/white x13 / Current colour	CORNICE	8	10 phases	original: Stone / Cream/white x9 / Current colour
WALL	2,4,6,7	17 phases	original: Warm mid green / Green / Cream / White / Cream / Yellow	DOOR	9	16 phases	original: Beige / Dark green / Cream x11 / Pale beige / Current colour
STAIR	5	19 phases	original: Dark grey / Beige / Stone / Pale green / Pea green / Beige / Dark buff / Pale green / Beige / Stone/beige x3 / Dark brown / Sky blue / Dark grey / Black / White x2 / Current colour				

*Figure 4.11
Memory of
Surfaces ceiling
installation.*

*Source: Picture by
the authors, 2016*

*Figure 4.12
Vernacular brick
infill, Holkham,
Norfolk.*

*Source: Picture by
the authors, 2012*

Figure 4.13 and 4.14 Memory of Surfaces main stair and service stair installations.

Source: Picture by the authors, 2016

it is relatively worthless. The readability of historic buildings so important to Morris is actually the legacy of bricolage. We are keen to draw a distinction between collage and bricolage – ostensibly similar but politically wide apart.

Figure 4.15 Memory of Surfaces wall installation with 'as found' exposed plaster.

Source: Picture by the authors, 2016

Collage as an operation is the self-aware cutting together of pre-existing realities in order to disrupt the meaning of both and create a third. Collage has its roots with Picasso in 1911 and was widely used between the 1930s and 1970s (when the practice of (photo)montage surpassed constructed collage) and came to be experimented with in the fields of cultural critique (Benjamin, 1983; Blöch, 1935; Brecht, 1963; Kracauer, 1963), history (Benjamin, 1983) and history of images (Warburg). This approach, indebted to a large number of artists and directors, was iconological: the heterogeneous archive of physical printed and published information left to us by history, loaded with objects, facts, actions, people, was used to elaborate an analysis of history, of meanings and of representation (Pinotti Somaini, 2009: 29, 2016: XVII). The juxtaposition of fragments was a resource (Schlögel, 2011), a way to take a political position though reworked visions. We have seen the consequences of collage as a process in relation to Battersea, when decoupled from any radical pictorial agenda it simply levels difference and juxtaposes naturally what is unnaturally contrived. Bricolage, however, is not interested in meaning without operation. Bricolage addresses action in a less theoretical way than collage but is no less powerful or questioning: it is linked to the recognition, awareness and practicality of materials. If awareness is the first condition for change, the installation was a reflection on how the science of surface analysis is also a craft, and how that craft can translate into art provoking the 'truthfulness' of materials and their story. Bricolage was, in the case of *The Memory of Surfaces*, both scientific action and artistic invention, its result open to interpretation – a fiction telling a truth. Bringing the subjective and objective into the same plane is a constant triumph for art and is constantly avoided by politicians.

In a way, *The Memory of Surfaces* installation was flawed – a fabrication that both makes and fakes. In questioning authenticity and memory this work becomes part of the problem it discusses, the physical nature of visual memory and its illusion. There is an issue, we think, with the perception of the physical presence of historic buildings – visual appearance creates triggers of recognition and associations that are easily divorced from the depth of the material seen and the labour required to fabricate it. In a rather obsessive manner the project delaminated these surfaces and was critical of the status that the visual achieves.

4.2 Clandon Park and the 'phoenix concept'

The issues around 'authenticity' are present in every architectural conservation project – one might extend this to every architectural project given that we respond to and recognise all images and ideas in relation to our past experience (if Locke is to be believed). One project where the different interpretations of 'authenticity' are in plain sight is Clandon Park, our second case study.

> Clandon Park was conceived to impress and dazzle. Commissioned by a politician and courtier, Thomas, Lord Onslow, and built by Italian, Swiss and English craftsmen, Clandon was designed for entertaining royalty in the countryside. Created in the 1720s by the Venetian-born architect Giacomo Leoni, an authority on Andrea Palladio, the new Clandon swept away an extended Jacobean hunting lodge, and signalled the arrival of a new style in architecture. The house captured the moment when the Baroque was making way for Palladianism: the most astonishing set-piece interiors were concealed within its austere red brick form.
> (Ghosh, 2017: 7)

History is far from the fixed reference point that many feel is a necessary underpinning to culture. History is the documentation of change, not stability, and the loss of a Jacobean hunting lodge now would be subject to proving overwhelming public benefit, while in the 1720s it was simply in the way of the political ambition of one man. That the Jacobean hunting lodge was to be replaced with a stylistic copy of an architect dead for over 140 years would also seem indefensible, but this was Palladianism – a style inextricably linked to the exercise of British privilege in the 18th century. The use of Palladio's *Quattro Libri dell' Architettura*, translated by Leoni into English, provided a pattern book for the aristocracy, a style that framed the political engagement between royalty and the political élite through set piece social theatres. A series of such houses were built within a carriage ride from Westminster, with Clandon built for politician and aristocrat Lord Onslow being one of the most significant and earliest Palladio-inspired houses.

Relatively little work was undertaken at the house: some additions ('intrusions' as termed by the National Trust in the competition brief of 2017) being were removed by the Trust after the donation of Clandon to the nation by Lady Iveagh in 1956, when it was extensively 'restored' and redecorated in consultation with the renowned decorator John Fowler. Fowler used pioneering 'paint scrapes' to chart the history of the decorative treatments of the house through its history. His methods were relatively crude and assumptions were sometimes proven to be inaccurate after follow-up research.

On the 29th April 2015 Clandon Park suffered catastrophic damage by fire, caused by arcing within a defective electrical cabinet, the opening of which caused an influx of oxygen that generated a fireball (belatedly electrical regulations IET (18th Edition BS 7671) requiring the technical prevention of this came into force in 2018). Without arcing protection or adequate compartmentation the fire reached the roof where high winds accelerated fire spread across and throughout the building. Clandon Park is one of the latest in a series of fire-related building losses which highlight not only the fragility that historic buildings have regarding fire vulnerability, but also the financial environment that exists around heritage. The knowledge of a building's fire frailty is often available, but the monetary means to address such vulnerability with highly bespoke, intricate fire protection measures is not. Added to that, the means by which effective fire prevention technology is installed is contested. Fire systems are invasive as original fabric is punctured, lifted, injected and replaced with fire retardant simulacra.

The framework of conservation thinking underpinned by Morris is hard-wired to retain 'as existing', with the outcome of this debate making the process of protecting buildings from fire even more problematic. This combination of requisite knowledge, requisite funding and unanimity of philosophical approaches means that fire management comes down to a game of percentage chance of a catastrophic fire happening. Clandon did not have the requisite fire breaks, nor mist systems in place.

The 'phoenix concept' is rooted in the idea that monuments are permanent, therefore even catastrophe cannot eradicate their presence. There is also, it appears, a more prosaic financial driver in the shape of insurance claims – it is interesting to note a *Guardian* article following the fire where the descendant of the commissioning patron, Lord Onslow, voiced his opinion on the fate of the ruin, and the Director General of the National Trust's reply:

> The fate of the Surrey mansion has sparked controversy, with suggestions from Lord Onslow, whose ancestors built it in 1720 and generations later donated it to the National Trust to preserve it, that the building should be left as a romantic ruin and the money spent on more worthy concerns. However, Ghosh said that although his opinion had been considered, it was based on a misunderstanding: 'If we did not rebuild and restore it in some shape or form, we would not get the insurance money,' she said.
>
> (Kennedy, 2016)

History is a process that Morris determined to be intrinsic to the life of the building, so absorbing catastrophe is surely part of that process of producing 'permanence'. The Palacio Pereira already discussed some of the tactics available to integrate catastrophe into the building fabric; Clandon Park followed suit with a competition to revive the insured phoenix again. What is of interest is not the various merits of the shortlisted practice teams and their concepts but how the brief was framed and the reception that brief received from interested parties in the debate. On the National Trust web page *Clandon Park appeal*, an interface collecting donations from the public, former

*Figure 4.16
Clandon Marble
Hall surviving
statue.*

*Source: Picture
by the authors,
2019, courtesy the
National Trust.*

director Helen Ghosh stated clearly: "Returning parts of the house to its 18th Century glory whilst at the same time creating a building of beauty and relevance for the 21st century" (National Trust, 2015), – and again:

> We concluded that the principal state rooms – given their historical and cultural significance, and because so many original features survived – should be restored. However, the upper floors were so badly damaged – and of generally

lower architectural and historical significance – that here a restoration seemed less meaningful. However, these spaces might be re-imagined in the light of Clandon's present-day needs.

(Ghosh, 2017)

Underpinning this 'phoenix project' was an acknowledgement that pre-fire visitor numbers were around 56,000 per annum; to manage the costs of restoration and long-term viability this number needs to triple. The cost of the project was estimated at £30 million in 2017. Prosaic visitor numbers matter to the philosophy of the National Trust, whose remit is to ensure the properties and places it is custodian for are genuinely public and accessible; the communication of the memory of surfaces to the public is paramount. This memory is, through the lens of Morris's philosophy, bound up in the events that both created those surfaces and in cases such as Clandon, destroyed those surfaces. The current Lord Onslow's logic in arguing for the retention of the scorched ruin appears watertight to a follower of Morris, for whom 'Paladianism' was a curse and the honesty of what the fire revealed would always surpass the folly of restoration. However, it is important to acknowledge the continued presence of Viollet-le-Duc within the conservation world, albeit via the terms of building insurance. Clandon is selectively apportioning honesty and deceit according to the lavishness of the décor and the status of the original spaces. This form of ideological compromise prioritises Viollet-le-Duc in the ground floor 'theatre', restoring the Marble Hall, State Bedroom and entry sequences, with Morris relegated upstairs with the necessary 'state of the art' facilities to create a self-funding venue with technology 'of its time' in spaces left with the scars of fire still visible.

The announcement of the brief for the competition received a highly critical response from the Georgian Group[4] – the statutory consultee on buildings from the Georgian Period in the UK, and originally a sub-group of the SPAB. The initial groups' separation in terms of chronology (SPAB previously focussed on pre-Georgian buildings), latterly becoming ideologically distinct – the Georgian Group is avowedly 'Viollet-le-Duc' in its belief in the restoration of 'splendour' as a de facto position when dealing with Georgian buildings. It is instructive to take extensive quotations from their editorial response to the National Trust's approach to Clandon and the architectural proposals that followed:

> The images presented by the NT (National Trust) from the finalists' proposals, however, embody a jumbled retreat from the Trust's curatorial duty as custodians of nationally important – in this case Grade I – Listed Buildings. It is a retreat which many observers believe has been apparent for some time: an embarrassment over the ownership of 'elite' houses; a focus on the 'accessible' and the 'relevant'. Clandon looks set to suffer – irrevocably – from a continuation of that trend.
>
> (National Trust, 2017: 4–5)

There is an assumption that the built manifestation of an historic 'élite' is now a victim of political revisionism/correctness, and that contemporary viewpoints that question the sources of the wealth that generated buildings such as Clandon Park are less important that the buildings themselves. The cause is truly divorced from aesthetic effect as fortunes from slavery that enabled commerce or military extortion should not, if one follows this Georgian Society argument to its logical conclusion, alter the way we see the building, which is a 'thing as such' and not a document of social context. The élite nature of the building appears to extend to an exclusive connoisseurship of its 'beauty' (which is considered unquestionable, despite the absence of Palladio's refinement in Leoni's 'Palladianism'), given that 'accessibility' to its 'relevance' is an unwelcome trend that is clearly diluting rather than widening social knowledge. Custodianship of a building means, for the Georgian Group editorial at least, the preservation in perpetuity as originally conceived as though it was a sculpture or painting. Time and understanding are irrelevant to the spectacle of the building. This position generates problems as it simplifies them.

"The Trust is intent on not restoring the building" and this is "a betrayal of the trust placed upon it by both its members and the nation as a whole" (*ibidem*), claimed the group. The editorial elevates its argument to a matter of national principle and makes the case on moral terms. Note how ethically and morally inflected the language is, recalling the use of political dialectics first identified by Orwell in *Politics and the English language* (1946), which conflates morality and the summoning up of national identity and indignation. "The purpose of salvaging artefacts from the fire 'should, of course, be to inform a scholarly restoration of the lost fabric'" (*ibidem*), they continue. The dismissal of any dialectical position is clear, lamenting "an approach which will not seek to repair lost fabric, but to create new interventions, despite the existence of a 'full photographic record of the pre-fire interiors'" (*ibidem*).

Compromise is the mechanism for dissatisfying everyone and pleasing no one, it seems.

Of interest in the debate here is the 'scholarly restoration' of what? In the mid-1970s John Fowler, the celebrated historic decoration expert 'dressed' a number of the Clandon rooms, including the State Bedroom. Amongst other things, the fire revealed the original blue painted timber panelling to the walls – far more austere than Fowler's idea of what a state bedroom should look like. Additional timber grounds were nailed into the panelling to install his red-flocked wallpaper on a hessian backing. Does the Georgian Group reinstate the 1970s Fowler décor, or the blue panelling?

When referring to repair, the Georgian Group editorial used a quotation by Andrea Palladio (source unquoted) defining the belief in the "entire and complete body":

> Beauty will result from the form and the correspondence of the whole, with respect to the several parts, of the parts with regard to each other, an of these again to the whole; that the structure may appear an entire and complete body, wherein each member agrees with the other, an all necessary to compose what you intend to form.
>
> (*ibidem*)

This ideology informed 'Palladianism' and justifies full recreation rather than acceptance of loss and the keeping of the consequences as an unequivocal narrative of its loss as a museum piece. The object of reverence can become a facsimile with full moral authority because it appears as it was. The morality of appearance is unquestioned:

> To do anything other than a comprehensive and scholarly restoration at Clandon would not only set an unacceptable example for other owners of

*Figure 4.17
Clandon state
bedroom
panelling with
wallpaper
fragments.*

*Source: Picture
by the authors,
2019, courtesy the
National Trust.*

fire-damaged listed buildings, but would also imply insincerity from a charity whose chief purpose is the protection and celebration of the historic environment under its care.

(*ibidem*)

Moral and ethical argument combine – 'insincerity' is the hallmark of the un-restored – to restore is 'honest', yet for Morris the exact opposite is true, where imitation of previous styles is both fraudulent and preventing the contemporary artistic voice being heard:

It does indeed seem strange to me people cannot see how the times have changed, that they should insist on these lifeless pieces of reproduction. The workman of to-day is not an artist as his forefather was; it is impossible, under his circumstances, that he could translate the work of the ancient hand-icraftsman; and sure, I am that if he were artist enough to be able to do so, he would refuse to try it. I say the workman of to-day is no artist; it is the hope of my life that this may one day be changed; that popular art may grow again in our midst.

(Morris, 1879)

To make matters worse, the notion of 'sincerity' is somewhat bereft from buildings like Clandon. To side with the Georgian Group for a moment, is Clandon a building that exhibits the kind of honest handicraft that Morris constantly referred to in medieval building, or was it simply a stage set made of plaster and imitation? If its 'true' purpose is an elaborate play of appearances for the benefit of social status and ostentation, where is the honesty that Morris's visible, crafted repair would contribute to? Should we not simply re-dress the brick enclosure and reinstate the photograph?

Current thinking on the presentation of our monuments is predicated on the simulation of narrative. The period furniture assembled for the purpose of describing an 'authentic' atmosphere of inhabitation so typical of historic properties throughout the UK falls within Morris's distrust of 'the idealization' of restoration. Is the simulation of our environment a legitimate business? What are the parameters of fictions in order to sustain facts? Does the use of period décor, the proliferation of 'heritage paints' and back catalogues of Liberty and Morris and Co. wallpaper and fabric speak of a positive re-engagement with the past, or a flight from the here and now?

Restoration to an intellectually predetermined point in time negates that story of occupation, creating a spectacle from history and allowing a narrative, selected by authority, to stand as a 'truth'. Without daily necessity to engage, our environments quickly assume the status of scenography. Clandon asks us to consider the validity of scenography, its strategy of both re-providing the originally ostentatious scenography of 'public' rooms while retaining fire scarring on the upper floors could be argued as a healthy or heinous compromise, depending on your allegiance to either Morris or Viollet-le-Duc. It is the author's suspicion that Morris would simply stop the rain coming in and leave the shell as an epitaph to a social order he would willingly have swept away.

The notion of misremembering

The inspiration for neoclassicism that passed through the interpretation of Palladio's writings defines the composition as a whole, and all parts to it. As revealed by the debate at Clandon Park, the use that current restoration practice often makes of this concept is worryingly linked to a static notion of history intended as a snapshot of exact past to recover as it was, where it was. Is this the definition of 'halcyonism' and how does society now deal with the irrevocable loss of this concept, indeed, was it ever anything but a proposition as opposed to a reality?

Listed building status confers a duty to preserve and protect – does this extend to replication? What are the ramifications for this? Replacing lost fabric is a duty – is it? Craftspeople will be failed in their skills development if restoration is avoided – how far is this true? Is the Palacio Pereira team's refusal to fully restore but emphasise strategic intervention throughout to create scales of completeness more effective than the '50% approach' at Clandon, where a contemporary staircase is dropped more or less elegantly into the building shell while other rooms appear as though nothing at all has happened since 1730? Most importantly, how is an approach formulated when so many variations on the theme of 'conservation' are available? Any skilled technical imitator can totally restore a building to its original semblance, any architect can design an incongruous stair. How is an approach formulated when so many variations on the theme of 'conservation' are available?

If we revisit the ICOMOS guidelines in more detail, to discern how its language shapes or is shaped by contemporary heritage development, we find as many loopholes as solutions:

> Point 2: Conservation of cultural heritage is now recognized as resting within the general field of environmental and cultural development. Sustainable management strategies for change that respect cultural heritage require the integration of conservation attitudes with contemporary economic and social goals including tourism.

And again:

> Point 3: The object of conservation is to prolong the life of cultural heritage and, if possible, to clarify the artistic and historical messages therein without the loss of authenticity and meaning. Conservation is a cultural, artistic, technical and craft activity based on humanistic and scientific studies and systematic research. Conservation must respect the cultural context.
>
> (ENCoRE Guidelines for Education and training in the conservation of Monuments, Ensembles and Sites, 1993)

The tone of ICOMOS is accepting of the realities of cultural commodification. Development is recognised as a driver, contextualised within a social narrative, but the narrative portrays the public as passive consumers of heritage rather than participants. The relation to the ordinary practice of realising art through manufacture has shifted from Morris, for whom the engagement of people through their work ensured cultural relevance of the buildings and spaces they needed, used and maintained. The emphasis is on science and systematisation; craft is simply the delivery mechanism for academic/professional study – yet this is a fundamental reversal of pre-Renaissance practice, where it was craft that set the realisation and scope of the work, with academia studying the results.

There is a question around engagement that impacts directly on how we identify with memories and what we remember.

> Point 4: There is a need to develop a holistic approach to our heritage on the basis of cultural pluralism and diversity, respected by professionals, craftspersons and administrators. Conservation requires the ability to observe, analyze and synthesize. The conservationist should have a flexible yet pragmatic approach based on cultural consciousness which should penetrate all practical work, proper education and training, sound judgement and a sense of proportion with an understanding of the community's needs. Many professional and craft skills are involved in this interdisciplinary activity.
>
> (*ibidem*)

Is 'cultural consciousness' enough to connect people with history through the medium of buildings, or is ICOMOS only speaking about the 'cultural consciousness' of the conservator, rather than the local community to whom the building notionally belongs? Conservation is often articulated as a professional sphere, not a shared one. Indeed, all too often the notion of heritage is used to reinforce the legitimacy of regeneration projects. Its use concerns marketing matters but involves as well the political and normative level that sustains urban change. The frequency and global extension of this phenomena reflects on the political and economic deviations that the promotion of legacy and on its spatial consequences entail. Among them the financialization of space and the marginalisation of social groups, the aesthetic consumption of the past, the increasing coding of both images and spaces. The difficulty in trying to actively narrate through conservation is that concepts such as memory, tradition, originality and heritage, like almost all the definitions we have explored so far in this book, are ambiguous. Traditional references themselves have been widely used to instil values and behaviours whose implicit continuity with the past was expressly crafted. In the book *The invention of tradition* historians E.J. Hobsbawm and T. Ranger (1983) define 'invented traditions' as a set of activities generally regulated by norms that have symbolic nature. Although this mainly applies to rituals and commemorative actions, the use of invented traditions can also be functional to architecture. The choice of the gothic style for the reconstruction of the British Parliament in the 19th century, or the choice to rebuild the Chambers according to the previous plans after WWII are some examples. Most of all, invented traditions well exemplify the process of selection through which materials from the past are chosen to build adequate narratives for the present. Despite this, people consider those buildings as unquestionably original.

For Morris, the social relations of working people were intrinsically bound up in class struggle and the emancipation of their class from the generation of surplus for the middle/governing class. Their identity originated in the fabric of ancient buildings, and their future lay in the repair and sympathetic adaptation of those buildings alongside the making of new ones according to contemporary needs through skill and material knowledge.

How does a community remember? What evidence sustains itself better – by words, orally or written (these are purportedly more accurate, unless censored, but requiring tenacity or analytical perspective often eluding non-specialist researchers), images (the camera never lies, of course), and our environment (used, cherished and overlooked in equal measure)? The latter is of interest: environment is as much a document as a book, but easier to access and potentially as readable if interpreted. The key question is how to interpret, and more importantly, how to enable others to interpret? In this context of historical narrative and its reception, the position Morris took against the passive spectacle of restoration is relevant, for how do we engage with the fabric of our surroundings if we have no tactile experience of them?

Lessons learned

It is useful to investigate how the mechanisms of conservation retain within and enable the promotion of heritage as a spectacle – and how the observation by Morris of the value of craftwork can help to reinvest both the preservation and the adaptation of historic fabric with new social agendas that are not inextricably linked to commodity. Can this way of understanding the memory of surfaces as both physical and political evidence be translated to the scale of buildings and places – not as critique but as proposition? To do this, the means by which decisions are made regarding conservation and its social purpose require investigation. *The Memory of Surfaces* began to question the role of scientific practice and process in the way we perceive the decorative surfaces of heritage.

To deepen the understanding of surface into structure, the role of the architect also comes into question. How is heritage understood, what is its role in the making of meaningful spaces for people, how does the past become engaged with the present and what priorities are required to negotiate the difficult debate on 'significance' – for the professional or for the passer-by? History is by definition a snapshot of past evidence, and by necessity also a matter of interpretation and selection (of old documents, texts, materials) made by people for other people. How comprehensive that snapshot is, how thoroughly it is recorded or how the ordinary is sifted out to make way for what the historian considers 'significant' is an inherent issue. As we see with the contemporary debates around gender, colonialism and political interference in all spheres of artistic and cultural production, what we once saw as objective facts are being seen as ideological interpretations. *The Memory of Surfaces* finds no solutions to these newly opened wounds but was fully engaged in expanding the questioning of 'authenticity' that is now rightly to be contested.

The case of Clandon Park revealed some ambiguities embedded in the definition of heritage and in the shaping of an authorised discourse that can be adopted by official bodies to spur restoration. Indeed, shaping of material and cultural significance is dependent on selected narratives that are based on a number of factors, not least on economic convenience. In any society, the shaping of heritage narratives is mainly carried out by dominant classes which have the ability to inform a so-called authorized heritage discourse (Smith, 2006): the answers to the demands of the present are satisfied by creating a bespoke vision of the past which can be continuously reviewed and changed in time. George Orwell's much quoted comment 'who controls the present controls the past' implies an active role in its construction rather than a flattened approach to conservation. Foucault (1994) suggests that power needs to be examined at the point where its intentions are invested in its real and effective practices: acting on the significance of material and immaterial resources, those in power can influence what is remembered and therefore what is forgotten (McDowell, 2008), reinforcing the idea that 'heritage is not given, it is made' (Harvey, 2001: 336; Brett, 1996).

The care for the retention of 'authentic' materials is often supported by an ideological approach arguing that true conservation always refers to the original state of the building, as in the case of the Georgian Group. This attitude has recently shifted to support more sinister operations. The main common intervention of real estate in London, for example, consists in conserving the aspect of the historic building, restoring and repositioning original materials in place and then modifying the interiors, adapting them to the new uses – which is generally inhabitation. The spate of 'death mask' architecture in London (façade retention, with a new building cowering/lurking behind) is testament to this concept at its worst. As Waterton and Watson (2011) noted, the discontinuity between the former and the new is sealed, frozen through appearance. English Heritage, in particular, is watchful to assure that everything is "as true as the original as possible" (*ivi*). Despite the sentiment one would ask what the line is that separates 'false history' with renewal when economic advantage is at the heart of the project. The same care for materials, it can be argued, can be seen as truthful and respectful maintenance of original qualities, but also a guarantee of value: when unique features are restored and maintained, they not only preserve but gain significance though time. The wooden panels, in some cases removed, restored and reassembled as much as the columns, the sweeping staircases, the ballrooms and great halls, all bear intrinsic historic value and at the same time contribute to the authenticity of the product on sale, or in Clandon's case, its ability to fund its own maintenance in lieu of state support.

Alongside spatial changes come an interlaced system of norms and regulations, promotion of social practices and policies which affect not only the way construction is enabled but also its social returns (Söderström et al., 2012). Conservation guidelines and frameworks such as ICOMOS play a great part in this, addressing narratives that are the precondition for action. Too easily, however, they promote a univocal interpretation of heritage, excluding of the plurality of voices that normally inform the reading of space, or at best considering them as simple receivers. Once again, we open the question of heritage financialization via scientific recognition and the unsolved crisis of societal inclusion in the recognition and utilisation of shared patrimony.

> united in that communion of happy, reasonable, honoured labour which alone can produce genuine art, or the Pleasure of Life.
>
> (Morris, 1884)

Handcraft is the means of reconciling history with the present. If we assume Morris' thought, we can appreciate the record of accumulated work on a building as the means of understanding its value. 'Restoration', as defined by Morris, is the removal of the marks of time and hand, both of which define our humanity. Skilled and technically informed craft-based interventions that are clearly of their time are the means by which use value is sustained, and memory is owned. Morris linked the arts to architecture in a seamless way, the usefulness of art and the art of usefulness being inextricably bound together within a narrative of common cause and common participation. In the Victorian age of rampant scientific endeavour, the supposed pre-Raphaelite retreat from modernity requires further reflection in light of the issues Morris first raised around 'authenticity'. We suggest that modern science per se was not the issue for Morris, nor was style, with the British re-adoption of 'Gothic' in the 19th century finding no favour with Morris, for whom it was the framework of capital rather than aesthetics that underpinned the role of making in society. Craft, as Morris well understood from his mastery of weaving, dying, printing, bookbinding, furniture and textile design is also a material science – the issue is the quality of our engagement with materiality, our gain, our benefit, our social bonds that derive from it.

If craft in a contemporary setting is only the delivery mechanism for professional evaluation, how can people relate to the interventions made by 'conservation' within their environments? Is the role of the professional another iteration of the middle/governing class that takes decisions on behalf of a grateful population? Are 'heritage interpretation' panels on the construction site hoarding enough to secure engagement of local people for whom that building is part of their memory landscape? Communication is both liberator and gaoler of meaning, for surely it helps conceptualising the value of heritage, but we should remember that interpretation is always linked to selection, and potentially to exclusion. In this sense, the selection operated by official bodies, international standards such as ICOMOS, and professional architects holds responsibilities beyond the simple provision of guidelines.

The memory of surfaces requires handling with care. No rule is a given, other than that the relationship between memory and surface is fluid and fragile. How we determine a technical course of action should by definition relate to a strategic awareness of the history, and therefore memory of the building, its language, its materiality and its social context as well as its purpose and its use (which are not necessarily the same).

In Chapter 5 we look in detail at one material, terracotta, in a way that attempts to bring these disparate aspects into a common appreciation, We look at how historic political legacies inform the use and status of a material and how that can be challenged, how 'significance' is defined professionally in relation to conservation, and how that intellectual understanding of significance becomes translated into practice. Later in Chapter 6 we question further the notion of how the engagement of people in their surroundings can refocus professional practice around issues of heritage.

Notes

1 Dr Helen Howard works at National Gallery and is expert in the technical examination of European Old Master paintings, medieval wall painting and polychrome sculpture.
2 Marco Maggi (1957 Montevideo, Uruguay) is a New York and Uruguay based artist whose work incorporates common materials such as office paper, aluminium foil and graphite to create micro drawings, sculptures and macro installations. (https://en.wikipedia.org/wiki/Marco_Maggi)
3 John Locke (1632, Wrington, England–1704, High Laver, Essex), English philosopher whose works lie at the foundation of modern philosophical empiricism and political liberalism. For more information visit: www.britannica.com/biography/John-Locke
4 The Georgian Group is an English and Welsh conservation organisation created to campaign for the preservation of historic buildings and planned landscapes of the 18th and early 19th centuries and founded in 1937. For more information visit: https://georgiangroup.org.uk/

Bibliography

Books, journals

ABC Radio Australia (2009) *UNESCO Warns Malaysia over Penang Heritage Listing.* [Online] Available at: www.radioaustralia.net.au/international/radio/onairhighlights/UNESCO-warns-malaysia-ov erpenang-heritage-listing (Accessed: 4 April 2009).
Benjamin, W. (1983) *Das Passagen-Werk*, Frankfurt: Suhrkamp.
Blöch, E. (1935) *Eredità del nostro tempo*. Translated by L. Boella, Milano: Il Saggiatore, 1992.
Bourdieu, P. (1979) *Distinction: A Social Critique of the Judgment of Taste*. Translated by R. Nice, London: Routledge, 1984.
Brecht, B. (1963) *Gesammelte Werke*, Suhrkamp: Frankfurt.
Brett, D. (1996) *The Construction of Heritage*, Cork: Cork University Press.
Edwards, J. (2015) 'Why Building Conservation Needs BS 7913', *IHBC Journal Context*, 141, September: 45–46.
Foucault, M. (1994) *Biopolitica e Liberalism*. Translated by O. Marzocca, Milano: Medusa, 2001.
'The Georgian News', e-Newsletter, September 2017 Editorial, pp. 4–5.
Ghosh, H. (2017) 'Clandon Park: An Architectural Marvel', in *Clandon Park International Competition (National Trust)*, pp. 7–9. [Online] Available at: https://competitions.malcolmreading.co.uk/clandonpark/assets/downloads/Clandon-Park-Search-Statement.pdf (Accessed: 30 April 2019).
Harvey, D.C. (2001) 'Heritage Pasts and Heritage Presents: Temporality, Meaning and the Scope of Heritage Studies', *International Journal of Heritage Studies*, 4 (7): 319–338.

Hobsbawm, E.J. and Ranger, T. (1983) *L'invenzione della tradizione*. Translated by E. Basaglia, Torino: Einaudi, 1987.

Kennedy, M. (2016) 'Clandon Park's Marble Hall to Rise from Ashes of 2015 Blaze', *The Guardian*, 18 January. [Online] Available at: www.theguardian.com/uk-news/2016/jan/18/clandon-parks-marble-hall-to-rise-again-from-the-ashes-of-2015-blaze (Accessed: 30 April 2019).

Kracauer, S. (1963) *Das Ornament der Masse, Essays*, Frankfurt am Main: Suhrkamp.

Lévi-Strauss, C. (1962) *The Savage Mind*, Chicago: University of Chicago Press.

McDowell, S. (2008) 'Heritage, Memory and Identity', in Graham, B.J. and Howards, P. (eds.), *The Ashgate Research Companion to Heritage and Identity*, Farnham: Ashgate Publishing, pp. 37–54.

Mohamed, B., Omar, S.I. and Zainal Abidin, S.Z. (2015) *The Perils of Tourism Growth in a World Heritage Site: The Case of George Town, Penang*. 5th International Conference of Jabodetabek Study Forum, At Bagor, Indonesia.

Mohsit, M.A. and Sulaiman, M.B. (2006) 'Repeal of the Rent Control Act and Its Impacts on the Pre-War Shop Houses in Georgetown, Malaysia', *Journal of the Malaysia Branch of the Royal Asiatic Society*, 29 (1): 107–121. [Online] Available at: www.jstor.org/stable/41493817 (Accessed: 4 March 2019).

Morris, W. (1879) *Seconding a Resolution against Restoration*. Speech at SPAB, London, 28 June. [Online] Available at: www.marxists.org/archive/morris/works/1879/spab3.htm (Accessed: 30 March 2019).

Morris, W. (1884) *Art and Labour*. Speech, Leeds, 1 April. [Online] Available at: www.marxists.org/archive/morris/works/1884/art-lab.htm (Accessed: 1 May 2019).

Orwell, G. (1946) *Politics and the English Language*, London: Horizon.

Pinotti, A. and Somaini, A. (2009) *Teorie dell'immagine*, Milano: Raffaello Cortina Editore.

Pinotti, A. and Somaini, A. (2016) *Cultura visuale. Immagini sguardi media dispositivi*, Torino: Piccola biblioteca Einaudi.

Schlögel, K. (2011) *Marijampole, oder Europas Wiederkehr aus dem Geist der Städte*, Carl Hanser Verlag GmbH & Co. KG, Verlag: Berlin.

Smith, L. (2006) *Uses of Heritage*, London: Routledge.

Söderström, O., Klauser, F., Piguet, E. and Crot, L. (2012) 'Dynamics of Globalization: Mobility, Space and Regulation', *Geographica Helvetica*, 67: 43–54.

Walston, S. (1978) 'The Preservation and Conservation of Aboriginal and Pacific Cultural Material in Australian Museums', *ICCM Bulletin*, 4 (1): 9. doi:10.1179/iccm.1978.4.4.002

Waterton, E. and Watson, S. (eds.) (2011) *Heritage and Community Engagement*, London: Routledge.

Websites

Building Conservation 'Conservative Repair'. [Online] Available at: www.buildingconservation.com/articles/conservative-repair/conservative-repair.htm

The Courtauld Institute of Art. [Online] Available at: https://courtauld.ac.uk/study/student-life/east-wing-biennial

ENCoRE 'Guidelines for Education and Training in the Conservation of Monuments, Ensembles and Sites (1993)'. [Online] Available at: www.encore-edu.org/ICOMOS.html?tabindex=1&tabid=190

Historic England, Heritage Definitions. [Online] Available at: https://historicengland.org.uk/advice/hpg/hpr-definitions/

National Trust, Clandon Park Appeal. [Online] Available at: www.nationaltrust.org.uk/appeal/clandon-park-appeal

SPAB 'Preventative Maintenance'. [Online] Available at: www.spab.org.uk/advice/preventative-maintenance

SPAB (1877) Manifesto for the Society for the Protection of Ancient Buildings. [Online] Available at: https://www.spab.org.uk/about-us/spab-manifesto

Technical Preservation Services 'Restoration as Treatment'. [Online] Available at: www.nps.gov/tps/standards/four-treatments/treatment-restoration.htm

Online dictionaries and definitions:

Australian ICOMOS, "preservation", https://www.gdrc.org/heritage/icomos-au.html (accessed June 1, 2019).

Oxford Dictionaries, "bricolage", https://www.lexico.com/en/definition/bricolage (accessed June 1, 2019).

Oxford Dictionaries, "conservation", https://www.lexico.com/en/definition/conservation (accessed June 1, 2019).

Oxford Dictionaries, "memory", https://www.lexico.com/en/definition/memory (accessed June 1, 2019).

Oxford Dictionaries, "protection", https://www.oxfordlearnersdictionaries.com/definition/english/protection (accessed June 1, 2019).

Chapter 5
History and material significance
Craft and a sense of place

Approach

Fundamental to Morris's approach to architectural heritage is that the building is a document both of the society that built it – shared common skills, meanings and habitual life folded together into a fabric – and of the place in which the building is made. The specificity of material to a locality, for Morris, made buildings almost geological extensions of their territory. The direct translation of the ground into the building through the use of quarried stone, extracted clay-fired brick and timber grown on site created a form of material romance that the industrial revolution had already dismantled. With bricks shipped by rail to clay-less industrial towns, iron columns cast in Glasgow and erected in shopping colonnades of Johannesburg effectively undermined the material narratives of place Morris extolled. In truth this idealisation of place was a myth; Venice itself stood in the lagoon only because of stone from Istria and timber from Slovenia, Montenegro and Croatia, so if the most revered city in Ruskin and Morris's lexicon was a transnational assembly, is there any usefulness in ascribing value to material in relation to place?

In this chapter we are not so interested in arguing for or against Morris's valuing of materiality as an expression of place. We are interested, however, in the narrative that material provides, and how that narrative generates a relation between us and our surroundings. Understanding materials and techniques give us the ability to see through appearance into the history of a structure or landscape. The ability to see beyond a surface is potentially valuable in an era dominated by the superficial. Buildings as places are a form of human geography, a technical geology, a politically motivated ecology where legislation, entrepreneurship, infrastructure and circumstance contrive to create what should appear to be an inevitable means to inhabit the landscape or city we live in.

When approaching heritage buildings now, one of the primary drivers for assessment is the understanding of materiality, although as we have seen this form of 'reading' shifts from wider cultural significance to diagnosing causes of decay without really elaborating on the socio-political significance of material itself. The presumption to operate a 'like-for-like' approach to repair and alteration invests the building with a form of physical continuity that is at odds with the absolute shifts in technical and social change that separate its past from its present. If the material romance of place was relatively arbitrary, if material stories are frequently fictions that relate to hard-nosed economics or cultural appropriation, why then is there a reverence for original materiality and an impulse to define imitation as 'honesty' when the clay that made the bricks has long gone, and 'authentic' heritage London stock bricks are excavated and fired in Eastern Europe?[1] Can an understanding of the nature, processes of manufacture and built presentation of construction materials contribute to the development of a narrative for the building that can influence how that building is perceived, used and altered in the future? The significance of any material is a complex set of references, both conscious and habitual which are unfolded in order to demonstrate how the built fabric, social purpose and cultural identification are engaged with each other, and are readable in multiple ways. The ability to discover wider frames of reference within the materiality of a building is critical to evaluating not simply the significance of its fabric, but the significance the building as a whole has to society.

Chapter 5 explores the relationship between meaning and surface and investigates how official narratives linked to originality and authorship are increasingly excluding communities in the definition of their own heritage. Craft, manufacture, material specificity and social appreciation are some of the topics we will deepen, revealing that aesthetics is not simply appearance (Pye, 1968) and functionality is not simply technical (Benjamin, 1936). The case studies presented here, the Grade I listed church of St. Pancras and the Whitechapel Gallery, reveal ideas about the practicality of art and the fetishisation of craft technique. Their stories are representative of how the changes that always concern architecture have material and social consequences born out of selection and constraint and affect the way we understand and engage with place.

GLOSSARY

Conservation: *noun - a careful preservation and protection of something especially: planned management of a natural resource to prevent exploitation, destruction, or neglect; the preservation of a physical quantity during transformations or reactions (Merriam-Webster Dictionary, online). The processes of looking after a place so as to retain its cultural significance (Australian ICOMOS).*

The emphasis on the establishment of equilibrium outside of external influence is important, in social terms this exclusion is problematic as importance is interiorized and the building or space becomes mute in its dialogue with its surroundings.

Maintenance: *noun – Middle English from Old French, from 'maintenir' (see maintain) (Oxford Dictionaries, online). Means the continuous protective care of the fabric and setting of a place, and is to be distinguished from 'repair', which involves some aspect of restoration or reconstruction (Australian ICOMOS).*

Maintenance was a core activity for Morris as a means to 'stave off decay' and sustain historic buildings through regular care by local people. The engagement with a building was indented as a way to foster a specific beneficial social relations between the building and the community, and between members of that community.

Reconstruction: *noun – late Middle English: via Old French from Latin 'constructio' (n-), from 'construere' (to heap).*

Reconstruction operates at two scales – at a building scale or structural scale:

- at a building scale this means returning a place to a known earlier state and is distinguished from 'restoration' by the introduction of new material to constitute the fabric of a building that appears to be from a previous time. The more 'accurate' the reconstruction, the more historically appropriate the materials for the reconstruction will be. On occasion the unavailability of compatible material will require the use of similar material – such as the use of French rather than British limestone for the new pediment within the Foster and Partners Great Court redevelopment for the British Museum.
- at a structural scale this approach allows for the use of technically advanced materials to sustain the continued use of older, potentially weaker fabric, requiring a comprehensive understanding of chemical as well as tectonic compatibility to avoid the risk of interface failure. Common examples include the use of resins or metals within stone, brick or timber structures to secure their performance as structures, the presence of this technology usually remains hidden to 'preserve' the appearance of the historic.

Restoration: *noun – late 15th century, denoting the action of restoring to a former state: partly from Old French, partly an alteration of obsolete restauration, from late Latin 'restauratio'(n-), from the verb 'restaurare' (Oxford Dictionaries, online): returning the existing – fabric of a place to a known earlier state by removing accretions or by reassembling existing components without the introduction of new material (Australian ICOMOS).*

Historic England define this state as being "...a known earlier state, on the basis of compelling evidence, without conjecture. "The Institute of Historic Building Conservation (IHBC) state that "Restoration aims to achieve a high level of authenticity, replicating materials and techniques as closely as possible. Where necessary, modern works, such as replacing outdated utilities, or installing climate controls, alarm systems, and so on, are undertaken in a concealed manner where they will not compromise historic character." (IHBC Conservation)

The key concepts within Restoration, described by the IHBC require the prioritisation of 'historic character' over new building additions or requirements. 'Historic character' is effectively an ideal condition that absorbs material alteration without visible alteration. The identity of 'Historic character', however thoroughly defined only provides evidence of appearance, and the result of 'restoration' is without question a pretense, as the work is new. The basic principles that should be taken into consideration, particularly for structural restoration are: having sufficient respect for the original materials; respecting the valid contributions of all periods on the building; replacement of missing parts must integrate harmoniously with the whole; additions should not detract from the building, its setting or relation with surroundings; use of traditional techniques and materials; modern techniques and materials are admissible where traditional alternatives are not feasible.

Restoration is often a course of action taken due to the presence of decay and can be executed in either a reversible or irreversible way. External buttressing, ties and stitching are considered reversible structural techniques, however they all result in visibility, and therefore actually fall outside the definition of Restoration as not compromising the appearance of 'character'. Irreversible techniques include the introduction of high performance grouts, high tensile steel reinforcing bars or using bonded epoxy dowels to secure surfaces, all of which retain the impression of continuity.

The impression of continuity needs careful evaluation, not seeing does not mean not changing – stress patterns, thermal expansion, chemistry, mineralogy can all be subject to incompatibility or even failure in the short or longer term. On occasion the use of modern materiality is a necessity – either averting catastrophic failure or dealing with unacceptable toxicity such as cyanide or arsenic in historic paint.

Alongside this official definition (IHBC) Morris and Webb (1877) provided a more radical and different perspective in the SPAB Manifesto: "For Architecture, long decaying, died out, as a popular art at least, just as the knowledge of mediaeval art was born. So that the civilised world of the 19th century has no style of its own amidst its wide knowledge of the styles of other centuries. From this lack and this gain arose in men's minds the strange idea of the Restoration of ancient buildings; and a strange and most fatal idea, which by its very name implies that it is possible to strip from a building this, that, and the other part of its history – of its life that is – and then to stay the hand at some arbitrary point, and leave it still historical, living, and even as it once was".

5.1 St. Pancras Church, London

Award-winning conservation work by the author on the Grade I listed St. Pancras church in London prompted a reflection on the materiality of terracotta in relation to practical conservation methodology, issues of repair or replacement, authenticity and appearance, manufacturing and the ethics of architectural reproduction, and was presented to the Society for the Protection of Ancient Buildings as technical continuous professional development (CPD) jointly with Historic England. The chapter elaborates on how an awareness of heritage values can inform and develop a conservation project and how it can be structured to gain community benefit through identifying and working with heritage significance.

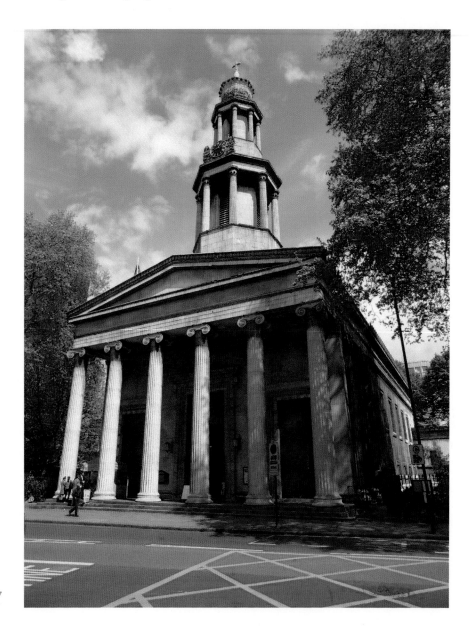

*Figure 5.1
St. Pancras
Church
elevation.*

*Source: Picture by
the authors, 2019*

The ancient parish of St. Pancras in London was geographically extensive, reaching from Oxford Street to Highgate. By the early 1800s demographic shifts saw the Southern end of the parish overpopulated, and the decision was taken in 1816 to build a new church in Euston Square and leave St. Pancras Old Church as a 'chapel of ease'. An open competition attracted over thirty submissions and the successful design was by a local architect and his son, William and Henry Inwood. The church as we know it today is the result of that competition: the west end delivers the basic arrangement of a portico, while the vestibules and tower are reminiscent of the design by James Gibbs at St. Martin's in the Fields (1722). However, St. Pancras is in a Greek revival style using the Ionic order, the Inwood's project drawing heavily on two ancient Greek monuments on the Acropolis in Athens for their inspiration. The octagonal domed ceiling of the vestibule and the pinnacle of the spire is a direct imitation of the Tower of the Winds, a marble tower in the Roman Agora in Athens that functioned as a 'timepiece'. At the east end of the church is an apse, flanked by the church's most identifiable features: two tribunes designed in imitation of the Erechtheum, with entablatures supported by caryatids. A stone sarcophagus is located behind the figures in each tribune, upper levels of which were designed as vestries, a collision between the culturally significant and the prosaic provision of service spaces. At a detailed level the Greek lexicon is extensively quoted, with the cornices studded with lion's heads, antifixae lining the parapets and sima demarcating the corners of the portico.

Following submission of the scheme to the competition, Henry Inwood travelled to Athens to study directly the inspiration for the church. While he was there the

Figure 5.2 Inwood perspective 1819 from 'St. Pancras Church 1937', booklet.

Source: Picture courtesy the Society for the Protection of Ancient Buildings

As designed 1819.

commission was awarded, allowing him the opportunity to bring back to England plaster casts of details of the Erechtheum, and some excavated fragments that may or may not have been legally acquired. The building is in brick, faced with Portland stone, except for the portico and the tower above the roof, which are entirely of stone. All the external decoration, including the capitals of the columns is of terracotta, including the caryatids, constructed in sections around cast-iron columns and modelled by John Charles Felix Rossi, the son of an Italian émigré who learned his craft with Coade and who provided all the terracotta on the building.

The first stone was laid by the Duke of York at a ceremony on 1st July 1819, carved with a Greek inscription, of which the English translation is: "May the light of the blessed Gospel thus ever illuminate the dark temples of the Heathen." This is an interesting reference to one of the underlying issues with 'Greek Revivalism' in the early 19th century – the adoption of pre-Christian iconography, and explicitly the direct quotation of 'pagan' Greek architecture for the building of churches. This theological fault line has further political ramifications that this chapter will go on to explore.

The church was consecrated by the Bishop of London on 7th May 1822. The total cost of the building, including land and furnishings, was £76,679, making it the most expensive church in London since the rebuilding of St. Paul's Cathedral by Wren. St. Pancras was designed to seat 2,500 people, with the crypt, extending the entire length of the church, designed to contain 2,000 coffins. Fewer than five hundred interments had taken place by 1854 when the practice was ended in all London churches. Ironically, following the exhumation of over ten thousand bodies from St. Mary's churchyard adjacent to Euston due to the arrival of the High Speed 2 railway, the crypt may finally fulfil its repository purpose. One of those souls to be reinterred is Charles Felix Rossi.

Over time, the Grade I listed building has suffered a number of structural and environmental challenges. The church was closed for two years from 1951 for structural

Figure 5.3 Detail of elevation terracotta enrichment.

Source: Picture by the authors, 2016

renovation made necessary by dry rot and war damage to the main roof, requiring a new roof and suspended plaster ceiling. The North Chapel was added in 1970 and the interior was 'restored' in 1981. The commissioning of 'The Portico project' with Heritage Lottery funding in 2016 sought to address fundamental issues of decay identified over three statutory quinquennial (five yearly) inspections. The environmental challenges, in particular, relate to the material decay of the building's fabric. Classical architecture is a Mediterranean language with details derived to correspond with a fair climate – the inability of this language to deal with the North European climate should not be underestimated, as the visual purging of guttering in key visual locations together with the highly articulated mouldings and projections make water management highly problematic. London's rain is heavily acidified by atmospheric pollution and has, since the completion of the building, caused erosion of the alkaline limestone with the loss of between 10–20 mm of stone across the whole building and in particular the upper surfaces. This loss of surface depth and projecting drips lead to the exposure of iron cramps within the walls to water saturation, causing the iron to become affected by corrosion, which in turn expands and fractures the stone, advancing water ingress. The loss of projecting drips to clear water from the walls hastens erosion locally. Finally, post-war repairs and alterations to the rooves had created weathering issues and water ingress problems where oversized lead bays had failed due to inadequate movement joints on the portico, creating material stresses, cracking and a series of inadequate temporary repairs.

The following description of the condition of the building fabric written for the winning entry of the project for the John Betjeman Award for Church Conservation (2017)[2] demonstrates the detailed understanding of the diagnostics of decay. This, as our discourse highlights, is not enough in itself, and the case study moves through diagnostics to a wider understanding of material and cultural significance of terracotta. The

Figure 5.4
Stone decay to edge of portico.
Source: Picture by the authors, 2016

analysis is based on a year-long investigation led by Chandler's practice 'Arts Lettres Techniques'[3] and 'B2 Architects',[4] who were appointed to deliver the restoration project. Moving beyond the restoration itself, the case study explores the wider implication linked to the significance of a material – in this case terracotta, its traditional value and the role a material plays in shaping not only architectonic form, but also cultural meaning.

A statement of need

Arresting decay was primary, and the means by which this was best addressed required a careful judgement that weighed up the ability to preserve original fabric with the necessity to dismantle and reassemble. Every original element was retained and protected. Only one new piece of terracotta was needed within the limited area for this project, made and fired by skilled craftspeople at Darwen Terracotta in Lancashire. Replacing missing pieces that impact on the appreciation of the whole and establishing a recipe for future replacements would seem incontrovertible; however, taking the philosophy of leaving 'as found' would prevent such replacement of lost fabric. Why was replacement considered appropriate here? Firstly because St. Pancras has some of the finest terracotta enrichments in the country, secondly it is hugely important to ensure our specialists in terracotta can contribute to work of this quality, or it will become a skill of the past and thirdly maintaining the visual continuity and coherence of Inwood's design similarly requires a continuity of decoration – missing elements create points of absence more significant than the continuity of the enrichment, which is the wrong emphasis. Preservation and repair are more sophisticated than simply 'not touching'. If following Morris's line of thought means anything, it is to ensure that craft and care are constant companions for a building. Where the challenge really resides is in how the act of replacement is undertaken, where original fabric can be sustained, and where sustaining material failure creates unacceptable risk.

In three consecutive quinquennial inspection since 2002, reports warned of consequences of the "extreme length of the lead bays" – double the Lead Sheet Association recommended length on the roof of the portico.[5] The resulting thermally induced cracking of the lead was only noted – shorthand for not having enough budget to address the inevitable water ingress and the threat it posed to the timber roof structure below. A series of welded repairs were made to the lead during this time, with the outer bay adjacent to the pediment being covered with a layer of asphalt-based roofing felt which was only partially successful in preventing water ingress to the timber framing and top face of the plaster soffit below. It was clear that the roof had been modified at some time after construction as each of the antefixes along the flank of the portico has a specially detailed rebate with fixing holes to accommodate the end of each timber roll. With the introduction of a shallow gutter behind the antefixes at some point in its history, they were left to sit in isolation surrounded by an asphalt-covered cementitious render, allowing water penetration and unmanaged run-off to corrode the leading edge of stone and the terracotta enrichment directly below. The line of terracotta enrichment below the antefixes, exposed to the sun and rain on southern edge of the portico, thanks to corroded iron cramps have all fallen in the past onto the public realm below. It was critical therefore to secure the terracotta on the northern edge of the portico roof.

In parallel to the poor condition and performance of the lead, the erosion of the Portland stone copings around the northern and southern porches has allowed water ingress to the parapet walls, advancing iron cramp corrosion on the inner stone faces of the parapet cladding and eroding/loosening a band of terracotta enrichment on the outer face. A visual evaluation revealed shell inclusions and the bronze cramps on the upper surface of the copings projecting up to 10 mm, left marooned by the dissolving action of the water, indicated how much of the surface has been weathered away by highly acidic rain (the Euston Road is one of the most highly polluted urban thoroughfares in Europe). The erosion of the stone on the inner edge of the copings was so pronounced that they were almost flush with the inner face of the parapet, the lack of projection therefore shedding nothing. The terracotta displayed a variety of conditions depending partly on orientation and partly to inherent variation in the terracotta blocks themselves. The general erosion of the coping stones was in some locations exacerbated (on joints for example), which created particularly significant damage when the terracotta was constantly saturated, and consequently encrusted with black carbon deposits that hasten the loss of surface integrity through concentrating acidic contact. The terracotta enrichment below the coping stones is restrained back to the wall structure using iron cramps, the water accelerated decay causing the fracturing and loosening of these elements with many pieces of terracotta falling to earth as a result. As part of the Heritage Lottery–funded project the team prepared an illustrated and measured catalogue of 32 architectural elements in storage at the church that had descended from the building since 1952, including a 48 × 58 × 32 cm terracotta antefix. The restoration project envisaged the placement and re-fixing of these elements where possible when a wider programme of repair is able to secure funding.

The loss of the surface, or 'fireskin' of some, but by no means all of the terracotta elements is indicative of inconsistent manufacturing. The fireskin is the semi-vitrification of the surface of the terracotta under firing that, when optimised, creates a block that is incredibly durable. When inconsistently fired, as was the case in coke- or wood-fired kilns of the early 19th century, the fireskin can be fragile or porous, vulnerable to freeze/thaw conditions.

The complex relationship between lead, stone, terracotta, iron (and acidic rain) has shifted the physical quality of each in relation to the other, their altered states over time posed technically interesting challenges: the question for the consultants was how to link these diverse materials and causes of failure together in a conservation strategy. The starting point is usually 'what would William Morris say', knowing that he could give one of two answers – leave the fabric alone, or add to its history using integrity and without artifice. In the case of 'leaving alone' the context is usually 'why make change'? If the answer is material failure then repair and secure the fabric, being honest and minimal in its execution. Doing nothing hastens decay, so lead, stone and terracotta all required specific, considered responses to particular circumstances.

A statement of action

The primary protective surface is lead, specified as a matching code 7/8, the thickest available allowing for the longest length (bay) to be used. With the existing lead skin removed it became clear that the original supporting larch boarding and connecting timber rolls were sufficiently sound to be allowed to dry out and retain in situ. The timber rolls were unique in section – reminiscent of a triangular ridge rather than the

recognisable rolled profile, so the ability to re-use was significant. A good deal of time was spent on the roof assessing the way water was behaving around the antefixae at the edge of the portico, and a lead detail for each terracotta antefix was devised to utilise the rebate set into the upper rear edge shaped for the original lead roll to fix into. The two holes provided in the terracotta to make the fixing for the roll was re-used to screw in a hardwood block that gave a ground for clips securing each sheltering lead cloak.

For all the writing in the charters devoted to material forensics and craft-based historic skills, the contemporary condition of professional specification determining contractor's costs and liabilities have in reality skewed the roles of architect and artisan. Rarely can the constraints of contemporary building contracts leave space for deliberation and shared problem solving. The intricate lead detailing at St. Pancras was a rare moment when the skills and open mindedness of the lead workers allowed for site refinement of the details to achieve better than designed.

Lead drips were then dressed between the antefixae, even between the final antefix and the sima (lion head) enrichments at the corners (sima normally perform the function of water discharge like a gargoyle, here they are simply decorative). The development of these details was drawn as part of the contract tendering, but were developed on site in collaboration with the lead workers, who contributed a great deal to the definition of the architect's ideas. These drips are imperceptible from the ground and will over time allow the stonework and terracotta to dry out below. A future and more extensive façade repair programme can then consolidate these areas.

Arresting the fracturing and spalling at the top of the inner parapet stonework directly under the copings was difficult, the minimal removal of damaged stone around the corroding iron cramps to affect repair difficult. Lifting and resetting the existing copings allowed not only minimal removal of stone to achieve cramp replacement,

*Figure 5.6
Completed lead
cloak to portico
antefix.*

*Source: Picture by
the authors, 2016*

but also for the cleaning and re-securing of the water-affected terracotta on the outer face of the wall using non-corroding stainless steel cramps. The requirement to lift the coping stones was an issue for the team – clearly they had never been disturbed so their removal and replacement was invasive. The deciding factor was the ability to deal with the totality of issues: water ingress, corroding iron cramp removal and the deterioration and falling/eroding terracotta elements. With all three tasks requiring urgent attention, the careful numbering, lifting and resetting of the coping stones in lime mortar was specified, and the scaffold installed to facilitate it.

Figure 5.7
Completed lead
cloak and drip to
portico sima.

Source: Picture by
the authors, 2016

There were a number of cramps holding the inner parapet wall cladding that had not yet corroded to the point where stone was being pressurised by iron expansion. These cramps were left in peace. Only cramps with evidence of localised cracking, iron oxide leaching or spalling would be cut out and replaced. Where no evidence of corrosion was seen, iron cramps were left in peace, with a proviso that future water saturation would be dealt with. The resetting of the copings allowed for the insertion of a lead drip to the inner face of the parapet, a non-original detail which would augment the ability of the eroded copings to throw water clear of the inner face of the parapet wall, the new stone repairs and the remaining iron cramps, prolonging the life of all three. A number of coping stone edge pieces were reinstated in a matching stone, located to correspond to areas where significant localised erosion had created enhanced water run-off that threatened or had already made significant damage to the material below it. The eroded profiles were respected but not imitated, the new pieces unmistakably new, sitting slightly proud of the adjoining original material.

A sequence of carefully executed cleaning procedures was developed in collaboration with Sally Strachey Historic Conservation[6] on a terracotta element that had fallen from its location due to complete cramp corrosion and washed-out lime bedding. Based on the results of this ammonium carbonate poultice and Thermatech (pressurised steam) cleaning trial, a process was determined which removed the majority of the carbon crust and associated blackening while ensuring that the fireskin was not eroded and the age of the terracotta not erased.

With the risk of future cramp failure causing the loss of historic details and risk to passers-by, an in-situ cleaning operation was discounted in favour of the more interventionist approach. The architects specified the recording, numbering and careful removal of the terracotta elements while the coping stones were being reset, with each piece cleaned as per the trial. The elements were then re-fixed in place using stainless

Figure 5.8
Dismantling
terracotta
enrichment
below the
parapet coping
stones showing
accumulation of
carbon deposits.

*Source: Picture by
the authors, 2015*

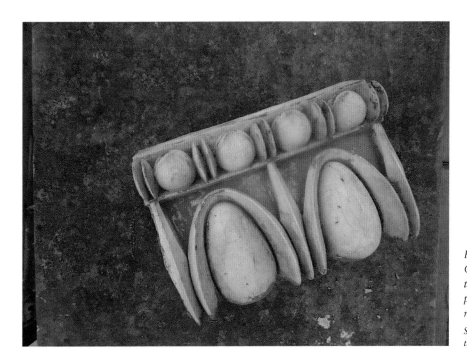

Figure 5.9
Cleaned
terracotta
piece prior to
reassembly.

*Source: Picture by
the authors, 2016*

*Figure 5.10
Re-assembly
of copings
and terracotta
enrichment.*

*Source: Picture by
the authors, 2016*

steel cramps with a lime mortar bedding specified with regard to the long-term hardening of the material beyond the strength stated in its technical specification. Evidence shows that the 'hardness' of lime-based mortars proves to be far higher that stated, meaning that over time the mortar becomes more durable than the masonry it is bonding, creating erosion issues for the masonry itself. The binder should be sacrificial, therefore softer than the material it binds.

The challenging climatic conditions, combined with access to a wide range of deterioration problems in a single site where the terracotta quality was exemplary, attracted the interest of Historic England. While research into the diagnosis and replacement of terracotta is already established, the consolidation of the surfaces and the range of potential repair materials available has never been systematically applied and monitored to assess long-term effectiveness. The opportunity to develop a programme of trials became part of the conservation project, the repair samples executed at the base of the tower monitored every six months for two years (short term) starting from mid-2019, then in 2026 and finally in 2031. The trials will look at permeability, hardness, colourfastness, thermal expansion, surface quality and the relation of the surface of the repair to the terracotta adjacent to it. Surface repairs matter in order to consolidate the original material and avoid the necessity to remove eroded terracotta pieces and renew them. Some of the trial repairs are surface applied, other deeper repairs require the drilling and insertion of stainless steel dowels to act as armatures for the repair. Mortars have traditionally been used to create surface repairs, however the bond between lime and terracotta is unreliable because terracotta does not behave in the same way as stone either thermally or chemically. In addition, the recent advances in epoxy resins and acrylic polymers in relation to UV stability and thermal movement require a re-evaluation at a practical, as well as a philosophical level, accepting the retention of historic fabric through the use of technically advanced contemporary materials rather than 'like-for-like'.

The necessity to rely on craft skills able to tackle material matters drives the long-term sustainability of heritage technology and the competence in applying it and opens the debate on the relationship between craftsmanship and practices of renewal, fabric sustainability and skilful intervention. Creating a toolkit for consolidating historic terracotta is therefore part of establishing a range of options, with St. Pancras contributing to best practice:

> The intention of this research is also to encourage fine scale repairs to architectural terracotta, avoiding in some instances the need for replacement, and as a consequence provide opportunities for economic, craft based repairs that can re-establish the visual integrity of details on this and other historic terracotta buildings.
>
> (Willett, 2019)

After the portico project at St. Pancras won the SPAB John Betjeman Award for Church Conservation in 2017,[7] and Historic England worked with the author to establish a long-term terracotta repair trial, it seemed prudent to reflect on both the philosophical and practical implications of the work by exploring what Morris had to say about terracotta. His perspective was less than positive; in fact Morris issued a challenge to the use of terracotta that requires a response:

> Now there is, by the way, another kindred material to brick, and that is the cast brick they call terra-cotta. I cannot abide it, I must say. I do not think I need treat it any further, and I will tell you why. . . . It is used for nothing else except ornament, and I am rather inclined to think that of all things not wanted at the present day, and especially in London outside a house, the thing that is least wanted is ornament. That is to say, as long as there is a huge congeries of houses, as in London, the greater part of which are lamentably and hideously ugly, I think one ought to pitch one's note rather low, and try, if one can manage it, to get the houses and buildings to look solid and reasonable, and to impress people with their obvious adaptation to their uses; where they can be made big to make them big, and not to bother about ornament.
>
> Such ornament as there is, to keep it for the inside, where at all events it can be treated with delicacy, and you do not feel that you have something which after all, whatever value there is in it as ornament, will presently disappear, and you simply get something which is of no particular use, except for collecting dirt.
>
> You know perfectly well how that cast stuff is generally used; I noticed some as I came along just now, and I said to myself: After all, these things are not a bit like cast work, or moulded work at all; they look like a bad imitation of carved work. It has a fatal ease in the matter of ornamentation, which makes the material, it seems to me, decidedly bad for its purpose. I think it is very much better if you want to have brick ornament on a building to get cut and rubbed brick.
>
> (Morris, 1881)

Morris felt the work of architecture, made with skill, for utility and within a craft-based employment structure created art by default – not by design. The process of terracotta was neither moulded nor cast (actually, its manufacturing process requires both), but results in an imitation of carving, leaving us with an open question around

authenticity, reproducibility and honesty of expression. Integrated within this philosophical evaluation is a practical one – Morris balanced these two issues throughout his
writings on conservation and politics and is in some sense his greatest legacy. The criticism about 'collecting dirt' is an observation on what is an inappropriate delicacy of
articulation for a building exterior, with the implication that the level of detail should
be reserved for the interior. This is a highly provocative observation on appropriateness
of craft – is the external elaboration of a façade in terracotta less worthy than the one in
stone? Would the appearance of a department store such as Harrods in Knightsbridge,
which is entirely clad in terracotta, be more appropriate in another material? Or rather,
was Morris simply unhappy at the decorative excesses of late 19th-century commercial
taste that vied with cathedrals for ornate presentation and intricate sculptural excess,
only affordably and executed in a fraction of the time? Surely, there are many reasons
why terracotta has been preferred to other materials, one of them being that

> When there are many molded and decorative features which would neces-
> sitate much hand work for dressing and carving, if stone were used, the
> advantage in terra cotta in point of cost is evident. Further economy may be
> obtained by repeating the detail of the ornamental features, so as to require
> the fewest possible different pieces. Very often suitable designs may be found
> in catalogues of terra-cotta manufacturers, by using which the cost will be
> considerably less than when new patterns and moulds must be made for
> the work.
>
> (The Colliery Engineer Co., 1899)

Terracotta was indeed a cheap alternative to stonework and a focus of Morris's com-
bative desire for craft-based building construction using the primary materials of stone,
brick and timber. His attitude was drawing on the achievements of medieval guilds to
find true architectural languages for material. However, the arguments are wider than
technical preference. Terracotta is not simply an industrial replacement for ancient
handcraft. It was actually used in Mesopotamian and Egyptian art, in the Greek,
Minoan and Etruscan civilisations, adopted by the Romans and revived in the Italian
renaissance by Palladio, from whom Inigo Jones then Kent and Burlington delivered a
civic expression for the emerging British Empire. So what historical truth do we look
for, and how far back should we look? Perhaps 'authenticity' is the wrong critique to
apply to terracotta, for if we look back to the original Greek temples that inspired St.
Pancras, we find the original use of terracotta for fine ornamentation. For example,
Charles Waldstein in one of his *Essays on the Art of Phidias* (1885) discovered the
use of terracotta as a means of finalising the design of the marble frieze on the Parthe-
non, comparing the identical terracotta figure in the Louvre to the original in London
(neither, ironically, in Greece). Still in the 1st century AD, terracotta was part of the
material lexicon of the Greek temples, a refinement of the ceramic process specifically
for architectural decoration. What this tells us is that the Inwoods's use of terracotta is
far from inauthentic or simply a cheap substitute of a nobler material. On the contrary,
Inwood was using terracotta exactly as an original material, part of the craft processes
needed for construction, and linked to the same classical culture that, together with the
style, mastered different materials to shape the building.

The execution of the acroterion in terracotta, to adorn the parapet line of Greek temples, utilised the hollow construction achievable using fired clay to develop a pragmatic,

lightweight method of realising architectural statuary with the ability to create serial decoration economically. This original application of fired clay remained pertinent in the 17th, 18th and 19th centuries, showing a continuity of practice and its efficacy. So was imitation or historicism really the key to Morris's objection to terracotta?

We need to remember that for Morris, politics, art, materiality and conservation are all entwined.

Greek sculpture is fundamentally associated with the culture of perfection – a benchmark of naturalism in art that shaped the post-enlightenment view of the way statehood is manifest through art. The crafted work of the European Middle Ages so beloved by Morris was eclipsed by the Enlightenment's rediscovery of the Greek model. The acute replication of reality in Greek sculpture gave the polis its language as a political model of 'democracy', its perfection of appearance effectively sidestepping fundamental issues of empire, social hierarchy, gender suppression and slavery. As such every European empire or aspirational empire has adopted this principle in the way it defines its own cultural output – Roman, British, American, Napoleonic France, Stalin's Russia, the Third Reich. Given the unforeseen political legacy of Greek art, it is therefore unsurprising that Morris, as a pre-Raphaelite saw this in an unfavourable light. Both politically and artistically the periodic revivals of Greek aesthetics regarded the medieval period as a 'dark age' between periods of 'civilisation', invariably serving socio-political ends that Morris considered corrupt and exploitative. He addressed this explicitly:

> Meantime to the cultivated Greek citizen there seemed nothing wrong or burdensome in chattel slavery, and all that it gave birth to: to him it was part of the natural order of things and the greatest minds of the day could see no possibility of its ever ceasing. So might our citizen have argued, not without the agreement of many cultivated men of the present day, who, I observe, do think, and not unnaturally, that the cultivated gentleman of Greece or England is such a precious and finished fruit of civilization, that he is worth any amount of suffering, injustice, or brutality in the mass of mankind below him.
>
> (Morris, 1884)

So, both artistically and politically Morris had issues with terracotta. This makes winning the Society for the Protection of Ancient Buildings 'John Betjeman Award' in 2017 interestingly ironic by applying principles of repair that Morris advocated to material that he himself detested. However if, as he states, a building is a document to learn from, then St. Pancras also gives us a socio-political narrative readable through attention to detail, material and technique.

St. Pancras attained its Grade I heritage status as an unrivalled example of 'Greek revival', with Inwood undertaking direct inspiration/imitation from the Acropolis in Athens. The relationship between inspiration and copyism is an interesting one, in that the caryatids studied by Inwood on the Acropolis are now all replicas – castings rather than stone, executed in the manner of terracotta while the originals are protected from the acidic air of Athens in the Acropolis Museum – except for one, which ironically stands 900 metres away from St. Pancras Church in the British Museum. So the cast terracotta caryatids on St. Pancras mirror their cast sisters in Athens in more than simply inspiration or imitation. Executed in terracotta by former Coade employee John Charles Felix Rossi in 1822, each of the St. Pancras caryatids, unlike the originals, hold either an extinguished torch or an empty jug, reflecting their position as guardians of the dead.

In acknowledging that the use of terracotta at St. Pancras was not simply imitative, but part of a long-term, interpretative, adaptable and nuanced heritage of Greek decoration, we should look in detail at the craft within the technique, not merely at the stonecraft that it supplants. Terracotta is a curious hybrid process: the use of moulds to generate the clay 'building blocks' imply casting; however, the creation of the moulds involves full scale carving, along with the requisite skills in handling clay ware, glazing and firing and careful assembly on site. Terracotta has a complex process when originating a new project, which is even more intensive when, as at St. Pancras, we

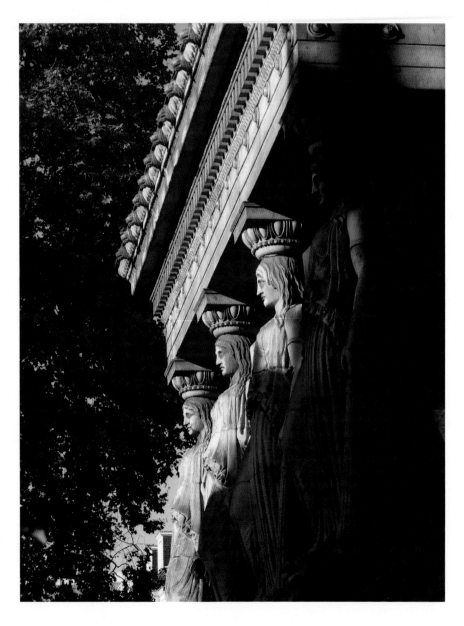

Figure 5.11 Caryatids above the North crypt entrance.

Source: Picture by the authors, 2019

are extending the act of replication. The process of making a single 'building block' of terracotta used in the portico project can be summarised as follows:

Survey and modelling – detailed measurements and profiles are taken from an original – drawings are developed and inform the carving of the block through the making of zinc profiles that define its parameters. Modelling clay is applied and sculpted to refine the deep detail.

Moulding – a plaster 'negative' is cast to form a mould in sections that disassemble and contain 'joggle joints' to ensure accurate reassembly after each use. Disassembly of a mould that contains a complex three-dimensional 'carving' requires the mould to be designed with extreme care.

Pressing – clay is applied by hand 'pressed' into the detail of the mould to a uniform thickness of around 35 mm, with supporting webs or ribs of clay internally to prevent slumping. The clay is seasoned by exposure to the air then ground and mixed with water and materials known as "grog", that when fired produce a partial vitrification of the surface that increases the durability of the terracotta. Grog consists of very fine white sand and powdered pozzolans. The mixed clay is then layered, cut into sections and remixed through a pug mill, creating a uniform mixture for application in the moulds. The blocks made by Rossi were solid, creating issues with duration of firing and uneven heat flows through the clay in the kiln. In modern manufacture the lessons learned from industrial clay wares in Staffordshire using slip casting are applied – reducing the thickness and increasing the evenness of the block walls by using a clay slurry that 'dries' against the plaster mould as a shell, as with a toilet pan, saving material and more importantly time (and skill) in the pressing process.

Hand finishing – the clay is left in the mould for between 12–18 hours up to five days depending on the scale and complexity of the piece, to semi harden prior to its removal. Once removed the block has the joint lines from the mould carefully pared away and the surface smoothed.

Drying – originally air dried, modern manufacture uses drying facilities, with the original taking weeks to dry this is now a matter of a few days.

Terracotta is unglazed clay – the option to apply glaze to colour and crystallise the surface creates faience.

Firing – coke or wood fired kilns were Rossi's means, the unevenness of heat circulation in relatively primitive kilns was little different from those used in ancient Greece. Impurities in his solid blocks could easily cause fractures when firing, and uneven colouration was part of the process of uncontrolled heat. Modern kilns circulate 1170 degrees C of heat precisely for approximately four days, giving even and predictable colour and efficiency – so efficiently that the terracotta panels used on the Francis Crick Institute (2017) needed six separate colours to be made fractionally differently from each other in the German factory to achieve/imitate the differentiated appearance of what we assume to be the 'real' appearance of terracotta.

Clearly there is a craft in designing for manufacture in terracotta, there is a craft in drawing, the craft of manipulating plaster and forms, in applying the clay, glazing and firing. When St. Pancras was built the industrialised process of manufacturing

Figure 5.12
Original and replica terracotta piece prior to firing.
Source: Courtesy St. Pancras Church, 2016

terracotta was only relatively precise. As we will see with the weathering of St. Pancras the firing was anything but industrialised as we understand the term. Consistency of dimension is relatively precise; however the deterioration of one block in relation to its immediate neighbor, which is still as perfect as the day it was fired, indicates that firing technology is anything but accurate. The process is a hybrid, geometrically determined with relatively high tolerances that account for shrinkage of a fired clay when aiming for a set of closely fitting blocks creating architectural decoration. It is a strict three-dimensional reproduction of a two-dimensional design process, taking handcraft skills not as the origination of the work but as the execution of a carefully orchestrated, semi-industrialised, semi-craft process. Handcraft contains both the precision of practice and the flaws of human error – the balance of the two creating for Morris, art. The removal of error by the replication of what solely craft made in the medieval period was anathema to Morris, as was his observation that 'design' as a two-dimensional practice took away the craftsperson's freedom to express themselves in the execution of the work – hence his disdain. In reality, there is the same relation between terracotta processes as there is in hand-blocked wallpaper or tapestry weaving – the minute differences between one terracotta block and another creating diversity within a whole.

However, the modern manufacturing methods as used at the Crick Institute prove Morris, nearly two centuries after Rossi fabricated the caryatids and mouldings for St. Pancras, to be correct.

Terracotta is both imitative and authentic – in that imitation is as intrinsic a fact to materiality as is authenticity. If our built human history is bound together with material imitation, is it possible to ascribe robust notions of value to any heritage? Is materiality simply a spectrum of the inauthentic?

We would propose that losing a single truth that underpins heritage means that multiple and overlapping narratives become possible. As with the amplification of the significance of terracotta, deeper and more challenging reflections on meaning and relevance become possible when the narrative is democratic rather than exclusive. St. Pancras case study revealed that 'authenticity' as we know it is strictly linked to a dominant narrative that selects and pairs images and meaning. This strategy addresses a more general growth in aesthetic reflexivity (Kearns and Philo, 1993) that brought important consequences in the appreciation of the notion of authenticity. In our case, the use of terracotta was not more authentic than the use of stone in relation to classical architecture, being both part of the craft process leading to construction and in the construction itself. This teaches us that the link between craft and sense of place is not as determined as one may think, and that the de-layering of building techniques can open wider issues on style and significance.

Considering the link between collective and dominant narratives, observing the validating use of the concept of 'authenticity' and understanding material significance against wider political, social and economic contexts, may help us to broaden our understanding of place specificity, and their potential meaning to the community. The use of terracotta in a second case study illustrates how the reflection on significance within its use at St. Pancras enabled an alternative reading of another culturally significant building – the Whitechapel Art Gallery.

5.2 The Whitechapel Art Gallery, London

Heritage as built fabric depends on its status through cultural consensus. If a building has significance through its original purpose, and its historic form was derived from that purpose, what happens to its heritage status when that purpose shifts? Who are the subjects that can redefine its significance and how?

The Whitechapel Gallery has a complex history in what was originally a simple building. To understand its heritage significance fully, its programme of exhibitions across a century is more revealing of the shifting nature of significance than any physical mapping, which by definition only registers significance changes in built fabric. As authors, we are conscious of appearing to depart from the emphasis Ruskin and Morris placed on built fabric, but we rather see this as an extension of their radical re-designation of materiality, intended as a document to be read. For this reason it is important to explore not only the meanings associated with the physical duration of built fabric, but also the ephemeral meanings associated with the cultural dimension of the building itself. Both materials and social significance layer over time, in so much that the buildings can be seen as complex texts that can be read at many levels. Alterations to the building create a sequence of distinctive moments that are drawn, documented and mostly remain visible – what is important however is what they signify sociologically, not merely architecturally. The Whitechapel is an excellent example of a building that grew physically as its ideological underpinning and social priorities reconfigured.

Figure 5.13
Whitechapel Art Gallery façade.

Source: Picture by the authors, 2019

We explore the sociology of the building primarily through the 2012 intervention to the Whitechapel Gallery façade by Rachel Whiteread, looking at the professional translation of social intent into artistic signature. As we will see, this created a short critique in relation to the process of engagement and embedding of social capital in the fabric of a place. The case study review of Whiteread's intervention is critical of the use and misuse of 'craft' as played out within a material process – glazed terracotta, and the relationship that this particular work has to wider relations with cultural significance, locality and commodification.

"The Whitechapel Gallery was founded in 1901 to bring great art to the people of east London" (Whitechapel Gallery website, 2019). Its opening resulted from the experience of a couple, Canon Samuel Augustus Barnett, vicar of St. Jude's, Whitechapel, and his wife Henrietta, who organised an art exhibition at St. Jude's School House, Commercial Rd, in 1881.

> They saw art as a teacher and believed that art 'would educate people so that they might realise the extent and meaning of the past, the beauty of nature, and the substance of hope'.
>
> (John Passmore Edwards webpage, no date)

The gap between the founding concept of Canon Barnett and the current Gallery website is instructive. Whilst not at odds with part of the original mission statement, the Whitechapel Gallery was previously more than simply a conduit for 'elsewhere' art into East London. With the voices of Ruskin and Morris coming clearly through Barnett's statement, we will look at the shifting role the Gallery has played in the heritage of the East End and draw parallels with the form and materiality of the building as it too shifted in response. In 1881, Samuel and Henrietta Barnett enacted their belief in the transformative potential of art for the impoverished community they were surrounded by, establishing salons and exhibitions where "the paralysing and degrading sights of our streets" (Survey of London, 2016) in Whitechapel could be ameliorated.

The Barnett's vision was linked to a legacy of thinking around the status and impact of art. Following the Enlightenment, the definition of culture as secular defined a separation from the spiritual; however with the fine arts the mechanisms of art production and its consumption by the growing middle classes still relied upon the ritual and reverence that spirituality demanded to establish its comparative importance. As Carol Duncan notes in *The Art Museum as Ritual* (1995: 424), the veneration of artwork saw a new category of secular culture stepping in. This demanded the redefining of 'art' – a category – from a labelling category to a concept with agency. 'Art' was intended as a homogeneous concept that in the 18th century was believed that it could improve the viewer spiritually, morally and emotionally. This revelatory experience counted on a series of references that would tap into the viewer's personal and cultural experience, with the gallery drawing on the classical language to access the iconography and status of 'the temple' – the National Gallery, Tate Britain, The National Gallery of Scotland, The Louvre, so it goes on. It is clear that the way museum and exhibition were organised posed some issues on the selected narratives and on the powers of the ones who hold them. If it's true that the open nature of these spaces favoured social mixing and the access to art, it is also true that contents and messages were carefully selected by the few. E.A. Coombes (1992: 490) suggests that from the 1850s, museums were considered "the most democratic and socialistic possession of the people. All have equal access to them; peer and peasant receive the same privileges and treatment". However, opposing that view, Bourdieu and Darbel (1997) note that this is the means by which the bourgeoisie maintain control of the role and significance of art, and that their privileged access to cultural education means that the peer 'gets' far more than the 'peasant'.

The self-reflexive nature of the art museum and its operation as a self-justifying, socially corrective device is only partly applicable to the Barnett's endeavour. The particular emphasis on engagement, practice and participation provided a radical tendency that makes the Whitechapel Gallery a very particular example that, in its early years of operation at least, provided an alternative to the criticism levelled by Bourdieu and Darbel. Intrinsic to the Barnetts's mission was the provision of an art school and an education in the importance of participating in craftwork. This intention, to bring the source of inspiration and the means of work to engage with it, provided a rich backdrop to the formation, realisation and future of the gallery. By February 1894 the brief for a picture gallery, art school and accommodation for the Whitechapel District Board envisaged art, practice and local governance coming together. However, questions around the social role of craft were even then being raised, Barnett noting the closure of C.R. Ashbee's Guild and School of Handicraft on the Mile End Road in 1895. The establishment of the Cass Institute nearby, which contained an art school, further questioned whether the local population or those from further afield would actually use Barnett's school. In the end, the Whitechapel Art Gallery was established as a charity in 1899, its trustees indicative of its mission statement – bringing together long-term partners such as Henrietta Barnett with local institutions such as the adjoining Free Library, Toynbee Hall and London Parochial charities, along with the London County Council who funded exhibition and examination space for its crafts colleges and the Royal Academy from whom the inspirational 'elsewhere art' was to come.

> Despite the rather dimly lit rooms (in St Jude's School), hemmed in by other buildings, the exhibition attracted 10,000 visitors. It included one room entirely filled with items from the South Kensington Museum, paintings lent by artists and collectors, including work by G.F. Watts and John Brett, middle eastern and western ceramics, including Staffordshire, Wedgwood and contemporary work by De Morgan and others, and art-needlework and Morris & Co other textiles. Costs were low with catalogues a penny and several days with free entry. By 1886, visitors had reached 46,000, and three rooms were added to the school to expand the shows.
>
> (*ibidem*)

The realities of the sites available, medieval in scale and layout with complex plots and ownership issues, became a reality check to the elaborate early designs for the project, which were exhibited at the Royal Academy in 1896 by the architect Charles Harrison Townsend, who had been engaged in the Barnett's philanthropy since 1877. Townsend deployed the compositional arrangement of twin flanking towers and a terracotta façade he had previously employed at the nearby Bishopsgate Institute, here framing a proposed mosaic frieze by artist Walter Crane in the upper section of the elevation. The grandeur of the watercolour rendering and the declared budget of £10,000 proved incompatible, and the financing of the project was subject to constant compromise as Barnett sought to secure funding.

The shift to a smaller site that the demanding benefactor Passmore Edward favoured, and which gave a frontage to Whitechapel High Street was under the Barnett's consideration by May 1896 and is the location that we know today. This was a narrower, shallower site requiring two nave-like galleries stacked with committee rooms above the entrance and caretaker and service rooms above that, hidden behind the Crane frieze. A funding shortfall in the 1890s was overcome by a range of benefactors sympathetic to Barnett's ideology, together with local Anglo Jewish patrons in business locally.

Completed and opened in 1901, the façade is dominated by the offset entrance arch above which a series of leaded light windows signalled the presence of the committee rooms – the institution overlaying the public entrance. Behind Crane's as yet unrealised frieze depicting 'Poetics', 'Truth', 'History' etc. paying homage to the seated figure of Art, were the caretaker's office, storage space and a WC, lit by concealed side windows. This juxtaposition of high intent and low pragmatism is ironically appropriate for the building. The façade was realised in buff terracotta by Gibbs and Canning of Tamworth and include a relatively plain shallow relief of trees in a Secessionist manner banding the base of the tower elements. The choice of terracotta delivered a presentation that was pristine within the context of dirt and poverty – the orchestration of the façade with twin towers offered a literal bastion for art within the underprivileged surroundings to elevate the population. In contrast to the pristine buff terracotta, none of the proposed internal adornments were realised: the office floors used rubberised matting, the galleries used woodblock and ornamentation was achieved through the use of red linen from Liberty's around the walls. The first director was Charles Aitken, a former art lecturer at the Regent Street Polytechnic and the Social and Political Education League, who put in place exhibitions of local artworks with two or three themed displays a year, such as *Scottish Artists* (1902) or *Dutch Art* (1904), and included works by acclaimed artists such as Constable, Reynolds and Turner. This provided the local audience with a selected, organised understanding of a theme or collective category of art that formed a superstructure allowed to understand the commonalities and differences within a group of artists working in a particular place or on particular subjects. The exhibitions attracted as many as 200,000 people and were free, with catalogues for one penny. In 1906 *Jewish Art and Antiquities* was accompanied by a series of lectures from the Chief Rabbi, bringing the spectacle of fine objects into an intellectual and social context. During this period the upper gallery hosted displays of work from local schools, gymnastics, singing, first aid and dressmaking, with a library of prints and photographs of art for children to borrow. In a time before cheaply available mass media, the communication role was intrinsic to the pedagogic role – the future of an increasingly social media and technological change were to bring significant challenges to this multi-modal mission.

Tension between community and culture

The earliest expression of tension between the local and the 'elsewhere' came in 1907 via the inclusion of the New English Art Club in the *Spring Exhibition*. The presence of an increasingly identifiable, European-influenced 'avant-garde' became even more noticeable in the 1910 exhibition *Twenty Years of British Art (1890–1910)* organised by Aitken, who then secured the directorship of the Tate Gallery. Was the inclusion of the 'avant-garde' part of the pedagogic remit of the Whitechapel Gallery to broaden the local community's horizons, or a means to transform the local gallery into an international stage? Aitken and his successor Gilbert Ramsay's proposals for an exhibition of *Twentieth Century Art* caused Henrietta Barnett to write to Aitken and Ramsay cautioning

> not to get too many examples of the extreme thought of this century, for we must never forget that the Whitechapel Gallery is intended for Whitechapel people, who have to be delicately led and will not understand the Post-impressionist or futuristic methods of seeing or representing things.
>
> (Survey of London, 2016)

Henrietta's comments appear at odds with the aims of the original trustees "to open to the people of East London a larger world than that in which they usually work. To draw them to a pleasure recreating their minds, and to stir in them a human curiosity" (*ibidem*) and throw into question how 'free' is speech and how open the world of the working East End ought to be. What is the optimal balance between international awareness and the security of locality?

How is this tension played out through a long view of the gallery's history? The gallery archive lists the full itinerary of exhibitions from the beginning in 1901. It is very instructive to see the subjects of the exhibitions, in particular the balance between Barnett's 'Whitechapel People' and the imported 'larger world'. The list is a 'texture' of specific use and a document of the attitude the curators had towards art as something made or something merely seen. Perhaps the equal valuing of the local and the international was an inspired original move and making a distinction between the two sowed the seeds for division where only one side would be likely to win.

Some representative years are included here, sourced from the Whitechapel Gallery archive,[8] with observations on the exhibition agendas: the bold headings highlight the provision of local engagement, its early prevalence and its later decline:

1914

LCC Schools Needlework: 29 January – 28 February 1914
Twentieth Century Art: 8 May – 20 June 1914

1921

Modern Dutch Art: 17 January – 26 February 1921
Women's International Art Club: 17 January – 4 June 1921
Polish Art: 9 May – 4 June 1921
Knox Guild of Design and Craft: 5 September – 1 October 1921
Toynbee Art Club: 5 September – 1 October 1921

The first material change to the galleries happened in 1924; the lower galleries "which had become very depressing in appearance" were whitewashed and the walls matchboarded and painted with cream Sanotex "which gives a good background to all works of art" (Survey of London, 2016).

Figure 5.14
Whitechapel Art Gallery: exhibition of artwork by school students, 1913.
Source: COLLAGE: *the London Picture Archive, ref: 210347*

1939

> *Spanish Art – including Picasso's Guernica*
> *Artists International Association: 9 February – 7 March 1939*
> *Lyndham T Vints: Collection of Oil Paintings: 13 April – 13 May 1939*
> *Angela Antrim: 25 May – 24 June 1939*
> *Contemporary French Painting: 25 May – 24 June 1939*
> *Herbert E West: Collection of English Watercolours: 25 May – 24 June 1939*
> *East End Academy: 6 November – 22 December 1939*

After the war a succession of directors sought to provide ever more challenging, pioneering exhibitions. Visitor numbers fell to less than 13,000 in 1947, turned around by then-Director Hugh Scrutton with access to state funding via The Arts Council, LCC and local London Boroughs.

1956

> *Pictures for Schools: 10 February – 4 March 1956*
> *Josef Herman: 14 March – 23 April 1956*
> *Nicolas De Staël: May – June 1956*

Charles Howard: June – July
This is Tomorrow: 9 August – 9 September 1956
Merlyn Evans: October – November 1956
Jewish Artists in England 1656–1956: 8 November – 9 December 1956
East End Academy: 29 December 1956–27 January 1957

The appointment of director Bryan Robertson ushered in a 17-year tenure that intentionally shifted from the local to the international, emphasising the solo genius – Rothko, Pollock, Riley – and creating a platform for radically new thinking, such as *This is Tomorrow* in 1956 that opened the doors to both 'pop art' and the 'as found' of the Smithson that fed into Team 10 and the challenge to modernist orthodoxies.

1964

Robert Rauschenberg: 4 February – 8 March 1964
The New Generation, 1964: March – May
Franz Kline: May – June 1964
Painting and Environment: Nigeria, Uganda: 12 May – 25 July 1964 Young Commonwealth Artists 21 August – 13 September 1964 Mary Potter: 7 October – 8 November 1964
Jasper Johns: 2 December – 31 December 1964

An international 'elsewhere' agenda continues. In 1971 the then-leader of the Greater London Council, Conservative Desmond Plummer, observed "I very much doubt the value of this Art Gallery and am dubious of its management" (Survey of London, 2018).

1972

East London Open and Strike for Kids under 12: 7 January – 9 January 1972
Leon Kossoff: 19 January – 20 February 1972
Joseph Beuys: 27 February – unknown date
Systems: 8 March – 9 April 1972
David James: 18 April – 27 April 1972
John Peek: 18 April – 27 April 1972
Pre-Raphaelites; 16 May – 14 June 1972
John Davies: 21 June – 16 July 1972
Patrick Heron: 21 June – 16 July 1972
This is Whitechapel (Ian Berry): 28 July – 3 September 1972
Bill Woodrow: 28 July – 12 August 1972
Alan Charlton: 8 September – 15 September 1972
Peter Logan: 26 September – 15 October 1972
Decade '40s: 1 November – 26 November 1972
Evelyn Williams: 1 November – 26 November 1972
Spike Milligan: 5 December – 23 December 1972
Michael Perton: 5 December – 23 December 1972
Prints and how they are made: 5 December – 23 December 1972
Llewellyn Xavier: 5 December – 23 December 1972

State funding facilitated an extensive programme under director Nicholas Serota. In these years solo artists dominate, while the freedom afforded by state funding and the ability to charge entry fees for the first time, overturning Barnett's constitution, brought back financial stability and some form of a local agenda. However, craft is hardly represented.

1983

Francesco Clemente: 7 January – 20 February 1983
Barry Flanagan: 7 January – 20 February 1983
Auschwitz Exhibition: February 1983
Whitechapel Open and A Child's View of Docklands in 1961: 9 March – 10 April 1983
Terry Atkinson: 27 April – 5 June 1983
Bruce McLean: 27 April – 5 June 1983
A Visit to Bangladesh: 27 April – 5 June 1983
Purbo London: 27 April – 5 June 1983
Malcolm Morley: 22 June – 21 August 1983
The New Whitechapel: 22 June – 21 August 1983
Georg Baselitz: 7 September – 30 October 1983
Work From A Salvation Army Hostel: 6 September – 2 October 1983
Richard Hollis: 3 October – 30 October 1983

The international solo artist dominates the developing itinerary, with craft activities entirely lost and the use of the Gallery as a platform for local art production relegated to secondary shows in separate rooms developed in the early 1980s behind headline artists in the formal galleries.

Constant façade, shifting spaces, shifting content

While the exhibition's purpose was changing, shifting from local to global reach, the fabric of the building was also undergoing modification. The first major alterations, coinciding with the arrival of Nicholas Serota, were prepared in September 1976. The adjacent George Yard Mission Infants School building to the west of the gallery was acquired more than fifty years after it was first mooted – proposing a ground floor bookshop and lecture hall with side gallery to Angel Alley, linked to the gallery via two bridges. The scheme filled in the main lightwell adjacent to the front stair with a new lift, shop and store with office above. Finalised as a plan in 1979 by Colquhoun and Miller, a further three years of fundraising culminated in a new design in 1982–3, and built between 1984–5 at a cost of £1.6 million. A four-storey extension abutted the old lightwell with storage, loading and AV facilities connected via a new east-west stair designed in a post-modern idiom with banded brick and referential but simplistic detailing. Despite the expansion, the gallery was convoluted and had to close for approximately ten weeks a year to re-hang. This required the loss of the original front stair, replaced with the new bookshop. The commercial investment that enabled the 1980s redevelopments gave way to Heritage Lottery funding streams in the 2000s.

In 2003 the Passmore Edwards Library to the east of the gallery was announced as being vacated by 2005, allowing for a new acquisition. The new director – Iwona

Blazwick – marshalled donations from artists such as Damien Hirst to build both funds through auctions of donated artworks, and a revitalised brand, bringing Michael Craig Martin and Rachel Whiteread as 'artist advisers' on a fashionable architects shortlist to pitch for the redevelopment scheme. Eventually, the respected Belgian arts specialist architectural practice Robbrecht en Daem was chosen to execute the project, completing the internationalisation process. The closure of the Whitechapel while the Robbrecht en Daem project was built required an 'off-site' strategy, ushering the shift to a branded agenda that both reinforces the Whitechapel 'brand' while bringing in corporate sponsors. Max Mara presenting cosmetics for women as well as art by women to address the gaze of others is an example – the confluence of which gives pause for thought.

The 'regeneration' project itself was a mixture of major intervention and 'preservation' aesthetics. Significant elements within the 1985 gallery scheme were removed, including the staircase, the entrance and the bookshop, losing the café overlooking Angel Alley for more gallery space. Elsewhere the fabric of the gallery the architects inherited was respected. Within the library conversion the approach was interventionist and the spaces were comprehensively repurposed and the building's presentation radically altered, as the major funder – the Heritage Lottery Fund – required archive and study spaces that were added to the top floor behind the gable that had been removed in the 1970s. The absence of the local is conclusive under Iwona Blazwick's directorship. On 4th April 2009, the adjoining Passmore Edwards Library, decanted to an 'Ideas Store', was incorporated into the gallery at a cost of £13.5 million, doubling the size of the available exhibition space, funded largely by the Heritage Lottery Fund.

The former reading room was stripped of plaster back to brick, retaining the columns and pilasters as 'traces' of its former identity almost in imitation of the nearby Wilton's Music Hall or the Neues Museum in Berlin, where Tim Ronalds and David Chipperfield/Julian Harrap respectively chose to retain wear and repair as an aesthetic form. The tendency to relish in the ruined is now a frequent tactic for renewal projects on public buildings such as the Bristol Old Vic and Battersea Arts Centre (Haworth Tompkins Architects, 2018). Effective in foregrounding 'heritage', this method is the antithesis of restoration, but neither is it conservation in the case of the gallery, where the reading room had its plaster previously. The blurring of retention, reinstatement and imposter ruination creates either a multi-dimensional response to the existing building, or an incoherent aestheticisation, depending on your point of view. If one expands a critical evaluation to its breaking point this heterogeneous approach is entirely aligned with a social media age, a post–post-modernity where value is relativised to the point of atomisation and whatever creates reaction is valuable – both culturally and financially. The project was capped, without irony it seems, by a copper and steel weathervane by artist Rodney Graham depicting Erasmus riding backwards on his horse reading a copy of his book *The Praise of Folly*. The Whitechapel reopened in 2010:

2010

British Council Collection: Thresholds: 9 January – 14 March 2010
Melanie Manchot: Celebration (Cyprus Street): 13 January – 14 March 2010
Art in the Auditorium: Charly Nijensohn and Nova Paul: 21 January – 18 April 2010

Where Three Dreams Cross: 150 Years of Photography from India, Pakistan and Bangladesh: 21 January – 11 April 2010

John Latham: Anarchive: 2 April – 5 September 2010

Art in the Auditorium: Lars Laumann and Aïda Ruilova: 20 April – 5 July 2010

Robbrecht and Daem: Pacing Through Architecture: 24 April – 20 June 2010

Rachel Harrison: Conquest of the Useless: 30 April – 20 June 2010

The Bloomberg Commission: Claire Barclay: Shadow Spans: 26 May 2010–1 May 2011

Artists in Residence: The School Looks Around: 10 June – 2 August 2010

Keeping it Real: An Exhibition in Four Acts: Act 1: The Corporeal. The D. Daskalopoulos Collection: 10 June – 5 September 2010

Alice Neel: Painted Truths: 8 July – 17 September 2010

Jake and Dinos Chapman: Children's Art Commission: 7 August – 31 October 2010

This is Tomorrow: 9 September 2011–6 March 2011

Keeping it Real: An Exhibition in Four Acts. Act 2: Subversive Abstraction: The D. Daskalopoulos Collection: 17 September – 5 December 2010

Art in the Auditorium: Stephen Sutcliffe: 1 October 2010–2 January 2011

Walid Raad: Miraculous Beginnings: 14 October 2010–2 January 2011

Richard Wentworth: Three Guesses: 6 November 2010–6 March 2011

Keeping it Real: An Exhibition in Four Acts. Act 3: Mona Hatoum: Current Disturbance: 17 December 2010–6 March 2011

The exhibition timeline demonstrates clearly the changing priorities for the Whitechapel Gallery. In 1910 five exhibitions were put on: two were local, three had themes such as *20 Years of British Art, Country in Town* and *Shakespeare and Theatrical Memorial*. In 1975, of the thirty exhibitions listed, twenty-four were solo shows, and by 1986 of thirteen shows six were solo, four were themed and three were local. In 2011, of the twenty shows fourteen were solo works (two sponsored by international brands); the local content was entirely missing. The original purpose of the gallery was as a carefully organised conduit of 'elsewhere' art in order to stimulate local engagement in order to enrich and to produce. As we have seen through the timeline, this heritage of producing heritage has given way to showcasing the production by others, increasingly for others as the local community gives way to tourists visiting the blockbuster shows by headline artists. If focussing on locality was originally intended to feed local heritage, how did this transform in time, embracing more international needs? It is interesting to see how the Whitechapel Gallery sees its own heritage: "Throughout its history, the Whitechapel Gallery had a series of open exhibitions that were a strong feature for the area's artist community" (Whitechapel Art gallery website).[9] The website appears to make a distinction between the local 'community' and 'the area's artist community'. In fact, the exhibiting artists *were* 'the community' in the early decade of the gallery, which, through its East London Art Club was a platform for local people. They were supported by teachers like Slade graduate John Cooper who helped them to make art that later became part of the Tate Gallery collections, the Courtauld Institute of Art and the Duveen Gallery. The principle that incoming artists and local people can create genuine work was evidenced by the recognition of community artists such as Elwin Hawthorne and Walter Steggles,[10] who went on to represent Britain at the Venice Biennale in 1936 alongside Walter Sickert and Barbara Hepworth. It is of interest to note that the current British Council online timeline for the Venice Biennale has a selective entry for 1936:

> Famous artist and sculptor Barbara Hepworth's work was shown for the first time at the Biennale alongside artists who had previously exhibited in Venice, such as Augustus John, Walter Sickert and Ethel Walker.
>
> (Venice Biennale website, 2019)

It is interesting why Hawthorne and Steggles were omitted from the 'official' Biennale history when Osbert Sitwell opened their East End Group exhibitions, Prime Minister Ramsay MacDonald attended them and author Arnold Bennet gave financial support. The process which allowed Hawthorne and Steggles to become artists does not exist anymore, which is of greater significance than the omission of their names. One can only conclude that the selective history of 'professional' and amateur is the official history of art. The current Whitechapel Gallery website notes that "by the early 1990s these (local) open shows became less relevant as emerging artists moved to other areas" (Whitechapel Gallery website). Remarking on the gentrification of the East End, artist Rachel Whiteread commented that Dalston, where she started her art career "was a hinterland that couldn't really exist in a city that's constantly expanding. 'I can't help but wonder, though, where on earth young artists work now?' She makes a face. 'I've heard . . . [she lowers her voice a little] that they're all down in Deptford'" (Cooke, 2012).

Whiteread obviously opens another issue on both the exclusivity of the art offer and housing availability, the places where community can inhabit are at stake because of the progressive gentrification of the city. The idea of 'artist' as part of a local community seems to have shifted. What both the Whitechapel Gallery website and Whiteread refer to is the 'artist' not as a longstanding member of the local community – as were Hawthorne and Steggles, but as art students and graduates arriving with degrees from 'elsewhere', often benefitting from relatively privileged family upbringings in places like Muswell Hill. Living in cheap rent areas was a choice based on a career as an artist, rather than 'no choice' birthplace and demographics. The East End had its own abilities to record and express itself artistically through the support of institutions like the Whitechapel Gallery; however the definition of an artist not as an amateur making 'art' but as a 'professional' making 'Art' marks a major shift in the value of the practice, and redefines for whom it is valuable.

When the Whitechapel Gallery's role as educator and enabler shifted to being promoter and showcase, the requirement to 'import' art became an inevitability and was mirrored by the introduction of 'emerging artists'. Along with the idea of 'emerging artists', the infrastructure for hosting established artists was also shifting. In the early 1970s, new venues such as the Hayward Gallery had advanced the marketplace model in London and amplified the need to 'compete' for hosting artists of note. This was done by offering gallery interiors and environmental control required by the monetary inflation of the post-war art market and the ever more demanding preconditions for lending works. So, to survive, the showcase must compete for its content and therefore, as with Premier League football teams, must attract leadership to deliver curatorial strategies that succeed. Nicholas Serota was such a 'manager', and the coincidence of his diplomacy and the availability of new funding actors enabled the Whitechapel Gallery to commence transformation into an internationally competitive art institution.

Throughout the changes, and up to 2012, the Whitechapel gallery retained the same presence on Whitechapel High Street across a century – albeit an incomplete one. With the whole façade acting as a picture frame for the allegorical frieze by Walter Crane that never was, circumstances dictated a completion was required. The occasion came with the proposal to regenerate Whitechapel High Street for the Olympic Games in East London in 2012. The project was called *High Street 2012* and supported the renovation of "London's oldest high street" (Mayor of London, 2012) through the financial support of the mayor, the Department for Communities and Local Government, English Heritage, Transport for London, Heritage Lottery Fund and London Thames Gateway Development Corporation. Under the pressure of urban representation (rather than 'regeneration') how would the gallery respond? One of the options was to finally install the Walter Crane frieze – why not install it in 2012 as part of the drive to present East London to the world via the Olympic lens? What are the heritage arguments around this? Clearly the documentary evidence exists to determine both the detail of the Crane's proposal and the organisation of the façade around its place. In terms of 'restoration' the critical criteria is infallible documentary evidence; however a broader question to ask is what purpose is served by completing a project over a century old, and could its completion in a contemporary way add to the history of the building by adding to its legacy? Eventually, the answer to 'filling the void' was challenged by the commissioning of a site-specific installation by artist Rachel Whiteread. The decision to add a contemporary artist's work into the void accords with Morris's approach to building historic layering: for him the building would be a document to be added to. In the case of the Whitechapel Gallery, this choice seems to have philosophical as well as branding appeal, because the overriding Olympic message was one of a forward-looking nation at ease with its history and ready to meet the future.

We can see Rachel Whiteread as the most public part of the transformation of the Whitechapel Gallery into an internationally significant venue for internationally significant art. Initially acting as an artist advisor, Whiteread already collaborated to the transformation of the building on the appointment of the internationally renowned Belgian architects for the 2007 project. A theme emerges here, one of a radical shift from local and embedded to international and competitive. How was the intervention intellectually framed? How did heritage issues inform the project, given that its cultural and architectural significance was listed at Grade II* in 1973?[11]

Whiteread makes clear the difficulties linked to compromise when notions of local and national representation, memory and heritage are involved. "I'm really happy with it. I had a few cross moments. A project like this takes four years. All the bloody meetings. I would start stamping my feet because you can't make a good public sculpture from meetings. But English Heritage are pleased now" said Whiteread (Cook, 2012). Compromise, she implies, ruins good art. Good art is the product of the artist, those around simply need to understand this, and their acquiescence will lead to the realisation that the artist was right. We will consider the idea whether this is the artist's remit in Chapter 6 where we will discuss some alternatives roles for the architect and explore alternative roles for the artist.

Whiteread's Whitechapel art project is composed of two elements, as a caption to her exhibition at the Tate Britain in 2017 for *Tree of Life* states: "Whiteread added bronze leaf casts covered in gold leaf across the façade, and added four terracotta casts of windows typical of vernacular architecture of the period of its creation". These elements – leaves inspired by the original Secessionist banding and terracotta windows imitating vernacular architecture, have underpinning ideas that are independent from each other and can be considered as two simultaneous installations. Concerning the gold leaves located across the façade, made in the Whitechapel Bell Foundry close by (since closed and the subject of a contested redevelopment), Whiteread stated:

> I was also thinking about the Arts and Crafts moment. I was thinking about the street. I was thinking about Hackney weed [aka buddleia], which pops out of buildings all over the place. I was trying to find somewhere where the old and the new worked together, and I was thinking about what it is that really makes something a presence among all the greyness – and that turned out to be gold leaf.
>
> (Whiteread, 2012)

The replication of the leaves from the terracotta banding and the scattering of the gilded bronze casts brought a modern, apparently dynamic layer to the formally organised façade attuned to the transformative agenda of the 2012 Games and utilising the artist's singular working method of casting. Whiteread rose to prominence through a series of works exploring the material manifestation of space through the casting process, representing space otherwise unacknowledged such as that under a bathtub, below a chair, within a fireplace. In casting the entirety of the interior of a terraced house – the project called *House*[12] – was a profound piece of sculpture that reinvested domestic space and memory with a genuinely new meaning. The extrapolation of that idea includes the casting of door panels, doorknobs, bookshelves staircases, sheds and more. What new meaning the casting process brings to these different elements is variable, the transparent cast of the Trafalgar Square 'Fourth Plinth' was a tour de force in resin casting and its transparent inversion of the plinth on which it sat spoke critically of the idea of the plinth destined to host an equestrian mounted general, yet the doorknob cast in rubber or numerous old windows cast in coloured resin appears arbitrary. Her casting of windows and the turning of a positive into a solid negative form was introduced to the Whitechapel. Using the casting process required in the manufacture of terracotta, the material relevance for the Whitechapel is possibly the only perceptible relevance in the fact that the whole façade of the gallery itself is realised in the same material. Casting is an intrinsic 'memory process'; it depends on an existing condition that becomes reinvested with new purpose through replication. The manipulation of the process can achieve deformations that subvert the memory function and introduce new ideas, casting what was solid as transparent resin or vice versa, making a brass doorknob into rubber to alter its nature and our memory expectations of the piece. These strategies of uncertainty, of 'making strange' or subverting expectations of memory underpin Whiteread's practice – the question is how this kind of technique reshape the rhetoric of legacy and memory when applied to a Grade II* listed building, what is the effect that it has on the narratives associated with the building, and how can these new narratives exploit material references to create meaning? Also, this operation forces us to reflect on the significance that this operation has and for whom.

The leaded glass patterned terracotta windows appear to replicate the first floor former boardroom glazing, making them an extrapolation of the materiality of the façade itself. In fact, the Tate exhibition caption is correct; the cast terracotta windows are from similar windows with a moulded architrave, whereas the Whitechapel windows are leaded light steel framed pivoting windows. Perhaps the lack of architrave was

Figure 5.15
Whitechapel Art
Gallery façade
detail of tree
frieze.

Source: Picture by
the authors, 2019

deemed too plain to act as the originator of the casts – we will never know, however the opportunity to provide a continuity of ideas with the cast leaves was passed up. Why are eight original windows augmented with four similar copies, and should this concern us? The discontinuity between the art of place and the place of Art is inherent in Whiteread's piece – derived from the physicality of the building but simultaneously little to do with its heritage as a community resource, taking the space of Walter Crane's allegorical representation of art in human form and converting it into a process driven 'signature' piece representing the artist. Whiteread's signature gives windows onto the rooms concerned with the pragmatic workings of the institution, but no matter, as they

*Figure 5.16
Whitechapel
Art Gallery
detail of original
and Whiteread
windows.*

*Source: Picture by
the authors, 2019*

are blind. The installation represents an idea from 'elsewhere', fashioned by one of only three craft businesses still expert in terracotta to enliven an already listed building for the spectacle of the Olympic Games held further along the Commercial Road (the Olympic Park is indeed along Commercial Road from Whitechapel). The commission stands as an imported spectacle underwritten with an imported signature. It is critical to look further into the intellectual role that art can play in issues of heritage and differentiate between the artwork as 'brand' and the artwork as social idea.

The philanthropic mission of its founders, offering opportunities to local people to become artists as part of growing a culturally richer community, established a model of engagement that started to lose sharpness with time, shifting from social intent into artistic signature. While the building changed and expanded, its popular character also transformed towards a more elitist conception of art. The fact that this coincided with the involvement of international artists does not necessarily mean the loss of engagement intentions and of interest in the context. Rather, it was the shift towards import and branding that characterised the change in character of the gallery. The necessity for the gallery to grow on the international stage by importing rather than producing and exporting art is also linked to the liveability of the area and the changes that inform its social and built fabric. Originally an underprivileged area of London, Whitechapel cyclically hosted immigrant communities and workers over centuries. It is characterised by mixed cultures and blended traditions and, as in other marginal areas, it hosted artist communities because of the affordability of the rent. The processes of gentrification that started in the last century impact local and artists' communities alike, fundamentally altering both existing buildings through hikes in the cost of inhabiting them, and with new buildings that cluster into 'areas of regeneration' providing unaffordable investment potential to 'elsewhere' investors. The change in the conception of the 'artist' as an 'imported professional' grew parallel to these urban 'regenerations' to the point where poverty and art practice were decoupled and 'creative districts' are now being created from scratch as part of wider regeneration programmes. However, none of the artists who settled in fringe areas in the past would be able to afford to live in a 'creative district' as such. That leaves us two options: either the artists who can settle there are a new kind of wealthier 'creative', or they are sponsored by someone. Surely art does not need to be poor to be valuable, and it is well known that many of the great works of art are born from patronage and commissions, but it is difficult to imagine the same freedom of action that produced, differentiated and radical creation within these 'artistic', pre-packaged enclaves with elite opportunities.

Lessons learned

The St. Pancras and Whitechapel case studies highlighted the necessity to reflect on the concepts of authenticity, craftsmanship, authorship and sense of place. The ways these concepts link one to another is not obvious and depend on our ability to read the transformation of the social and economic context in the layered history of buildings, which become – as Morris would put it – real documents of time.

The interventions undertaken at St. Pancras are an example of how materials choices have both philosophical and practical meaning that should be observed as part of the same concatenated process. On the one hand, the use of terracotta can be seen as referential to the craft process of Greek temples, and therefore recovering the originality of this material. In this sense, Inwood's use of terracotta is far from inauthentic or simply a cheap substitute of a nobler material. Moreover, the process of moulding that characterises terracotta opens on another issue, the one of reproducibility – which was one of the major debates in the last century's thinking and especially in the work of Benjamin (1936). Copying is an intrinsic action of creation, especially when multiple elements are needed, and foresees imitation as part of process. The concept of authenticity, therefore, expands and positions itself beyond authorship, where more complex connections between material significance and reinterpretation intersect. It would include both precision of practice and human error and question the way single artefacts can be understood as part of a wider process. The cautious project of restoration acted along this thin line, balancing between retention and modification, replacement and conservation. It also reasoned on the complex link between materials and their altered relationships over time, highlighting the necessity to rely on craft skills able to tackle material matters, and debating on the relationship between craftsmanship and practices of renewal, fabric sustainability and skilful intervention.

The story of the Whitechapel Gallery opens further reflections on how, over time, alterations to built forms reflected changing relations with communities, mediated by marketisation. The consistent material expression of the listed façade clothes radical changes between people and buildings and throws into question the appearance of heritage and what it delivers for people. The identity of local environments often remains consistent thanks to statutory protection, how people engage with it and what that engagement costs, redefining the communities they serve beyond locality. Thanks to a £36 million regeneration project along Whitechapel High Street, the façade of the gallery was adorned with a symbolic piece of art by Rachel Whiteread. The call for solo artist interventions is not negative per se, but became emblematic of the profes-sionalisation of competences linked to the production and appreciation of art. At the same time, the intent of community involvement, cultivation of local talents and direct engagement loses importance. This experience talks to us about legacy in a different, social way and is linked to the value of creation, and its ability to deposit meaning and retain value in time.

Narratives linked to heritage and sense of place are malleable. Inclusion and exclu-sion are part of the process and we should not be surprised that history is often used to communicate specific messages or promote chosen subjects. Particularly inside the neoliberal city, heritage rhetoric will

> focus on the positive, the distinctive and the heroic, while eluding the unpop-ular, the dirty and the unsavoury. The danger is that those elements excluded from official heritage narratives are threatened denied any place in social memory – making the process of remembering a politicized one that risks excluding some aspects of the past, some communities and some memories.
>
> (Atkinson, 2013: 384)

Freud taught that remembering and forgetting are intimately linked and that one action always involves the other, that memory is another form of forgetting and that forgetting is a way to preserve hidden memories. The narratives of heritage and place concern not only official political communications, but all the coding that informs our visual and written understandings of where we are. The often-simplified description of buildings that we see earmarked for transformation, alteration and regeneration projects, are part of a 'politic of memory', which is an arbitrary operation of selec-tion and exclusion with political intents and applied to the urban realm. The idea of originality and authenticity is here manufactured, and we have already observed how 'cut and paste' operations of selection and invention are used to inform bespoke narratives that reassure us while simultaneously undermining our relationship to our surroundings.

Within this context, development-driven regeneration rhetoric frequently recalls craftsmanship to validate the authenticity of the details which in turn underwrite the validity of the whole: "this historic site demands the most impeccable standards of design and craftsmanship that bridge contemporary living and past aesthetics" can be read in the brochure of some new project in town (190 Strand), that uses "strong, distinctive and earnest materials, (as) a nod to the area's artisan past" (City Island).

We should remember, therefore, the pedagogical role that buildings play, not only when they host instructing exhibitions, but also for their inherit nature as documents registering change, political intentions and economic trends. The collage of the past, selectively shown and hidden, borrowed or interpreted in many of the contemporary projects of restoration is blurring memory through aestheticisation, turning our atten-tion away from the implications of forgetting.

The Whitechapel Gallery case study opened the discussion on the mutability of a building and its content, interrogating how both materials and people are part of this process of change. The building is especially interesting for its forefront role in the process of inclusion of both the appreciation and production of art. The unique purpose of the Whitechapel was to attempt to grow an artistic culture from within its own community, without denying the value of accommodating incoming artists and ideas. In 1936 it succeeded, only to be surpassed by the burgeoning post-war markets in art and property. The formation of a legacy of place is a parallel process of built and social materials and can be understood in heritage terms only through the careful observation of both. This means that the awareness of how materials and historic fabric informs our understanding of a place and its significance, is not only linked to the buildings but also to communities and the part they can play in the shaping of the place itself. This understanding can critically inform the way new proposals can or should negotiate with the history we live in.

Materiality is both a physical record of an intention that informs a building's creation and a surface to be inscribed with the evidence of how that intention shifted as priorities and circumstance shifted. At the Whitechapel Gallery the only constant has been the terracotta elevation to Whitechapel High Street, as galleries, stairs, offices and retail have been imported and relocated. In 2012 this durable, terracotta reminder of a socially informed heritage was co-opted by an artist's brand. Its listed status failed to 'preserve' it, providing overwhelming evidence that contemporary 'participation' is intrinsically defined by buying a ticket.

In Chapter 6 we ask what 'participation without a ticket' can look like by staring out of the windows of the Whitechapel Art Gallery towards Altab Ali Park on the other side of Whitechapel High Street. Altab Ali Park is another project part of the High Street 2012 regeneration project led by MUF architecture/art, an office mixing the competence of artists and architects. Choose the window carefully, some of them have no view.

Notes

1 www.imperialhandmadebricks.co.uk/
2 The Portico Project: www.spab.org.uk/about-us/awards/john-betjeman-award
3 The studio Arts Lettres techniques is run by the author, Alan Chandler who is one of the two principals. For more information visit: www.artslettres.com/
4 www.b2architects.com
5 https://leadsheet.co.uk/
6 Sally Strachey Historic Conservation are leading consultants and conservators of historic buildings, monuments and sculpture. For more information visit: www.sshconservation.co.uk/
7 The John Betjeman Award www.spab.org.uk/about-us/awards/john-betjeman-award
8 Whitechapel Gallery Archives WAG/EAR/1/3 and Whitechapel Gallery exhibition archive: www.whitechapelgallery.org/about/whitechapel-gallery-archive/
9 Whitechapel Art Gallery Website: www.whitechapelgallery.org/about/history/
10 Spitafield Life, From Bow To Biennale: http://spitalfieldslife.com/2012/12/20/from-bow-to-biennale/
11 Historic England List entry: https://historicengland.org.uk/listing/the-list/list-entry/1065820
12 For more information on the *House* project by Rachel Whiteread visit: www.artsy.net/article/artsy-editorial-rachel-whitereads-house-unlivable-controversial-unforgettable

Bibliography

Books, articles

Atkinson, D. (2013) 'The Heritage of Mundane Places', in Graham, B.J. and Howards P. (eds.), *The Ashgate Research Companion to Heritage and Identity*, Franham: Ashgate Publishing, pp. 381–395.

Benjamin, W. (1936) *L' opera d'arte nell'epoca della sua riproducibilità tecnica. Arte e società di massa*. Traslated by E. Filippini, Torino: Einaudi, 1991.

Bourdieu, P. and Darbel, A. (1997) *The Love of Art: European Art Museums and Their Public*, Cambridge: Polity Press.

The Colliery Engineer Co. (1899) *A Treatise on Architecture And Building Construction Vol 2: Masonry*, Carpentry and Joinery. [Online] Available at: http://chestofbooks.com/architecture/Building-Construction-V2/index.html (Accessed: January 2019).

Cooke, R. (2012) 'Interview: Rachel Whiteread: I Couldn't Say No. It Felt Right to Do This One', *The Guardian*. [Online] Available at: www.theguardian.com/uk/2012/jul/07/rachel-whiteread-whitechapel-art-interview (Accessed: March 2019).

Coombes, E.A. (1992) 'Inventing the "PostColonial": Hybridity and Costituency', in Preziosi, D. (ed.), *Contemporary Curating' in the Art of History: A Critical Anthology*, Oxford: Oxford University Press, pp. 486–499.

Duncan, C. (1995) *The Art Museum as Ritual*. Reprint, Oxford: Ed. Preziosi, 2009.

Kearns, G. and Philo, C. (eds.) (1993) *Selling Places: The City as Cultural Capital, Past and Present*, Oxford: Pergamon Press.

Morris, W. (1881) *The Influence of Building Materials on Architecture*. 20th November 1891 at a meeting sponsored by the Art Workers' Guild at Barnard's Inn, London. [Online] Available at: www.marxists.org/archive/morris/works/1891/building.htm (Accessed: 1 May 2019).

Morris, W. (1884) *'Art and Labour' 1 April 1884: Before the Leeds Philosophical and Literary Society at the Philosophical Hall, Leeds*. [Online] Available at: www.marxists.org/archive/morris/works/1884/art-lab.htm

Morris, W. (1891) *The Influence of Building Materials on Architecture*. Meeting sponsored by the Art Workers' Guild at Barnard's Inn, 20 November. [Online] Available at: www.marxists.org/archive/morris/works/1891/building.htm (Accessed: March 2019).

Morris, W. and Webb, P. (1877) *Manifesto for the Society for the Protection of Ancient Buildings*. SPAB: London

Pye, D. (1968) *The Nature and Art or Workmanship*. Reprint, New York: Herbert Press, 2007.

Survey of London (2016) *Whitechapel Gallery: Prehistory and Early History Up to 1914*. [Online] Available at: https://surveyoflondon.org/map/feature/388/detail/ (Accessed: March 2019).

Survey of London (2018) *Whitechapel Gallery: Early History of the Site of the 1901 Gallery Building*. [Online] Available at: https://surveyoflondon.org/map/feature/388/detail/ (Accessed: March 2019).

Waldstein, C. (1885) *Essays on the Art of Phidias*, London and Cambridge: Cambridge University Press.

Willett, C. (2019) *Historic England Surface Repair Trials* (unpublished)

Webpages

Arts Lettres Techniques. [Online] Available at: www.artslettres.com/

Historic England 'Maintenance and Repair of Older Buildings'. [Online] Available at: https://historicengland.org.uk/advice/technical-advice/buildings/maintenance-and-repair-of-older-buildings/

B² Architects. [Online] Available at: https://www.b2architects.com/

Haworth Tompkins Architects [Online] https://www.haworthtompkins.com/work?status=completed

IHBC. [Online] Available at: www.ihbc.org.uk/

IHBC Conservation Wiki, Restoration. [Online] Available at: www.designingbuildings.co.uk/wiki/Restoration

The John Betjeman Award. [Online] Available at: www.spab.org.uk/about-us/awards/john-betjeman-award

John Passmore Edwards. [Online] Available at: www.passmoreedwards.org.uk/pages/history/Libraries/Whitechapel%20art%20gallery/history%201.htm

Lead Sheet Manual. Available at: https://leadsheet.co.uk/service/rolled-lead-sheet-the-complete-manual/

Mayor of London, Regeneration Project: High Street 2012, Newham. [Online] Available at: www.london.gov.uk/what-we-do/regeneration/regeneration-project-high-street-2012-newham

Sally Strachey Historic Conservation. [Online] Available at: www.sshconservation.co.uk/

SPAB Manifesto. [Online] Available at: www.spab.org.uk/about-us/spab-manifesto

Spitalfield Life. [Online] Available at http://spitalfieldslife.com/2012/12/20/from-bow-to-biennale/

Survey of London (2016) *Whitechapel Gallery, 77–82 Whitechapel High Street.* [Online] Available at: https://surveyoflondon.org/map/feature/388/detail/

Venice Biennale, UK at the Venice Biennale. [Online] Available at: https://venicebiennale.britishcouncil.org/history/1930s

Willet, C. (2019) *Historic England Surface Repair Trials Report* (unpublished).

Whitechapel Gallery Exhibition Archive. [Online] Available at: www.whitechapelgallery.org/about/whitechapel-gallery-archive/

Whitechapel Gallery Website. [Online] Available at: www.whitechapelgallery.org/

Brochures

190 the Strand. [Online] Available at: www.berkeleygroup.co.uk/media/pdf/s/f/190-strand-brochure-3.pdf (Accessed: 1 December 2018).

City Island. [Online] Available at: https://issuu.com/ballymoregroup/docs/0708_bm_lci_bro_art_lr__pages_

Online dictionaries and definitions:

Australian ICOMOS, "conservation", https://www.gdrc.org/heritage/icomos-au.html (accessed June 1, 2019).

Australian ICOMOS, "maintenance", https://www.gdrc.org/heritage/icomos-au.html (accessed June 1, 2019).

Australian ICOMOS, "restoration", https://www.gdrc.org/heritage/icomos-au.html (accessed June 1, 2019).

Merriam-Webster Dictionary, "conservation" https://www.merriam-webster.com/dictionary/conservation (accessed June 1, 2019).

Oxford Dictionaries, "maintenance", https://www.lexico.com/en/definition/maintenance (accessed June 1, 2019).

Oxford Dictionaries, "restoration", https://www.lexico.com/en/definition/restoration (accessed June 1, 2019).

Chapter 6

As found

Tactics for a way out of the heritage trap

Approach

What is the value of a *Conservation Plan*, what is the origin of this mechanism, and what are its limitations? Are the descriptive and analytical frameworks established by the conservation profession able to communicate significance to stakeholders and participants, or only other professionals? What are the opportunities for structuring the voices who own a direct stake in heritage places and how can they become orchestrated effectively to revalue the everyday and the ordinary? Communities can be allowed to want what they have, rather than necessarily aiming for what is expected from a professionalised heritage industry. Starting from these questions, we look at the role of the *Conservation Plan* as the pre-eminent tool for understanding heritage and determining what is done with it. Through observation and de-layering of the rules that refined and define them, we aim to redefine the mechanics of conservation empathy and address other possible ways to include community inputs that go beyond 'professionalism'. In order to do so, we analyse three examples – one built project in London, art installations and an oral history recording project. Their different nature highlights the possibility to adopt a sensible approach to context at different scales and according to different durations. They also highlight the ability of a project to develop their aims and understanding of significance through people's contributions, rather than proposing internally defined solutions. These projects open up the *Conservation Plan* as an open process in approaching and dealing with heritage and place transformation.

To develop the ideas around conservation empathy we look at three parallel disciplines with a set of overlapping concerns around the 'found object' – archaeology, landscape and art. The simultaneous observation of these disciplines allows the discussion on how architectural conservation can reflect on an expanded set of strategic and tactical tools.

In the 16th century, the increasing fascination with the ancient world brought to the expansion of collections that started by including rare objects, artefacts of great beauty, and eventually focussed on antiquity. A sense of elitist possession linked to found objects developed throughout the 18th century, and as an adjunct to politics, notions of memory, legacy, tradition started to invade the fields of knowledge and arts (Scott), and heritage started to be associated with values of recognisability, identity and legitimacy. Contemporary archaeological practice in the UK operates with inclusivity and engagement, acknowledging and responding to an inherent public fascination for the discovery of physical history. As a practice it has offset funding constraints through carefully orchestrated public engagement strategies that articulate 'history for all'. The raising of Henry VIII's flagship 'Mary Rose', unearthing hoards of Saxon gold and the last Plantagenet King Richard's body from under a Leicester car park offer good examples of this 'public archaeology'. The public and media interest impact was significant, although purists may dispute the 'watering down' of scholarship in such readily consumable reporting with the risk that facts become fictionalised, it is an opportunity to re-imagine how architects can communicate the inherent value of finding and revealing significance.

Learning from landscape broadens the focus on 'the heritage building' to include wider territories of ordinary life. We look at the root definitions of both *'paysage'* and *'landscape'* that define our wider surroundings as spaces that are activated over time, or observed in seconds. How landscape practice conserves while transforming and adopts strategies of seasonal change over centuries is highly informative around the thin red line between preservation and continued use – both of which are vital for heritage assets but are frequently considered mutually exclusive.

Art, on the other hand, is able to address the re-elaboration of fragments through the building of meaning. In our case, this is essential to the understanding of the city and its layering. Throughout the 1920s and 1930s the practice of (photo)montage surpassed the traditional visual arts as the experimental field of cultural critique and history (Benjamin, 1983; Blöch, 1935; Brecht, 1963; Kracauer, 1963). This approach, indebted to a large number of artists and directors, was iconological: the heterogeneous archive of information left to us by history, loaded with objects, facts, actions, people, was used to elaborate an analysis of the past, of meanings, and to represent the existing through the montage (Pinotti Somaini, 2009: 29, 2016: XVII). The juxtaposition of fragments was a resource (Schlögel, 2011), a way to take a political position through reworked visions, and the city often offered critical materials for this operation.

Altab Ali Park (2012) in London by MUF art/architecture, the 'Peoples Landscapes' project for the National Trust (2019), and the art installation *Ferramenta* (2018) by American artist Theaster Gates are our case studies, dealing with strategies for reappropriating ostensibly 'ordinary' spaces and revealing their social significance in order to ask us what we do next. They help to refocus our attention on the social stories behind ephemeral objects and familiar landscapes as a means to re-evaluate how we know the place we live in. In particular, they use the philosophy of 'as found' to inform projects that reflect on contamination and layering. Through operation of collage, bricolage and restoration they intervene inside existing buildings and places. All of our case studies explore the benefits of the techniques of archaeology, landscape and art for those who share the use and the memories of them. The case studies are exemplars for how to engage with people in order to rediscover places, set out in a way that allows communities and professionals alike to envisage how such an approach can enable physical and non-physical heritage to come together.

GLOSSARY

Anastylosis: *noun – archaeological term referring to reconstructing ruined buildings or monuments.*

A form of 'restoration' generally applied to monuments without current social use value – existing elements are re-used to reassemble a monument such as Stonehenge or the Acropolis. According to the Venice Charter of 1964, the building or structures original condition must be understood scientifically, with each recovered element's correct placement determined. Replacement materials must be limited to those that are necessary for stability, and should conform to the specification of the original material where possible. As with 'authenticity', anastylosis can reveal knowledge and appreciation of historic construction through its operation, while undermining material value through introducing unoriginal elements. As with 'restoration', the requirement to 'pick one' historic presentation results in the loss of the historic accumulation of styles or requirements so valued by Morris, and the justification for one period being more significant than another is invariably open to challenge. The act of reassembly is also contested, the inability to relocate building elements exactly delivers approximation rather than restoration, and any damage caused to the original pieces in the reconstruction is irreversible.

As Found: *expression coined by British architects Alison and Peter Smithson, as defined in 1990:*

> "In Architecture, the 'as found' aesthetic was something we thought we named in the early 1950's when we first knew Nigel Henderson and saw in his photographs a perceptive recognition of the actuality around his house in Bethnal Green: children's pavement play-graphics; repetition of 'kind' in doors used as site hoardings; the items in the detritus on bombed sites, such as the old boot, heaps of nails, fragments of sack or mesh and so on"
>
> "Setting ourselves the task of rethinking architecture in the early 1950's, we meant by the 'as found' not only adjacent buildings but all those marks that constitute remembrancers in a place and that are to be read through finding out how the existing built fabric of the place had come to be as it was. Hence our respect for the mature trees as the existing 'structuring' of a site on which the building was to be the incomer .... As soon as architecture begins to be thought about its ideogram should be so touched by the 'as found' as to make it specific-to-place".
>
> "Thus the 'as found' was a new seeing of the ordinary, an openness as to how prosaic 'things' could re-energise our inventive activity. A confronting recognition of what the postwar world actually was like. In a society that had nothing. You reached for what there was, previously unthought of things [...]".
>
> (A + P Smithson in Robbins, 1990:201).

Community value: The Localism Act 2011 puts into legislation an initiative to pass on to local people the responsibility for local oversight of heritage assets, safeguarding the communities right to know that a place of community value will be sold and holding the unlikely prospect that such a group will have the resources to purchase it, as there is no requirement on the seller to offer it to the community. Examples given by Historic England 'Informed Conservation' (2001) to which this notional opportunity to acquire sites of community value apply include pubs, shops and libraries, the inclusion of formerly civic amenities such as libraries is something of an indictment of 'post-crash' austerity politics.

Engagement: *noun – from 17th century French 'engager' (to pledge) – the act of engaging, the state of being engaged; an arrangement to meet or be present at a specified time and place; emotional involvement or commitment (Merriam-Webster Dictionary, online).*

From a simple prearranged meeting to an emotional commitment, 'engagement' spans the prosaic to the particular. In regards to community engagement, the heritage professional can conduct their work under either definition, the results however will vary dramatically. Historic England recognise the social and communal value of participating in heritage, acknowledging that the results of such participation 'may' have documentary value, but is more likely to be an exercise in social engagement.

History/Herstory: *noun – late Middle English (also as a verb): from Greek 'ιστορία' (historia) via Latin (finding out, narrative, history), aspect of discovery rather than simply sequential events underwritten by an authority as in 'histōr' (learned, wise man). 'Herstory' as a feminist concept questioning the dominant male narrative.*

We understand that History is a partial, partisan and contested concept and not a fundamental truth simply requiring presentation. 'Heritage' is a selective concept which does not necessarily involve history, 'history' itself entails a more careful observation of the facts and their implications.

Landscape: *noun – all the visible features of an area of land, often considered in terms of their aesthetic appeal. A picture representing an area of countryside/ the genre of landscape painting (Oxford Dictionaries, online). The definition of an extended territory identified by its appearance.*

Since the mid-1980s the issue of 'landscape' has returned to the architectural debate, often expanding to include – rhetorically – everything. We link 'landscape' to the reflections on 'paysage': a spatial extent, natural or transformed by man, which has a certain visual or functional identity. "All landscape words refer to the rural character of the land. However, while in English, German, and Hungarian an 'urban landscape' would mean a destroyed landscape (which eventually might not be a landscape at all), the French word paysage can refer positively both to the rural and the urban scene". (Drexel, 2013: 90)

Ordinary: *adjective and noun – late Middle English: the noun partly via Old French; the adjective from Latin 'ordinarius' (orderly), reinforced by French 'ordinaire', from 'ordo', 'ordin' (order) – with no special or distinctive features; what is commonplace, standard or habitual (Oxford Dictionaries, online).*

The commonplace frames our personal and social development, yet is relatively undocumented when compared with the lives, locations and significance of kings, celebrities and those of wealth. When significance depends on documentation, the weight of evidence places hierarchy and priority on the extra-ordinary, leaving the historical process of countless lives as unimportant.

6.1 Conservation Plan and the mechanics of conservation empathy

The *Conservation Plan* we refer to outlines the logical process of the Burra Charter,[1] and "how to prepare a Conservation Plan to guide and manage change to a heritage item appropriately" (Australia ICOMOS, no date). The first version, signed by James Semple-Kerr was published by the National Trust of Australia in 1982 and can be found now in its seventh edition as part of the Australia ICOMOS publications.[2] Although the concept of the Conservation Plan developed in Australia, it became adopted internationally as a methodology for the documentation of an historic building or place in order to establish a clear set of parameters for future maintenance or change. The format of the *Conservation Plan* has been thoughtfully debated and developed over a number of years to the point where there is a coherent set of principles that funders, heritage bodies and statutory authorities recognise and, so varying extents conform with.

In the UK, the *Conservation Plan* became an essential tool for the reshaping of the Heritage funding landscape[3] and is important because it has come to define how heritage is understood and who understands it. The application of this evaluation framework to projects of historic and common interest tells us something about the ways significance is created and people are involved. In short, it speaks about the tactics of conservation empathy. The invention of the Heritage Lottery Fund (HLF) in 1994 was a critical moment in the British neoliberal project. The concept of lottery players augmenting existing, centrally distributed heritage funding was the original premise; however in the intervening period the central funding has diminished (HLF published business accounting), in line with the ideology of empowering (or abandoning, depending upon one's viewpoint) the individual, leaving the only significant funding stream available to heritage being the proceeds of the lottery. The mechanism for accessing the funding stream available through collective proceeds of individual gambling shares the same structure of competitive chance as the lottery itself. Individual projects are required to structure bids for funding, clarifying their case for support through clearly argued narratives and evidence. Do the custodians of what they consider to be a 'heritage' building or place possess the skills necessary to define the significance of their cause and justify their ambitions for it in a structured proposal for project funding? Rarely is the answer – enter the professional adviser to bring rigour to the funding application, articulate its appropriateness and provide evidence of an enhanced 'community buy-in'.

The HLF places emphasis on understanding how the funding is both appropriate to the needs of the applicant, but also on how that funded project remains viable in the long term. This viability test introduced a set of considerations to conservation that were previously underplayed – with State funding there was little emphasis on how communities sustained their own heritage – 'heritage' was a right, was funded to fix and 'heritage status' was a given not needing to be earned or justified in some way. As a concept this position is ironic – the State as patron of heritage is a 'socialist' notion – yet the passivity created in the community whose engagement is rendered unnecessary to its state sponsored preservation runs counter to William Morris's view that community use and collective effort is what sustains ancient buildings' usefulness, beauty and value. The double irony of the HLF is not only its funding separation from the State, but that its source of funding comes from gambling, the vast majority of which is derived from the lowest socio-economic sector of society. The neoliberal project of divesting the State of the State leads to a system where the poorest are funding their own heritage maintenance through the attempts to accumulate capital without working for it, employing freelance 'experts' as little as possible to step in from another socio-economic 'elsewhere' to facilitate it. This convoluted set of shifting political positions makes the reading of heritage complex. When the HLF was one of a number of heritage funding sources there was a mixed economy where Historic England[4] budgeted for a range of restoration, conservation and interpretation projects annually, stepping in to salvage derelict projects where required. As the funding landscape shifted through the 2000s and radically fractured after the 2008 financial crisis, the HLF is left as the only significant funding body for UK heritage. How the HLF understands *Conservation Plans* therefore matters far more than it ever did, and as such how they are underpinned ideologically and politically is of critical interest.

The necessity for a *Conservation Plan* is not restricted to the HLF, although the requirements for lottery funding from 1994 seem to have set a precedent for how and why the *Conservation Plan* was adopted and adapted for the UK. Key to this act of importation was *The Oxford Conference* in 1996, hosted by Historic England (then English Heritage before quasi privatisation) to bring influential voices on historic buildings and landscapes together to formulate how to convene around a set of principles or methods, and also deal with the new (and soon to be only) funding mechanism for heritage.

The Oxford Conference was an important event for heritage in the UK, setting in train a series of ideas that underpin current processes, and most critically establishing the value of constructing a narrative. Based on the work of Australian Kate Clark and her knowledge of Australian practice, the use of the *Conservation Plan* in the UK benefited from the contribution of fellow Australian James Semple-Kerr, the author of the *Conservation Plan* (1982), who participated as a keynote speaker. Reflecting on the discussions from the *Oxford Conference* and the publication of its debates (English Heritage, 1999) clarifies which ideas were influential, but also highlights where we could be if other ideas had been adopted and developed into policy. Fundamental positions on the originality of fabric, the role that change plays in the significance of a site and how communities contribute (or otherwise) to the process of defining significance lead to very different forms of the *Conservation Plan*.

> The objective should be to . . . engage the minimum number of persons with the necessary skills between them directly relevant to the assessment of the particular place.
>
> (Semple-Kerr, 1999: 13)

Semple-Kerr, through the contributions to the conference debates, argued for a clear basic framework in order to establish the case for significance, and he advocates a singular investigator in order to control the quality and objectivity of the analysis and interpretation. The danger of this pragmatic approach, no doubt borne of experience with trying to marshal stakeholders and statutory bodies countless times, does however fail to identify what a 'community' contribution to the formation of the *Conservation Plan* looks like (more of this later). In advocating the lone conservation plan writer, Semple-Kerr develops a thesis for the writing of the plan as a 'negotiation' – "It is an informal process by which a competent and experienced practitioner becomes both conciliator and arbitrator" (*ivi*: 16). This is in particular regard to the political situations within places or groups that require the Conservation Plan in the first place. This observation was not well developed within the unfolding conference proceedings, the emphasis on decision making and evidence not exploring this 'negotiation' aspect fully, or what required arbitration. Does this refer to conflicting historic documentation? Are there alternative understandings that require mediation? Do the local people disagree with the specialist's findings? It is our opinion that this potentially crucial aspect of delivering a Conservation Plan that is not elaborated but clearly even an impeccably organised Plan framework that people 'buy into' does not guarantee an uncontentious conclusion. Semple-Kerr advocates that specialist inputs need to be identified by the Plan, then investigations made to add depth and precision to the overall evaluation. His position was in subtle contrast to the kind of professional 'team' advocated by English Heritage in draft documentation from 1997 that he quoted in his keynote address to the Conference: "no-one – not even an experienced conservation architect – can write a conservation plan by themselves. It is a team effort, and might well include: an architectural historian, archaeologist, architect, landscape architect/archaeologist, specialists, engineer, planner, operations manager/director" (Semple-Kerr, source unnamed, ref. p14, Conservation Plans in Action, HE, 1999). English Heritage – then a part of the 'civil service' would, inevitably, think like a herd rather than a lone wolf.

It is instructive to consider the ideological positions that come through this seminal conference. The Conservation Plan was enshrined as the pre-eminent tool for understanding heritage and determining what is done with it. The lone expert enveloping a powerful narrative to which specialist knowledge is co-opted into the *Conservation Plan*, in distinction to the multi-disciplinary team coordinated and directed to elaborate a fully scoped document resulting in a definition, rigorously researched, of the status and condition of a heritage asset, and a scope for how it is to be preserved or changed. The debates around who writes the Plan and who reads it are interesting given our twenty-year perspective – was this framework for narrating heritage value via 'the Conservation Plan' sufficiently open? Martin Cherry from English Heritage felt it was, predicting:

> In 20 year' time, will historians ask: why did Conservation Plans become an issue in the late 1990s? There will be a move away from designations and controls and movement towards the involvement and persuasion of the public, saying that not only does the public have a shared interest in sustaining the built and archaeological environment, but it also has a pivotal interest and involvement in determining their value and significance.
>
> (Clark, 1999: 96)

The relationship between the role of the State in determining heritage value and how that value is perceived by the public is a critical observation. What is fascinating is Cherry's use of 'involvement' and 'persuasion'. Have plans become the tools for involvement or a means of persuasion – for fundamentally one is inclusive, the other manipulative? How is a specialist report from a professionalised, accredited cabal of consultants really 'involving', or is this blending of inclusion and exclusion more fundamentally political?

The 'public' often risk being seen as simple receivers of a process. As a development of this traditional problem our neoliberal methodologies enshrine the concept of the individual as the driver for social, cultural and economic policy, with 'the public' effectively a pluralisation of the individual. The closer to the individual, the closer to 'the public' and the more 'democratic' the outcome, it is argued. Social structures organised centrally infringe on the right to liberty and remove rights from the individual. Progress towards 'involvement and persuasion' are therefore central to contemporary cultural management. In relation to heritage this concept is fascinating because heritage is only evident when recognised by social groups – its plurality of participation makes it significant. There is a paradox linked to belonging, for what is excluded by the system is simultaneously part of the system by virtue of its marginal position. This paradox reveals three major separations: the separation between the mechanisms and the outputs of space production (politics); the separation between personal and social development (community); and the separation between perceived and normalised privation, meaning that people are accustomed to give away some of their benefits in exchange for 'higher aims' – Cherry's "persuasion". For example, the restoration of heritage through privatisation may result in the widespread perception of increased urban quality, and the groups that suffer marginalisation feel a sort of compensation in the opportunity of living in a 'better' city. Clark herself saw this as an issue, cautioning against the grading of 'significance' as a way of inviting threat to elements deemed 'low grade' without full information. Clark noted the use of the term 'tradable assets' in sustainability, where one benefit is identified as of greater necessity than another and is 'traded' (Clark, 1999: 149). This brings public benefit and significance together, rather than keeping them apart, but what are the consequences of 'tradability'? Is this approach towards 'the public' and heritage value sufficient? Is Conservation Plan making still too reliant on material investigation and historical documentation at the expense of cultural value shared by those who inhabit or engage with the heritage being 'planned'? Are *Conservation Plans* at risk of being simply narratives of persuasion?

Clark herself recognised the importance of consultation and the need to "build it into the process" (The Oxford Conference EH p33), however the trajectory of this statement is of real interest. In her book *Informed Conservation* (Historic England, 2001) Clark effectively specified the mechanics of the *Conservation Plan* and its transfiguration into its policy form – the *Conservation Management Plan*. Consultation is however far from appearing 'built in'. *Informed Conservation* (6.8, page 69) addresses 'Stakeholder Participation' as being owner, advisers and on-site staff, who could support awareness raising of the Plan through a list of generic events. Clark notes "Public participation in environmental impact assessment is becoming increasingly important" (1999: 69), yet impact assessments are different to *Conservation Plans*. The clear impression is that the public, the majority to whom the cultural asset belongs and who recognise its value and buy tickets for its upkeep, do not take part in the definition of significance that the *Conservation Plan* needs to establish. 'Consultation' is not included in the *Informed Conservation* glossary of terms. Is this framing of significance significant? Taking the long view from twenty years hence, we can see that whilst acknowledging the role of 'consultation', there is underscoring it the acknowledgement that this aspect is a burden on the caseworker and on the 'consultees' (Clark: 33), yet no description of how such consultation is framed, best organised, articulated and embedded. 'Consultation' implies expert and in-expert on either side of a conversation; 'engagement' has synonyms such as participation, taking part, sharing, association, involvement. The choice of words articulates a way of thinking, in research terms a 'bias' that needs to be acknowledged in order to clarify the veracity of the outcome.

Ideologies – professionalism and economy

> The point is to focus on attitude and respect. The attitude says, 'we will observe to the best of our abilities what is there and use the best of our knowledge to understand and interpret it'.
>
> (Johnson, 1999: 23)

Professionalism and economy can be seen as the leading ideologies guiding the approach to heritage and defining how its value is created and managed. It is clear from any study on heritage that 'value' is a central issue to its definition, especially now that heritage is increasingly linked to social, political and economic trends. The centrality of the 'professional' as the preferential subject with the ability to deliver a result is a matter of global significance. This trend seems to safeguard the production of a certified product and its monetary usability. The conversations around *The Oxford Conference* – and therefore the *Conservation Plan* – highlight the urgency to engage with professional matters and the way value is recognised and made available.

The issue that a number of the original *Oxford Conference* attendees noted was that the *Conservation Plan* can easily become the justification mechanism for an already defined scheme. Also, there was a tendency within the language of the conference to create statements that reconciled aspiration with achievement.

> Essentially a Conservation Plan has four main sections, and it should be realised that what is important about a Plan is not its detailed contents: rather, it is the logical process that you need to go through to produce the final result. It would be impossible to present the contents of a Conservation Plan in any other order than the prescribed one, as to do so would be to break the intellectual chain.
>
> (Clark, 1999: 30)

Whilst the sequence of 'Understanding the site', 'Assessing Significance', 'Vulnerability' and 'Conservation Policy' is indeed logical, the devotional language around the structure and its validity is of interest. Each of these four core sections have a professional aspect hard to ignore: 'understanding' relates to archaeology, buildings, wildlife, collections – knowing "what is there" as a first step. This is very much a physical evaluation – where is the cultural or social evaluation located? While it is creditable that heritage inspires leading professionals, the tone of the transcript is perhaps less than helpful regarding clarity. The question becomes one of not only what *Conservation Plan* is, but when it is developed, who by and for whom?

'Significance' also begins with the 'objects' of understanding that can be identified – Site of Specific Scientific Interest (SSSI) status, listing, ancient monument etc. The level of detail that Clark imagines to be necessary "about where a new car park might be positioned" for example requires a focussed look at the site 'as found' not only by the heritage professional, but the community it serves. This is potentially a space for local voices to record contemporary social significance. Vulnerability of the site may come from external factors, or indeed from the proposal issues the *Conservation Plan* seeks to underpin. The judgement of the strengths and weaknesses of place, as much as the shaping of proposals, would logically have community input in their definition, but

Clark does not elaborate on this point. Policy is about how the custodians develop management mechanisms to sustain significance and shape development. Again, who constitutes 'the management' and how policies are agreed requires definition on a project-by-project basis, but it would be careless not to highlight who could or should participate in the community aspects of each of these four key stages.

The Heritage Lottery Fund (now the 'Heritage Fund') cuts across the existing agencies for heritage in the UK and profoundly shifted the care of historic places from state to individual gambling. The word 'enhancing' is key. Can an inheritance be enhanced? If so, is that enhancement physical through intervention that generates value, or through how its value is understood? Is enhanced value cultural, social, political, artistic or monetary? This question of enhancement becomes refined when considering the new National Planning Policy Framework 2018 (NPPF) which, like its predecessors develops a further privatisation of formerly State responsibility with a view to the economic enhancement of the built environment. The full scope of the NPPF July 2018 is outside of our focus, so we concentrate on section 16 – 'Conserving and enhancing the historic environment'. At the outset, in line four, it is stated that historic assets "should be conserved in a manner appropriate to their significance" (NPPF, 2018: 54, point 184). Delivery dependent on understanding is fine in principle, but are the mechanisms for understanding suitable, inclusive and accurate, or merely precise within their own frame of reference – likely to miss the target when deployed?

The NPPF echoes the language of the charters in its regard for significance and appropriate evaluation. What differs from the language of conservation is the repeated linkage to economy – where "local character and distinctiveness", "economic viability" and "enhanced significance" all sit within NPPF point 192. Are these points that authorities should take into account when determining applications compatible? Sympathetic use was an idea from Morris and Ruskin, but their view was framed by the idea that historic buildings were part of the social operation, maintenance rather than enhancement was key – enhancement needs careful handling.

The NPPF introduces a clear approach to threats for heritage buildings and assets, in that consent for the demolition of a building can be demonstrated as being acceptable is substantial public benefits can be delivered, and that "the loss is outweighed by the benefit of bringing the site back into use" (*ivi*: 56, point 195). This deferment to public benefit includes the provision of housing and employment – both of which are national priorities. Therefore, removing historic buildings for redevelopment becomes a much cleaner possibility. The NPPF has one caution to this green light – no local authority should consent demolition "without taking all reasonable steps to ensure the new development will proceed after the loss has occurred" (*ibidem*, point 198). Lose first, argue what is reasonable afterwards – the requirement to make a record of what will be lost and make that record public is also caveated by noting that "the ability to record evidence of our past should not be a factor in deciding whether such loss should be permitted" (*ibidem*, point 199) – so if recording is too complex that is not an impediment to demolition either. The last section confirms that the economic viability of the redevelopment effectively overrides planning constraints:

> Local planning authorities should assess whether the benefits of a proposal for enabling development, which would otherwise conflict with planning

policies but which would secure the future conservation of a heritage asset, outweigh the dis-benefits of departing from those policies.

(ivi: 57, point 202)

This framework effectively legitimises widespread regeneration decisions that retain visually significant buildings, leaving them restored and repurposed within an extensive redevelopment that delivers on the balance sheet of the developer and on a quota for homes built. It opens up the paid experts' role in writing the conservation appraisal to one of 'justifier', the impartial assessment of that appraisal undertaken by local authorities with a fraction of the resources and a fraction of the time. As with any system it is the context in which it operates as much as the rules themselves that condition the result. When administering a building contract, the architect switches allegiance from 'client' to 'contract' and its impartial and fair discharge between client and contractor. No such impartial role is required in preparing a *Conservation Plan* for a client, and the risk that the conservation assessment is simply the groundwork for the optimised redevelopment of the site is more than real. In 1996 Kate Clark noted that "there are probably only a handful of people in the country who are good at analysing buildings and landscapes. But often those people do not have the design or business skills needed to work up a scheme" (Clark, 1999: 32). Perhaps Clark was right – and perhaps the divorce between design skill and *Conservation Plan* development has proved to be a fatally weak link, the lack of financial aptitude allowing the development agenda to easily absorb the significance agenda and have heritage assessments align with development agendas rather than the other way around. The professionalisation, accreditation and specialisation of heritage raises standards of practice, but without design expertise to engage heritage, or engagement skills to properly test significance and change with affected communities, conservation architects risk becoming academic at best, puppets at worst.

Why should the reading of historic significance and value be divorced from design development? Is this a question of training? Clark (1999) noted that heritage professionals (who are not designers, it seems) should be closely involved in the preparation of the *Conservation Plan* but using an outsider to draw it together – thereby diffusing internal organisational tension perhaps. This is neither a reiteration of the Semple-Kerr 'negotiator' model nor advocacy for a multi-disciplinary team authorship. One could conclude that the rigorous orthodoxy of the *Conservation Plan* is ideal for neither the lone author or the team – in which case it is perhaps an intellectual construct overlaid onto heritage, rather than being the logical framework of operation that comes from the circumstances of the heritage projects themselves. If conservation is about understanding the nuances of the particular, how rigid should the methodology for that understanding be? Common frameworks are necessary when comparison across examples is necessary – as is required when evaluating HLF bids.

The funding mechanism orchestrates the means of understanding narrative, the standardisation around specialist fields of interpretation and the management of these fields. These points can easily become a means of excluding non-specialists – when a system is tailored to the requirements of the system, does it speak to anyone outside of itself? In the context of developing a funding bid, the costs of *Conservation Plans* are high and are not pre-funded under HLF rules. This is surely a mistake. If a *Conservation Plan* can provide a catalyst for community users and specialists alike to convene around the definition of a site's significance, then it in itself is a piece of heritage definition and mobilisation.

Stephen Johnson (HLF) saw no possibility of funding *Conservation Plans* at the *Oxford Conference* – the HLF (now HF) draws a distinction between the funding of projects and funding the applications for projects. The presumption is therefore that the project is the result, whereas it could be argued that engagement and shared knowledge in the development of a *Conservation Plan* may equally be a result worth achieving. It may be that the *Conservation Plan* shows that no change is necessary – so no bid is needed, but it brought a community together around the making of the Plan in the first place. Bringing communities together around structured, supported *Conservation Plan* development is potentially more effective as a catalyst to develop empathy for heritage amongst its custodians than funding a café attached to a rescued building that may or may not mean much to the community in which it sits, and may or may not make enough money to survive.

Wide consultation should follow the development of a heritage proposal along the lines of planning processes around major redevelopment or infrastructure projects, Clark suggested; however the resources required are seldom available to smaller, localised heritage projects. Should not the plan that identified the basis for the proposal Clark refers to here be within the scope of the community to engage with? The importance of dialogue and engagement is frequently mentioned in the *Oxford Conference* proceedings, but always obliquely, generally, and without really framing its role.

Clark (1999: 37) made a prescient warning when she noted that diminishing lottery funding and the rising costs of making applications causes the entire linkage of *Conservation Plans* to project funding become questionable. This is particularly interesting as two decades after the *Oxford Conference*, the income from the lottery has significantly reduced, as have success rates for funding applications despite the documentation process becoming known and best practice embedded. Success rates have dropped by 11% between 2017 and 2019, reflecting the decline in lottery sales from £434 million in 2016 to an estimated £190 in 2019 (HLF Annual report, 2019).[5]

If the impetus for the *Conservation Plan* was linked to funding streams, then that link is broken. If the *Conservation Plan* becomes an instrument that is funded, far greater numbers of communities could understand and engage with their historic and not-so-historic surroundings. The role of experts is critical, but only if those experts are also expert in communication, in listening and in translating fields of knowledge both ways. As we have seen, the charters and the standards, the architects' professional educational criteria and the guidance on *Conservation Plans* do not enable this 'translation' to happen; they do not even acknowledge that this translation is necessary. Instead, a more urgent need linked to economics has replaced the necessary dialogue on the historic city. Heritage has become increasingly marketed as a cultural reference to originality, a local quality that could be cared for thanks to regeneration, an asset to 'restore' (reinvent) in order to protect authenticity.

Within the context of the neoliberal city that increasingly uses heritage as a means of financial value, reviewing the outcomes of the *Oxford Conference* illuminates a series of interesting perspectives that can help reconsider the role conservation plays in architecture, and architects play in conservation. It also opens up a discussion over value at many levels and encourages the inclusion of communities as part of a professionalism linked to daily life experience and in-depth knowledge of the physical and social context. The greater the cost of preparing project documentation, the less likely they will reveal information that is in conflict with the developer's ambitions, we suggest.

6.2 Learning – from landscape, archaeology and art

Paul Walshe of the Countryside Commission[6] articulated (Conservation Plans in Action: 76–81) a different relation to heritage from that of Clark or the architectural wing of conservation practice. He noted the distinct role that landscape heritage has in dealing with the concept of change. Landscapes are constantly evolving according to two strategic conditions – naturally occurring events such as the increasing number of catastrophic weather events and the impact of blight such as Dutch elm disease, oak processionary moth infestation or ash die-back inflict profound changes to how landscape is characterised and recognised. The management of such events prompts human action as a response to change rather than to preserve. Allied to this natural change is the human aspect of long-term planning that designers such as Humphry Repton or Lancelot 'Capability' Brown set out over centuries of management for landscapes they created. For Walshe, Management Plans, unlike *Conservation Plans*, attempt to define relationships and context rather than 'fixed assets' and are more meaningful. The understanding of significance generated through human action is profoundly interesting in relation to the aspect of Morris's philosophy that promoted the valuing of incremental change and the readability of that change over time. The meaningful and skilled engagement with landscape is clearly comparable to that advocated by John Ruskin (1819–1900), who already offered a precedent to our contemporary idea of landscape conservation, describing his interest in the Lake District and its vernacular crafts (such as dry stone walling), suggesting the relationship between people and landscape be based on activity, locality and necessity. Morris developed this thinking in relation to ancient buildings, prompting a closer focus on landscape as a field that can offer new ideas to the conservation of built contexts.

'Place' comes from the Gallo-Roman 'Pagus' – site with its own identity. Pagus became '*pays*' or '*paysage*' in French, meaning a defined area with natural and human distinctiveness in material, diversity, practices and even language. '*Paysage*' has within its meaning the concept of a distinct working territory – rather than the French alternative of '*campagne*', which is a passive concept of aesthetic origin, akin to 'landscape' in the British sense of aesthetic presentation of nature for leisure or contemplation. '*Paysage*' has no equivalent in English, tellingly, being both 'not city' and a productive environment unlike 'landscape', which is scenographic in origin. This linkage of place and its distinctiveness to human action, and the reciprocity that this entails is interesting to consider in that it holds within it the requirement for active participation rather than passive, usually visual consumption.

This is interesting in that the visuality of 'landscape' is undermined by its loss of 'aesthetic appeal' – thereby giving primacy to appearance and sensation. The French '*paysage*' holds meaning as a functional identity not simply a visual identity – the term 'urban *paysage*' as meaningful as '*paysage de campagne*'.

During the XIX century this was a theme of much interest and writers such as Piepmeier (1980), Ritter (1963) and Simmel (1903) focussed on the relationship that society forges with landscape. Their analyses paid special attention to the social and political standing of the classes that were tied to the pragmatism of *paysage* and the 'nature' of landscape. It was argued that only the people outside of the processes of land production can perceive landscape aesthetically – and that landscape contemplation is therefore a privilege of the non-working class. While the act of contemplation is pragmatic disengagement (at least in the Western countries), a working relationship establishes a distinctly different understanding of a place.

Figure 6.1
Yorkshire,
landscape.

Source: Picture by
the authors, 2015

Paysage would appear to maintain a more robust, working relation to people than the purely visual landscape, however as economic models change, this cultural equilibrium becomes extremely fragile. When it fails, the impulse to retain the appearance of *paysage* can become manifest in tools such as 'Design Guides'[7] that provide definitions of appropriate walling material, plant species and weathervanes that local authorities develop to 'preserve' their heritage. The ambiguous value of this approach is summed up in Walshe's comment "People in new housing estates are now looking for the ghosts in their landscape. The thread linking them to the past of the landscape in which they now find themselves has been broken" (Clark, 1999: 79). His assertion is that design codes can ameliorate a sense of alienation by restating the past as the present is built. The same discourse underpins the construction of Poundbury near Dorchester and countless other modern/ancient villages scattered throughout England. The position of landscape heritage is inspiring in its willingness to think openly about change management and the continuity of change, but as soon as buildings become factored into the equation the fabrication of codes and symbols becomes the strategy, and the tactics become a mockery.

David Russell of the National Trust followed on from Walshe at the *Oxford Conference*: "The essential nature of nature is change. Ecosystems are always becoming something else." (*ivi*: 133). He argued that trees inspired cathedrals that, unlike nature, can achieve and maintain perfection, whereas trees cannot. Here the distinction between the natural and the cultural is arguable – a stone cathedral also changes, shifts, decays and requires maintenance and renewal – slower, less perceptible, perhaps less vulnerable now to catastrophic failure (although historically this is less true, as the collapse of many cathedrals throughout history attest), one can argue that a building is also a form of ecosystem. Rather than searching for differences between the natural and the cultural as Walshe suggested, perhaps the intellectual framework for dealing with landscape has something to teach those who specialise in the conservation of buildings.

The issue here is one of understanding the mechanisms of the *paysage* and the role that the activity of meaningful work plays within a place. Without some degree of authentic employment and engagement with a place, the parameters that defined its appearance and the logic of its making is lost to appearances.

The value of the *Oxford Conference* was in convening a range of differing interpretations around how conservation planning should evolve. David Thackray confirmed that the Burra Charter was highly influential in the making of the National Trust's seminal 'Countryside Policy Review' in which cultural significance was considered an important extension to the notion of 'heritage significance'.

> Cultural significance . . . underpins the Trust's various approaches to the development of 'Conservation Plans' for its properties, for it is in this breadth of definition that we can accommodate the range of significance or values that might apply to any one place, from the international and national significance to local identity and local distinctiveness. It challenges us to ask the question 'significant to whom?'
>
> (*ivi*: 57)

Thackray argued that in consultation, the National Trust felt that there was a "real desire for concise guidelines giving a clear overall framework for the process, but which are non-prescriptive and flexible" (*ivi*: 58). This antagonism between the authors of the *Conservation Plan* concept and the desire for clarity of participation is interesting. Following this necessity, Thackray reordered and re-prioritised Clark's 'four critical steps', demonstrating that the introduction of participation and engagement shifts the logic of the process. Firstly, Thackray states that 'Summarizing Significance' is "*the* most important part" of the *Conservation Plan*, expanding on Clark's 'Assessing Significance' (section 2) and incorporating her primary task of 'Understanding the Site' (section 1). Secondly, he points out the importance of "a long-term vision" that understands opportunities and constraints ('Vulnerabilities' section 3), and thirdly he positions the statements of policy ('Conservation Policy' section 4). His final category is the definition of medium- to long-term planning outside Clark's *Conservation Plan* which deliberately stops short of becoming a 'Management Plan' and opens a reflection on the necessities implied in the administration of the built landscape.

The properties of the National Trust and its breadth of custodianship open interesting challenges regarding the significance of place. To achieve viability and to fulfil its educational responsibilities, the Trust frequently assembles bequests of art or artefacts within its properties, which act as significant hosts to meaningful, but often utterly unrelated objects. An example is offered by Llanerchaeron House in Ceredigion, which houses the Geler Jones collection of predominantly local agricultural machinery, as well as the Pamela Ward collection of fine art objects. Does this act of bricolage create greater significance, or confuse the character and experience of the original buildings? Who takes the responsibility for this curatorial assemblage – a heritage specialist or a creative interpreter? Surely, the meaningful engagement with landscape heritage is not immune to uncertain result over significance. Oran Campbell noted: "If we look at the concept of cultural significance . . . the whole debate over whether the architect or the archaeologist should lead the process becomes irrelevant" (*ivi*: 99).

The real value of the *Oxford Conference* is in the conflicting positions that the debate around the *Conservation Plan* generated twenty years ago and how the range of enthusiasm and scepticism it articulated have all manifested themselves in the contemporary condition of 'value' definition. The involvement of perspectives from landscape and archaeology to address the then-new requirement for *Conservation Plans* that underpinned the operation of lottery grant awards was both inspired, if marginally too late. The ability to synthesise an inclusive and engaged mechanism to understand heritage significance had already been lost because the mechanism for awarding funds, procuring professional advice and evaluating competing applications already prescribed the tools required. We have re-examined the Oxford arguments in order to restate the intellectual lineage for the following case studies and represent the lessons from landscape, archaeology and art that architectural conservation can learn from.

Speaking to people

> We meant by the 'as found' not only adjacent buildings but all those marks that constitute remembrancers in a place and that are to be read through finding out how the existing built fabric of the place had come to be as it was.
>
> (Alison and Peter Smithson, 1990: 201–202)

How, then is an architect's role re-imagined so that the requirement to understand a place and deliver design responsibility is opened and shared with the community that the project belongs to, and that the making of the project itself is in some way the making of the community? Starting with the building and its community 'as found', the Smithsons's suggested, becomes the means of identifying the innate structure of a site and an underpinning for the accuracy and usefulness of a proposal. Their inspiration in developing this position was the work of their colleague Nigel Henderson, a documentary artist and photographer who lived with his wife Judith Stephen, an anthropologist, in post-war Bethnal Green.

This area was deprived long before the war, after it was a territory waiting for redevelopment and regeneration. Henderson recorded daily life on his street and in his neighbourhood with an unsentimental frankness that made an un-aestheticised document of daily life – a parallel to his wife's work as part of the Mass Observation project. Henderson's 'Common Practice' required knowing your neighbours, buying groceries in the market, listening. That was the time when

> the vernacular architecture was embraced by many modern architects as a reference able to clarify and elaborate on constructive and artistic techniques. It started an intense debate on techniques, and was often intended as a sustainable approach to the city; and eventually assumed as an expression of regional and local identities and as an alternative to the Modern Movement.
>
> (Secchi, 2005: 154)

The relationship with artists was often strong and productive, as they started to observe the surrounding with a special attention to the built, cultural and commercial vernacular. Photography, as a medium able to communicate quickly and widely, was used to document the relationship between historic elements and the emergence of a new post-war culture, and artists gaining sympathy with the ordinary developed a visual form of urban, social archaeology.

Henderson's understanding of place in the early 1950s informed the Smithsons's architectural strategies for the city, the highly influential 'Golden Lane Housing' competition vigorously questioning received wisdom on housing at the time, and defining the dimensions and the ownership of communal spaces from patterns of use inspired by Henderson's recordings.[8] It is important to note that the final trajectory of post-war housing, its antagonistic ideologies and underfunded realisation are our contemporary hindsight. What was provocative about the Smithson's methodology that still has relevance is the value placed on 'the found', that understanding value requires immersion and empathy and the acknowledgement that any process of renewal needed to secure that value rather than seek to automatically replace it. The responsibility for determining a project is the crux of the issue, the definition of a project via a lead professional establishes a proven system of decision making that undertakes physical survey and analysis to mitigate structural or operational risk, but is under little obligation to dedicate time to mitigating 'social risk' by engaging in meaningful community liaison. The giving over of responsibility to discussion, debate and collective discussion creates an alternative dynamic that is not currently part of an architect's toolkit as delivered by education or Continuing Professional Development (CPD). Conservation-based architecture is a practice that, at least potentially creates a different dynamic to new-build architecture – material and technical skill-sets are specific, the role of history and research is far beyond simply legislation and technical resolution, and the relationship with a small group of specialist craftspeople creates partnerships across disciplines rather than hierarchies. However, the core issue that the *Conservation Plan* debate brings to the fore is one of 'significance' for whom?

> We do not have the language to express social values as clearly as we should, and much of the intangible social value is related to the spiritual and social value of a place. It is only when we can interpret the heritage in terms of contemporary perceived spiritual values that the public will be more involved, and will itself associate with and 'own' the project.
>
> (Clark, 1999: 109)

Specialists in the 'as found' are archaeologists. Highly specific knowledge, applied professionally through strict operational methodologies characterise the field. With such a specialised practice it could be assumed that archaeologists and communities would be distant relations, however the reverse can often be the case.

By the 20th century there had been a profound shift from wealthy amateurism that operated effectively under centuries of colonialist rules to the specialised, scientifically trained professional. Archaeology undertaken by architects and amateurs such as John Soane or Henry Inwood (St. Pancras Church is our example, see Chapter 5), underpinned the widespread development of neoclassicism and the Greek revival in its enthusiasm for the architectural language of classical civilisations. The historic appropriation of the ancient into contemporary practice, the adoption of sacred sites by new religions, the re-use of buildings and materials from one era into another collectively created Morris's 'history in the gap' (SPAB Manifesto, 1877), an "interesting and instructive" spirit of layered deeds.[9] However, while the buildings from the past are often amalgamations of previous history, the amateur architect-archaeologists understood only appearance, overlooking change and focussing on the ideal of style. The rise of archaeology as a practice in the 19th century was an appropriation of faintly enlightened amateurism, increasingly the ordinary artefacts of daily life came to assume significance as part of a wider set of cultural investigations. The relics from princes, kings and empires still today retain a sensational value, however the historic detritus of the ordinary carries equal importance – a Neolithic refuse heap providing more concrete information than a gold helmet or a statue of a god.

Archaeology has an interesting ambivalence in the status of its finds and the status its practice has in the public mind. While the daily detritus informs us about historic societies, the public appears to respond to more predictable sensation and impressiveness. Archaeology as a practice has managed this astutely, capitalising on the sensation to support, energise and popularise history as social understanding. The discovery of Richard III's body in a Leicester Social Services staff car park in September 2012 transformed history into drama, the last Plantagenet discovered by an unconnected series of events by individuals, not state departments or museums. Richard III enthusiasts Audrey Strange, Philippa Langley, historian David Baldwin and writer Annette Carson collectively sought to fund the archaeology through appeals to television production companies, Leicester Cathedral and Leicester City Council's tourism office demonstrates an entirely lateral approach to heritage that in some ways proves that the neoliberal project is emancipatory as well as 'fatal' to the State. The risks in 'following a hunch' were mitigated through media, whereas state funding and the attendant bureaucracy would likely have concluded that the exercise was futile. At the opening press conference in 2012, archaeologist Richard Buckley admitted "We don't know precisely where the church is, let alone where the burial site is" (Rainey, 2012: 21). With the £35,000 archaeology fee paid by the TV production company, the chances of finding Richard on the first day of the dig was nil; however Richard was found on that first day. As genealogical DNA, radiocarbon and osteological examinations progressed, Richard was more certain, as was the public interest, with the Channel 4 documentary *Richard III, the King in the Car Park* (4th Feb 2013) watched by 4.9 million viewers winning a Royal Television Society award. The success of Leicester City Football Club in winning the Premier League title was also attributed to the discovery and reinterment of the King, which headlined on the media for weeks. What does this tell us about archaeology and public participation?

The strategy of the 'community dig' can teach architects how to engage and involve the understanding of where public interest can be harnessed and engaged. There is of course a danger in the sensationalism of discovery being valued above the careful grind of revealing and understanding methodically, however in a neoliberal funding climate being able to choreograph events and knowledge exchange to intrigue, educate and generate funding within the practice of expert discovery is a strategy that is missing within conservation architecture. One could argue for the forensic process of looking, writing and researching *The Conservation Plan* to become the architectural equivalent of community archaeology – a framework of knowledge requirements that trained people can help deliver through 'hands-on' and shared research. Building a *Conservation Plan* by building a local team could use common understanding as a means to create design empathy. From this position, 'new work', 'repair work' and 'no work' become clearer choices that have built in participation. The application for funding is therefore not driven by the design project, but by the place itself and by the will to rediscover its ordinary history along with the more sensational headlines.

The Chartered Institute for Archaeologists ran a series of discussion sessions in 2017 with Historic England. Their concerns included standards and guidance on best practice and reflected on the changing planning system and the threats to local authority archaeology services – much the same as the concerns over the loss of building conservation officers. Published in October 2018 with Historic England, the transcripts focus on the challenges of developer-funded projects in creating new historical narratives and digital publishing ("who are we writing this stuff for anyway")[10] and issues around realising public value of archaeological archives. The themes reveal a proactive approach to contemporary issues of 'audience' and 'funding', hard to find within conservation architecture circles where client requirements are framed tightly and public requirements are invariably shaped by the clients' brief.

In the many charters and frameworks that try to tackle our relationship with heritage, the role of people is taken into consideration but the tactics for engaging people in the understanding of those relationships requires urgent definition. The neoliberal discourse around the individualisation of people within physical communities through the loss of collective employment and the generation of digitally enabled communities that are increasingly susceptible to influence for commercial or corporate interests characterise contemporary social structures. When community does not revolve around a shared place or shared physical activity, and work is increasingly via data, how can physical history still be considered a meaningful inheritance? If the language of professionally defined 'significance' appears to speak to itself, perhaps language is the problem, rather than knowledge.

At the *Oxford Conference*, Simon Jervis of the National Trust identified the role of language in the way *Conservation Plan* operates:

> James Semple-Kerr placed great stress on brevity and lucidity of language. These are obviously very important if the Plan is to communicate at all. But they can be difficult to reconcile with flexibility. What is crisp often also tends to be rigid.
>
> (Clark, 1999: 114)

The more specific the language and refined the output, the less inclusive or nuanced the results, he suggests. In Semple-Kerr's defence, political essayist George Orwell critically opposed the use of jargon and intricate language as a tool of concealment and persuasion that was inherently political. Within diverse communities we are also not only talking about a fluency in English – how are languages selected? Who is disenfranchised? Who signs, or interprets, provides Braille copies, and who pays for the material costs of inclusion? The public realm has underfunded public advocates and over-funded privatisers – the point about the realm of urban marketing is the political reduction of language to signs – the apparent impression of layered meaning within a singular process of consumption.

Jean-Marie Teutonico from English Heritage (*ivi*: 121) noted of the Paul Getty Foundation practice of funding the developing *Conservation Plans* (in the USA called Project Preparation Grants), "if you are going to ask for proper practice, you have to fund it"; however "in recent years we have seen preparation proposals costing more and more, and engaging more and more consultants. In a way, there is a danger that they can become an end in themselves instead of a means to an end, and it has started to become something of an industry in the United States".

Graham Fairclough from English Heritage (*ivi*: 129) proposed that the developers and writers of *Conservation Plans* "must find a way to engage with community-based ideas of significance as opposed only to those of experts. There must be room for the commonplace as well as the special", in this way highlighting how content and language needs to merge.

> Above all, though, it is essential to take account of who it is that makes the many value judgements – whether on significance or future use. Is it experts or local residents, business or politicians? Or can we find a way to involve everyone, through, for example, focus groups, visioning conferences, real-planning techniques, and capacity building and awareness creating projects such as Village Design Statements?
>
> (Clark, 1999: 130)

All these techniques have in common an attempt to move away from consultation towards participation. Since 1996, when the *Oxford Conference* took place, how far have we come and where are we now?

If the commonly held understandings of heritage are vague, and the way it is framed through policy and professionalisation of expertise liable to mislead, active public engagement in heritage is a potential tactic to overcome passive consumption or indifference. How is 'engagement' understood and what are the current exemplars and guidance? Historic England has two models that have been published in 2017 – an education programme called 'Heritage Schools' and *Delivering Public Engagement, Skills and Training*.[11] Heritage Schools, reported by Nick Bell and Nicola How is a CPD programme for primary school teachers running from 2011 to enable teachers to reflect on local history to foster awareness of locality, promote pride in the community and engage with 'on the doorstep' resources and places across eight regions of the UK. Reported feedback on the value the project has for teachers is extremely high, a testament to the social value of local history and to the initiative itself from Historic England.

> Studying real people and places that pupils have a connection to, compared to more 'abstract' or 'distant' history has had a positive impact on pupils' engagement with the topic and their subsequent written work. Teachers frequently commented on and provided examples to show both the quality and quantity of their pupils' written work related to their Heritage Schools topic.
>
> (How and Bell, 2018: 6)

This toolkit for supporting teachers to link national histories with locality, and to bring literacy requirements of the national curriculum into some relevant and graspable focus for children appears vital – the toolkit and support is free to schools, but with Historic England becoming self-funding under the 'shrinking state' ethos and schools having per-head pupil funding cut drastically, will either Historic England or schools be able to work in the same way in the future? If the successes achieved in the 2017 report are financialised and grade boundaries proven to rise due to such an initiative then government may think this form of 'heritage' is viable – however it is only by financializing heritage that it becomes supported, and many forms of heritage simply cannot demonstrate an 'adequate economic return'.

In 2017 Historic England published *Delivering Public Engagement, Skills and Training* (Gunthorpe, 2017), which uses a case study completed in 2014 – Harmondsworth Barn, "The cathedral of Middlesex" according to Sir John Betjeman, to illustrate how to deliver public engagement, skills and training activities during conservation works in progress.

> Building on the lessons learned from this project, English Heritage Trust are continuing to deliver these activities in their projects to encourage the public to view conservation projects in progress, include the wider community in their work and to expand the range of opportunities for volunteers.
>
> (Gunthorpe, 2017: summary)

In principle, the initiative to bring people onto working conservation projects to see and understand how the project is managed, why it is necessary, and more importantly why it is significant, has potential strengths. A detailed analysis of the case study reveals, however, that a series of limiting factors undermine the initiative and serve as a learning opportunity to take this exercised forward.

The initial limitation comes in the organisation of the public engagement after the scope of work, contractor and funding is established. Whilst logical, the constraints around standard construction site practice make engagement highly limited, where people are recipients, not protagonists. The contractor has strict liability obligations, in addition to the programming of work to optimise the completion time. Factoring in public access changes the shape not only of the on-site work, but the tendering process before that, the definition of the work before that, and one could argue the development of the project through public consultation before that. In the case of Harmondsworth Barn, the building was acquired by Historic England in 2011, so the client permission was ostensibly straightforward. How permission is gained when the owner is a private individual or organisation could not be incorporated in the study. The proportion of the £480,000 contract allocated to cover the 'engagement and training' exercise was 0.5% of the contract sum, arguably too little to substantially deliver engagement across six 'hard hat tours' at £18 per head, which was combined with a full-time trainee placement and on-site training for six members of the project workforce. Seven Sunday public access days were also included and relied on the 'Friends' of the Harmondsworth barn to facilitate.

> The hard hat tours were successful in engaging groups which skills research shows are underrepresented in heritage construction, young people and women. 26% of those on the tours were female, and 50% were young people.
>
> (*ivi*: 5)

The photographic illustration of the visits showed only silver-haired white men on site, perhaps an unfortunate choice of image. That people should have access to heritage projects is fundamental, and Historic England attempted to elaborate this process with this project – what is apparent is that the success of a public facing project, as with Richard III, is in building interest before the project team is in place in order to make public interest shape the project itself. Conventional sites lack adequate facilities with equal access, lack seminar spaces, lack spaces that are not draughty or full of dust. Engagement requires as much design as a high-quality repair or technical intervention. That bookings were found easier with groups than individuals narrowed the kind of participant that was able to attend – how it was advertised is also a limiting to enabling factor, but that fine grain detail was missing from the report. When the case study succeeded was in establishing the benefits to visitor and contractor alike in human terms, if not financially:

> Feedback from Jeremy Ashbee, Head Curator Properties, who gave an intro-duction to the members tours, highlighted the benefits of the contractor lead-ing the tours. . . . 'The success of the tours was largely down to the engaging and professional manner of the contractors and in particular Dominic Bar-rington – Groves, the site foreman. If English Heritage staff had been doing this on their own, it would not have been so successful as the enthusiasm and expertise of the main contractor was vital.'
>
> (*ivi*: 13)

The authors' experience of leading 'hard hat tours' aligns with this assessment. The question is whether engagement is simply an engaging spectacle, or is also an oppor-tunity to proactively establish the project itself. When the HLF is calling for proof of community buy-in and benefit in order to fund, what future shape can engagement take? The Heritage Fund requires community benefit stated at the outset, invariably standard construction fills the central space of the project with peripheral activities such as at Harmondsworth undertaken, then the community receives the result to make a success, or not, of the consequences. The pointed question about how this tripartite system can be reshaped is partly answered in our case study – Altab Ali Park by MUF Architecture Art LLP, using archaeology as a tool for participation that frames the project itself.

Altab Ali Park, Whitechapel, London by MUF Architecture/ Art LLP 2011

The development of the park into an inclusive space for the diverse communities of Whitechapel drew on the archaeological heritage of the site to generate a series of public engagement events that cemented the physical history of the site into the social and cultural fabric of the place and its inhabitants. Specific historical events and ideas became common knowledge through archaeology workshops held with the Museum of London that brought five hundred schoolchildren into contact with fragments of history under the surface of the existing park as a prelude to redesign. Artefacts from the digs, as well as art projects with local artists and students, form permanent elements in the space. Most importantly, the Altab Ali Park project approached history beyond broadcasting generalisations by uncovering layers of history and embracing complexity as part of the understanding of place.

> Our ambition was to make accommodation for all users of the park without prioritising one over the other and to understand the site as a microcosm of

the wider neighbourhood of this part of London where historically many different cultural, religious and political influences have shaped the fabric and the people who live here, states Katherine Clarke from MUF (2012).

This approach is typical of MUF, a mixed practice of architects and artist,[12] and won them the European Prize for public space for the Barking Town Square in 2008. Here, as in our case study, the dense meanings that are deposited into a place were used to inform an ambiguous urban collage, accommodating the differences, conflicts and appropriations that deposited over centuries in the form of built materials or social resistances.

The history of Altab Ali Park is central to the understanding of place significance. It is located on Adler Street, White Church Lane and Whitechapel Road, not far from the Whitechapel Gallery. The park was formerly known as St. Mary's Park and was formerly the burial ground of Whitechapel parish church. The church here was the second oldest in Stepney and there are records of a church from 1329, built as a chapel-of-ease and called St. Mary Matfelon. It may have been known as 'White Chapel' because it was painted with whitewash, giving the area its name.[13] The Victorian church that replaced the original White Chapel was destroyed in air raids in December 1940 and what is left now is the floor plan and few graves.

The park was renamed in 1998 in memory of Altab Ali, a 25-year old Bangladeshi Sylheti textile worker employed in the area off Brick Lane where the Bengali community was expanding while the older Jewish immigrant population was receding. On 4th May 1978 Altab Ali was murdered by three teenage racists on his way home. The same day was election day with the far-right National Front running in every Tower

Figure 6.2
Church overlays showing the traces of pre-existing buildings in Altab Ali park.
Source: Image courtesy MUF architecture/art

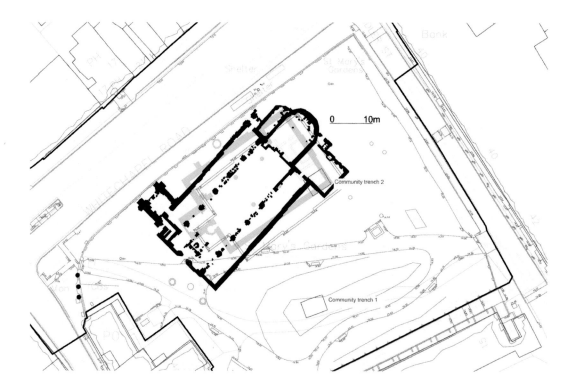

Hamlets ward and standing for election in forty-three council seats. The East End was characterised by many racist episodes at that time, and the killing of Altab Ali marked a turning point (Rosemberg, 2018). "Infamously, it was there in 1936 that Oswald Mosley's British Union of Fascists, in imitation of Germany's Nazis, had planned to march in protest at the area's large Jewish population" (Nye and Bright, 2016). Ali became a symbol of the need for resistance against racism and on 14th May 1978, 7,000 people marched from Alder Street to Downing Street and Hyde Park asking for the end of violence and in support of not only British Bangladeshis (Historic England, no date), but many diverse communities struggling for basic dignity in an aggressive racially conditioned environment.

Forty years from that time, prejudice is again on the rise in East London and the ethnic communities rooted here face new challenges (Rosemberg, 2018). Many of the streets around Brick Lane are transforming into wealthy ghettos and people are forced to move out (*ivi*). In order to keep the memory of integration alive and build on the legacy of movements that generated after Altab Ali's murder, the mayor of Tower Hamlets announced in 2015 that the borough would host an Altab Ali Commemoration Day. The idea is for the Commemoration Day to be a symbol of community co-operation against new forms of discrimination.

When MUF approached the area in late 2010 it was for taking part in the larger regeneration project called High Street 2012, promoted by the mayor of London and supported by investment from the Department for Communities and Local Government, English Heritage, Transport for London, the Heritage Lottery Fund and London Thames Gateway Development Corporation (Mayor of London, no date). The project aimed to rejuvenate London's oldest high street through seventeen individual creative projects,[14] "from works to the street and building façades, to cultural events and celebrations" (*ibidem*). The London 2012 Olympic and Paralympic Games was the catalyst of the initiative, wanting to create a vision for the six kilometre-stretch of the high street environment between the city and Stratford, home to Olympic Park, perhaps more cynically to present a pleasing face to a global television audience. Part of this ambitious vision was to use the temporary sporting event as stimuli to shape 'permanent' places, as in the case of Altab Ali Park, and to "increase the connection between individual places – making each one an attractive destination" (*ibidem*). History was a central concern, as was the appreciation of existing social and physical assets. The projects did not fail to address local association, historic cores, ancient market streets and new retail areas, multi-layered cultures and socially nuanced occupations. For example, the historic building part of High Street 2012's vision brought heavy changes to the façades of important buildings on Aldgate, Whitechapel, Mile End and Bow. Conservation architects teamed up with regeneration consultants and graphic designers "to negotiate the dual demands of historic conservation and contemporary requirements for shop front design. A dedicated council officer liaised between shopkeepers and planners" (*ibidem*), implying that the careful observation of local heritage could not separate built form from social meaning and the histories that deposited them both in place.

That was also the case for Altab Ali Park, an area dense with built remains and bearing a distinctive social significance. The area was home to the remains of St. Mary's Chapel, but its presence and that of the extended history of the site was poorly acknowledged. In 1966 the site had been laid out as a public garden, the footprint of the former church outlined in concrete blocks flush with the lawn. There were a number of monuments remaining, particularly near the entrance at the Whitechurch Lane and Whitechapel Road junction, as well as a number of chest tombs, including one tomb to the Mattock family. An old drinking fountain sat on the corner of Whitechurch Lane and Whitechapel High Street, with the inscription 'erected by one unknown and yet well known' stating that it was relocated from another site. There were the remains of old railings on the garden's side of the structure, and the arch at the entrance of the park created by David Patterson as a memorial to Altab Ali and other victims of racist attacks. The arch incorporates a complex Bengali-style pattern, meant to show the merging of different cultures in East London. Moreover, a Shaheed Minar was installed in place as a small replica of the one in Dhaka, Bangladesh and is a spatial trace of the realm of faith and an acknowledgement of the attachment to place. The monument, symbolising a mother and her martyred sons, is a commemoration to the victims of the Bengali Language Movement.

MUF wanted to create a commemorative park conceived as a matrix of the religious and secular history of the place. At the first sight, the redesign of the park appears as a landscape of incoherent fragments. Carved, 'accidental' Portland stone pieces mark the fragmented footprint of previous churches, and tree trunks laying among remains are designed so to enable play, for children and adults alike: one of the pieces is designed as a carrom board and another as a "marble run". Tiles mimicking the floors of forgotten rooms seem to indicate the place of ancient graves. There is a funerary urn from the 18th century placed opposite some logs. Some of the pieces are clearly old and coming from on-site excavation, others are replicas. The overall feeling is the one of a reconstructed scenography, where originality and fiction play hand in hand to disturb our all-too-linear approach to places and instil some questions. Ambiguity and contamination become fundamental values to nurture our understanding. Everything

Figure 6.3
Altab Ali park
after completion
with the Shaheed
Minar in the
background.

Source: Image
courtesy MUF
architecture/art

is orchestrated with care. To bring the footprint of the White Chapel lying under the grass back as an active presence in the park, a 38-metre-long bench makes a social space and gives views back across the park to the Shaheed Minar monument that is framed by a new landscape. An Alpana was planned here, as part of the final scheme, with the help of three Bangladeshi artists and students from Central St. Martins. On this side of the park the ground has been remodelled in a series of hollows decorated with scattered stones and logs, allowing a vantage point over the whole area. Katherine Clarke of MUF explains that

> the design of the park is a reaction against the Brick Lane curry house image of Whitechapel and tries to show that the history of the area is more nuanced and diverse. . . . "There is a tendency to see Whitechapel as homogenous in its identity, but you don't have to go far beneath the tourist view to find a place far more layered in its cultural and historical identity," she says.
>
> (Evening Standard, 2011)

In order to make explicit the layering of history inside the park, MUF activated a collaboration with the Museum of London. A series of 'community digs' were organised involving the archaeologists from the museum with five hundred school children and volunteers. The activity transformed the park into an outdoor museum. The church remains from the 16th and 18th centuries were revealed, together with a number of other artefacts including pottery pieces and objects of daily use. They were accurately named, group and categorised with the children's help and eventually transformed into new art pieces. One of them lays close to the entrance of the park where a square excavation, intentionally open, exposes part of the deeper ground of the park, and commemorates the archaeological activity. The art piece composed by the found objects has been positioned at the centre, surrounded by four coloured, 'sedimented' walls marking the limit between the terrain and the hole. The walls, realised in collaboration with the authors and the University of London, are designed to mimic a layered geological terrain, each stratum coloured with natural pigments and embedding some fragments from the excavation.

The found objects, in this case, offered the opportunity to engage actively with the history of the site and were used to support community activities of rediscovery, recognition and transformation. Rearranging their presence, mixing and matching the sources blurred the limits of recognisably (between original and orchestrated, among communities) revealing a vital, conflicting and complex place. Bricolage became a creative tactic of understanding, making clear that a good design is not necessarily coherent and unified, smoothed and pacified. Acknowledging multiple identities and different remains were part of the same operation, which stays open to future layering. "When I saw the church, walls come out the ground and understood how each object we found tells a tale about the way people lived it made me wonder at the bigger story and how I am part of that too" stated a pupil from Mulberry School who took part in the community dig (MOLA, 2012).

This opens up the question of how our relationship to the artefact is curated and when this can become a metonymy for wider stories and their significance.

In order to explore further the issue of curation of the artefact, and how that discipline can be reflected on conservation practice we propose to observe the 'True Value' exhibition by artist Theaster Cates. The aim is to expand on the everyday value of small scale.

Figures 6.4, 6.5 and 6.6 'Community dig' with children organised by MUF in collaboration with the Museum of London and artefacts chosen to be embedded into the new design.

Source: Image courtesy MUF architecture/art

Figure 6.6
(Continued)

Figure 6.7
Concrete beams
including
the artefacts
excavated during
the 'community
digs', MUF in
collaboration
with University
of East London.
The coloured
layers mimic the
historic layering
of the place.
Source: Picture by
Authors

'True Value' by Theaster Gates, Fondazione Prada, Milan 2016

The hardware store on the corner of 93rd and Halsted on Chicago's South Side was a kind of archetype, a place both unique to its location and yet found in city centres in almost every city anywhere. This store had its origins in the 1930s, the fruits of Italian migrant labour, providing the elements of everyone's life in small quantities and varieties – hoses, hooks and tools. This store has a wider significance in that the artist Theaster Gates purchased it and its entire contents from Ken, its second owner of 40 years, as no one else would take on what is now an anachronistic and unviable business model in an urban location surrounded by deprivation and social issues. The purchase of pieces of Chicago is part of Gate's practice,

> As Gates sees it, hardware stores are more than the sum of their stock. They are the gatekeepers of expertise, containing the objects that keep our crumbling world together that little bit longer. They represent the valuable knowledge of plumbers, electricians and builders, the "shamans" of this world, as Gates reverently refers to them. "I found myself preoccupied not with the painting but with the paint and the manufacturing of paint and the alchemy of pigments," he says in Milan. "Nowhere represents the 'before', the raw materials, more than a hardware store."
>
> (Ellis-Petersen, 2016)

The everyday value of small scale, local enterprise that services the small-scale acts of maintenance and inhabitation are everywhere being replaced by online services and courier deliveries. The network of human interaction that places such as Ken's hardware store enable disappear along with the store – the discussion of this loss is central to the project that Gates developed as he reworked the store and its 30,000 items for sale into an installation at the new Rem Koolhaas–designed Fondazione Prada in Milan in 2016.[15] The re-situation of the hardware store and its memories of self-help, community network and heritage within such an institution is both committed and problematic. It speaks about the loss of one form of capitalism – localised, low profit margins, networked relations of consumers and tradespeople, for another – large scale, high turnover, rapid replacement, generic. Along with local trade goes traditional local relations – between us and our fellow citizens and between us and the fabric of our surroundings that are replaced rather than fixed. "What happens to the legacy of those hardware stores when the last one finally disappears? What do we lose when craft no longer infuses our material lives?" (*ibidem*).

Gates concluded that the value of the hardware store lay not in simply maintaining it as an unviable business, but in converting it through art into a signifier for the issues it embodied. "Sadly, I just didn't have the capacity to keep the store going," says Gates. "But I started to think about what the truth of this hardware store going away means, not only for Chicago but for small, family-owned businesses that are being squeezed out around the world. Could the hardware store be a stand in for the failure of local economy globally?" (*ibidem*).

As Elvira Dyangani Ose, the show's curator noted,

> If there is a particular ethos that has characterized Theaster Gates's work in recent years, it is the formulation of the unimaginable as a common cause. It

Figure 6.8
Theaster Gates 'True Value'. Fondazione Prada, Milano, 2016. Photo Delfino Sisto Legnani Studio.
Source: Courtesy Fondazione Prada.

would be a misconception to believe that his attention to urban regeneration, social practice and blackness engages only the communities that his projects affect immediately. Instead, Gates's immaterial gestures – as much as the objects he produces and the experiences he generates – are essentially a 'call to arms', raising awareness of the need for what American theorist and poet Fred Moten calls the 'coalition', or the recognition that what affects those communities subsequently affects the rest of us too; the acceptance that we are all in this together.

(Fondazione Prada, 2016b)

Ken helped Gates to transfer the store to his Chicago studio, the process of moving the store recorded as an event but also as a documentary of Ken's reminiscences on video as part of the store's transformation into art. In a contemporary culture that values images and their dissemination, the conversion of an actual place and its significance into a sign of that significance is ironic. Is this act of 'museification' making a serious point, or simply making a spectacle out of its obsolescence?

What is achieved by transporting a hardware store to an exclusive gallery by a globally famous architect run by a globally famous fashion brand? In one sense the question is one of 'significance'. The loss of the store is significant to the people living on or near 93rd and Halstead, but the significance in attention that is now directed on that loss is huge following its relocation. A wider issue is how the context of our understanding affects significance, not simply the amount of significance that can be evidenced. Gates insists in interviews that his work is not about nostalgia but about power – who has it, and who lacks access to it. "Profit will trump humanity", Gates asserts, "So I think if there's anything nostalgic, it's that desire to see everyday people having control over their lives, a direct engagement" (Hellis-Peterson, 2016). The hardware store becomes part remembrance, part hunting trophy – evidence of what Gates believes is good in the world, but also the relic of its loss. The wider significance to Milan is the similarity of fate awaiting the Italian equivalent of this Chicago archetype – the *ferramenta* are, or were, intrinsic to the city. Part of the curation of the Prada show includes flyers to advertise Ferramenta Vigano, open slightly longer than the Chicago hardware store in the Corso Como area of the city, that is now part of the high value fashion district and under pressure from real estate dealing to vacate. "Gates operates on the conviction that everyday objects convey a deep understanding, not only intrinsic to their material aspect, but reminiscent of the experiences in which they have been immersed" (Fondazione Prada, 2016b).

The way the hardware store-as-art is described by the art press is interesting, invariably discussing the artist's own understanding as though the integrity of that knowledge alone secures the value of the work. This is in part a fundamental aspect of 'art publicity', where the artefact is a fragment of the artist and its 'value' relates to the integrity of its originator, rather than any actual meaning. Value in art is invariably tied to the monetary value of the piece, in turn linked to the monetisation of the individual artist. Gates appears motivated by an abiding social consciousness, but can the work achieve social consciousness when its significance is, at least in part derived from the global forces that are rendering the hardware store obsolete?

> *True Value* gathers materials, objects and tools removed from their original context and relocated in an art environment, sponsored by a fashion house instrumental in the reinvention deploying a framework to formulate a poetic and pragmatic space around objects of trade and human relationships those economic and labour exchanges create.
>
> (*ibidem*)

In addition to referencing the credibility of the artist's vision, the credibility of the gallery itself is also cited as intrinsically valuable to meaning – the 'framework' that renders the work poetic is the gallery setting itself – without which presumably there is only pragmatism. Gates, however, is actually interested in pragmatism, on the ground level resistance to corporate erasure, yet the work to attain significance is reliant on its enemy.

The experience of *True Value* poses wider question about art, even architecture's actual effectiveness in either debating or transforming urban blight when the context of producing either art or buildings is so linked to the financially empowered. The results of empowerment – the art piece or the building are invariably outside the reach or discourse of the majority of people, raising the question about the investment value of 'art about people' or buildings ostensibly about people but usually about investment. In this regard Gates's work displays a care for this concern. The recognition of value in the ordinary reads sincerely, the act of buying an un-saleable hardware store is a form of direct action that at least supports the owner's wish to retire, and the diligence with which the narrative is explored is both respectful and considered. The last element is the effectiveness in bringing that ordinary reality into a determinedly anti-ordinary setting. Does this re/decontextualisation achieve its stated aim of making the visitor – be they international art tourist or Milanese bystander – consider the fragility of the ordinary and the reality of its impending loss? In bringing these unacknowledged spaces and activities into the shadowless glare of the gallery, are we appreciating their role in underpinning who and where we are?

What matters is that that the actions of people have a physical and tangible reality. A 'sense of place' is often defined as 'intangible heritage' but this is contestable. Every sense depends on external stimulus: the identity of a street involves the loss of actions – the shopkeeping, the loss of places – the shop, and the loss of its stock – the materials with which we maintain our own places. Gates establishes a piece that discussed tangible loss through tangible rescue, making a valuable mirror to the collateral damage inflicted on human relations when capital jumps scale.

True Value was the name of the hardware store. The challenge for heritage professionals is to realise that the intangible 'sense of place' is actually intimately connected to real people, real activities and real places with material histories. The *True Value* of conservation is understanding the relations between all of these realities, and where necessary looking to engage with them in order to conserve buildings by conserving people, who Gates calls 'everyday shamen', and what they do – shaping our physical and social sense of community. Gates needed to relocate the hardware store to Milan to amplify its significance; this decontextualisation is a form of collage necessary to disrupt our overlooking of what is actually meaningful in the everyday. Using art practice to re-look and re-present reality that is ours, but that we ignore is an invaluable tool for engagement, but one rarely used by conservation professionals focussed on historical and material analysis. A notable example of institutional use of arts-based engagement comes from the National Trust, which developed a public programme in 2019 to mark 200 years since the Peterloo Massacre, appointing Turner Prize winner Jeremy Deller to assemble a series of artists to respond to the role that key Trust properties played in social protest and social change.

The People's Landscape, National Trust

The National Trust sought to commemorate the 200th anniversary of the Peterloo massacre (16th August 1819), where at St. Peters Field, Manchester, a crowd of over 60,000 peaceful demonstrators demanding parliamentary reform for representation were charged by cavalry, killing eighteen and wounding many others. The Trust has sites linked to the aggressors and the advocates within this seminal moment in social history, and through that realisation a wider set of socially significant sites were identified to elaborate our cultural connections to place. Through Arts Council and HLF Art Fund support, the initiative creates a connection across history, place and the arts that expands a sense of heritage as shared inheritance, an insight into the complexities of landscape beyond the appreciation of an image of British countryside and fine buildings, "to delve into the land that William Blake described as 'green and pleasant land' . . . to reflect on the radical histories of the people whose lives played out on this vast open stage" (National Trust website, 2019).

> People's Landscapes, is exploring the connections between our places and the rights and beliefs we hold dear today. Across the country, we are delving into

the deeper stories behind these places of change, through a series of events, walks and talks, including a collaboration with the National Portrait Gallery and projects supported by contemporary artists.

(National Trust website, 2019)

Bob and Roberta Smith worked with the Tolpuddle Martyrs' tree in Dorset looking at the transportation to Australia of six labourers guilty of forming a union to protest against their working conditions. Musician Jarvis Cocker worked with Kinder Scout and the mass trespass in 1932 that led to the legislation of 'right to roam' for ordinary people across a landscape privatised since the acquisition of the commons that heralded the capitalist state. Grace and Gary Winters explored the connection between the founder of Trust property 'Quarry Bank Mill', Samuel Greg, who witnessed the Peterloo Massacre of 1819 where a crowd of protestors in Manchester demanding political rights were charged by cavalry and who opposed the subsequent cover up and the head of that militia that charged the crowd. The same head of the militia lived in another Trust property – Dunham Massey in Cheshire, completing an intricate political dialogue between two properties that are proxies for opposing views of this significant historical outrage. Amber, a film collective, worked with local people in the former pit community of Easington, County Durham where the Trust are custodians of a five mile stretch of coastline once polluted by the mines activity; now that both pollution and pit are gone, exploring the best and worst of the closure for the community. In Croome, Worcestershire a house designed by 'Capability' Brown was converted into a boys' Catholic school from where accusations of child abuse have become public and an inquiry undertaken – a project carefully acknowledging this positive and awful past using oral histories to explore the meaning of 'home', illuminate issues of security and wellbeing. The Croome project is highly sensitive, celebrating the physicality of the building designed by a major figure in landscape design, whilst evidencing events that the building contained. Negotiating conflicted histories and voicing contemporary social concerns is critical if the Trust is "to become relevant to new audiences . . . we cannot simply expect them to come to us, sometimes we should be willing to go to them" (*ivi*).

The Trust has gone on record to deny a political driver for the People's Landscapes project, rather citing

> a conscious decision to find the stories that resonate most strongly from our places and to explore them, and to tell them in interesting ways with contemporary artists . . . if our places are to remain relevant now into the future, we need to be able to tell these complex stories . . . to those who may currently feel disconnected from our cultural heritage.
>
> (National Trust Website, 2019)

How interesting that artists, filmmakers and musicians are the communicators, not the conservation experts – despite the whole rationale for the *Conservation Plan* being about understanding and communicating heritage significance. "It is better that people be allowed to interpret and understand (a site) for themselves, as if it were their own discovery, rather than making it look as if some bureaucrat has imposed his will upon it" (John Orna-Ornstein, quoted by Esther Addley Guardian, 17 Jan 2019). This critical observation sits at the heart of the heritage question – who is heritage for and who is able to effectively shape the narrative that includes it and inform its meaning? If only heritage professionals recognise heritage value, the whole process becomes self-serving. This aspect of 'limited scope' was addressed concisely by the Lord Hankey back at the *Oxford Conference*: "We are still bad at understanding these human values, and the research and interpretation of these values should be better supported by the social sciences and by cultural anthropology" (The Lord Hankey, CPIA: 19).

Although the Trust's properties are the beneficiaries of rigorously researched preservation, the resulting work is precisely crafted sensation, with the contradictory nature of real lived events and their consequences over generations removed in order to essentialise a narrative of history. That this narrative is open influence for one particular constituency over another simply adds to the problematic nature of this practice of 'restoration'. The question for the Trust is how to balance preservation with a renewed relevance to new and existing communities?

How can the 'singular' emphasis on one selected and curated point in time (which has been the norm for presenting its properties to the public) deal with the evolving nature of historical understanding and interpretation, or bring new communities into the narrative? The implication of this 'singular' attitude is that memory is not grounded in actual lived practice but is frozen into a form of artificial synthesis that creates the outward impression of historical context but is, in short, a fabrication. More and more, organisations dedicated to preserving the cultural heritage such as the National Trust are shifting their own definition of 'custodianship' away from the Le Duc–informed preservationist approach. For Morris recognising the building as a 'document' was not to consign it to a passive academic role as an object of study, but as a diary of inhabitation written daily. Morris emphasised the ongoing maintenance, sensitive adjustment and meaningful use of a building as intrinsic to its value, writing passionately about the importance of historic accumulation of built form and its relationship with social life. Morris demanded an active engagement in the making of buildings from the constructor to the user: in his mind and in his own form of utopia they would be the same.

The 'People's Landscapes' project is particularly interesting because it tackles this crucial issue of history as a lived, complex iterative process in relation to the fixed and frozen artifice of the heritage setting. As noted by John Orna-Ornstein, the Trust's Director of Culture and Engagement and the figure behind the 2019 project 'Peoples Landscapes': "We recognise that many people want more than a cream tea. They want to feel connected to the Places they visit" (Addley, 2019). The People's Landscape has, in this context, the merit to unveil the link between oral narration and geography and to disclose the layering of stories that sits within the strata of places. It confronts us with the issue of communicating history in a complex way, exiting the simplification employed by current communication. As noted by Carlo Olmo (2018: 5), the problem of language is not secondary to contemporary democracy. We should recover the meaning of history, legacy and patrimony as opposed to the more marketable term 'heritage'; the meaning of identity, often rebuilt according to selected models from the past; the meaning of recognition as a matter of relationship, casual encounter as opposed to familiar homogeneity; and the value of social risk in the recovery and privatisation of a common good.

Redefining our vocabulary, recognising the complexity and difference of representation associated with places and supporting imagination should be considered as political actions charged in intentionality and social potential. The importance of plurality is clear: the stories that informed the places we live in represent a very broad variety of subjects and engagements, each one with its own system of representation that interacts with both the leading narratives and with unpredictable trajectories and

*Figure 6.9
Dorset,
landscape.*

*Source: Picture by
the authors, 2016*

local systems. Recognising the plurality of voices means revising our interpretative tools. It also means putting people back to the centre of the discussion, shifting from spectatorship to agency. Why can't *Conservation Plans* do this?

Lessons learned

The chapter proposed a critical overview of the heritage industry and its professionalisation that contextualises where specialist knowledge and skills are of real value but demonstrates that conservation is more layered than simply stone, lime and plaster.

Morris and the consequent elaboration of 'as found' rewrote the role that material history plays in socially constructed present. For Morris, material is a source of 'reflection' – a political consciousness manifest through a particular relationship to work and ethics. This work is, however, a marginal rather than mainstream phenomena. Our current relationship to history is fragmentary, a return to the appearance of history as consolation rather than as a meaningful social component of daily life. In a process of evolution from Le Duc rather than Morris, heritage is now a selective concept increasingly used to market the city. It must "produce memory and future, restore monetary value and culture, tell ethical stories and extol aesthetics" (Marini, 2017: 19); thanks to its instantly recognisable pre-existing value, heritage and its accomplice memory becomes a strategic communication device for place promotion and production, a spectacle of history rather than a common inheritance of meaning and identity.

Morris was a political contemporary of Marx, who articulated theoretically what Morris sought to address through material means. In 'The 18th Brumaire of Louis Bonaparte' Marx proposed that people made their own history, but they do this unknowingly. Within an industrialised capitalist society memory becomes a constantly rearticulated misunderstanding – the fabrication process of social relations, and the buildings such relations articulate are often dressed in a reassuring familiarity to maintain a sense of engagement and connection, despite the autonomous nature of accumulating surplus profit. What is the status of the historic building – does it anchor reality, underpin alternative realities, compromise new realities or is it simply a tool with which new realities are sold?

The diverse voices at the *Oxford Conference* were a prelude to the mechanics of evaluating heritage and justifying how and where change to historic buildings and places should happen. We show that the means by which this mechanism – the *Conservation Plan* – became determined was far from unequivocal, and that with hindsight the nuances of engagement and social practice within conservation have been at best sidelined, at worst ignored. The recovery of the range of perspectives that the *Oxford Conference* offered have been restated to underline the lack of inevitability in the current norms and structures of practice, that our own practice is as partial as any history. We have demonstrated the contested nature of what is considered 'significant' and proposed through our case studies how proven techniques from related disciplines can, when rigorously applied, rebuild social heritage.

The three case studies we focussed on (the National Trust's *People's Landscape*, Altab Ali Park by MUF and *True Value* by Theaster Gates) highlighted the centrality of heritage narratives. In particular, they revealed how the significance of place is both fragile and complex, requiring a number of differing viewpoints to be assessed before concluding its value. The rhetoric around significance is nuanced and serves particular interests, as every communication is addressed by specific subjects in so much that individuals, institutions or passers-by would tell the same story in different ways according to their experiences and aims. In spite of the reality that 'heritage narratives' may be faulty and partial, the imperfect nature of assemblage allows more voices to enter within the cracks. The Altab Ali Park project by MUF, for example, worked on historic fragments, selecting and discarding them within an open, inclusive process. The aim was not to rebuild a comprehensive image of history for the site but working on its layered significance. Accepting the inputs of different communities was part of the process and critical to the creation of new significance for the place.

Surely there is a need to expand the definition of both conservation practice and the heritage it is focussed on to include community engagement and place. Architectural practice engaged in heritage is not a distinct specialism applied to 'designated heritage assets' but a social practice working anywhere between the ordinary and extraordinary, acknowledging that every building or place could be positioned anywhere along that spectrum of meaning. Every place has as much history as any other, and it is the task of future frameworks, policies or professional actions to identify and clarify that very history. This requires engagement strategies currently unfamiliar to a sector that concentrates on technical and precedent based decision making.

> We need more, not fewer architects . . . there should be one on every street corner for life, offering a cheap service like doctors to anyone living in run-down communities. Architecture isn't about post-modernism, conservationism or eclecticism, it's about solving people's problems in the environment.
>
> (Hackney, 1985)

Within this context, echoing the context Rod Hackney proposed, we believe *The Conservation Plan* should be considered as a tool for engagement, underpinning community voice in how physical places develop their significance, not merely 'are significant' according to the evidence of the past. What it should be clear is that Heritage is about the future.

Within this context, and echoing the radical context that Rod Hackney proposed, we believe the role and ambition of *The Conservation Plan* should be reconsidered as a tool for engagement, underpinning a community voice in how physical places 'develop' their significance, not simply underline the significance accrued to date. Morris looked at the past as a layered accumulation of constant, sympathetic use, constantly evolving and adding to built fabric. When we detach or intercept use without sympathy, either towards the humble nature of materiality or the way the building operates socially, we are using *The Conservation Plan* to justify the elaborate preservation of a death mask, frequently obscuring the presence of financial return. Hackney challenged the elitism of the architectural profession, its distance from communities and its compromised role as a lackey to corporate or wealth interests. We too challenge the professionals to consider the ethics of selective preservation to make redevelopment palatable, we identify examples where empathy and engagement create heritage as much as preserve it, and ask the professions to consider whether their knowledgeable evaluation of significance adds to people's inheritance, or masks its theft.

Notes

1 The Burra Charter defines the basic principles and procedures to be followed in the conservation of Australian heritage places.
2 link to https://australia.icomos.org/publications/the-conservation-plan/
3 link to www.heritagefund.org.uk/
4 link to https://historicengland.org.uk/
5 link to www.heritagefund.org.uk/publications/hlf-annual-report-2017-2018
6 link to Natural England (nee Countryside Commission): www.gov.uk/government/organisations/natural-england
7 link to Village Design Guides: http://publications.naturalengland.org.uk/publication/2134081
8 In the early 1950s Henderson was a member of the Independent Group, which is regarded as the precursor to the Pop Art movement in Britain. He taught at the Central School of Art with Anthony Froshaug, Edward Wright and Eduardo Paolozzi. Together with the Smithsons, he took part in the exhibition *This is Tomorrow* at the Whitechapel Gallery in 1956.
9 "If repairs were needed, if ambition or piety pricked on to change, that change was of necessity wrought in the unmistakable fashion of the time; a church of the eleventh century might be added to or altered in the twelfth, thirteenth, fourteenth, fifteenth, sixteenth, or even the seventeenth or eighteenth centuries, but every change, whatever history it destroyed, left history in the gap, and was alive with the spirit of the deeds done midst its fashioning. The result of all this was often a building in which the many changes, though harsh and visible enough, were, by their very contrast, interesting and instructive and could by no possibility mislead" (Morris, 1877).
10 Engaging with Policy in the UK: Responding to Changes in Planning, Heritage and the Arts 27 October 2018, UCL Institute of Archaeology – video recording available online at: https://heritage-research.org/events/engaging-policy-uk-responding-changes-planning-heritage-arts/
11 For more information visit the web pages: Heritage Schools https://historicengland.org.uk/services-skills/education/heritage-schools/ and Delivering Public Engagement, Skills and Training https://historicengland.org.uk/images-books/publications/delivering-public-engagement-skills-and-training/
12 muf architecture/art: http://muf.co.uk/

13 St. Mary's Gardens was formerly the burial ground of Whitechapel parish church and referred to in the C18th as White Chapel Church Yard. The church here was the second oldest in Stepney and there are records of a church from 1329, built as a chapel-of-ease and called St. Mary Matfelon. It may have been known as White Chapel because it was painted with white-wash. It became the parish church for the western part of Stepney in 1338. The third church on the site was built in 1877 but this suffered a fire in 1880, with only its tower, vestry and church rooms remaining. It was, however, rebuilt by December 1882 and it could accommodate some 1,600 people, with an outside pulpit used for sermons in the summer. For more information: www.middlesex-heraldry.org.uk/publications/monographs/mdxchurches/mdxchurches-whitechapelstmary.htm

14 Consultants included EDCO Design, JMP, muf architecture/art, Rachel Whiteread, Alan Baxter, East Architecture Landscape Urban Design, PRP, Adams and Sutherland, Aecom, Minx Collective, Timorous Beasties, Julian Harrap, Objectif, Fluid.

15 Find our more on Fondazione Prada's website: http://artdaily.com/news/88558/Fondazione-Prada-presents-two-new-projects-by-Theaster-Gates-and-Nastio-Mosquito#.XKIRz-szbyt

Bibliography

Book, journals and reports

Addley, E. (2019) 'National Trust targets new audience with celebration of protest', *The Guardian*. [Online] Available at: www.theguardian.com/uk-news/2019/jan/17/national-trust-targets-new-audience-with-celebration-of-protest (Accessed: March 2019).

Alison and Peter Smithson (1990) 'The "As Found" and the "Found"', in Robbins, D. (ed.) *The Independent Group Postwar Britain and the Aesthetics of Plenty*, Cambridge and London: MIT Press, pp. 201–202.

Benjamin, W. (1983) *Das Passagen-Werk*, Frankfurt: Suhrkamp.

Blöch, E. (1935) *Eredità del nostro tempo*. Translated by L. Boella, Milano, IL: Saggiatore, 1992.

Brecht, B. (1963) *Gesammelte Werke*, Suhrkamp: Frankfurt.

Carman, J. (2014) *Cultural Value: Heritage Value: Combining Culture and Economics*. Arts & Humanities Research Council, Meeting Records. [Online] Available at: www.birmingham.ac.uk/Documents/college-artslaw/iiich/carman-AHRC-cultural-value-project.pdf (Accessed: 1 December 2018).

Clark, K. (1999) 'Conservation Plans in Action', *Historic England*, pp. 27–40.

Drexel, D. (2013) 'Landscape, Paysage, Landschaft, Táj: The Cultural Background of Landscape Perceptions in England, France, Germany, and Hungary', *Journal of Ecological Anthropology*, 16(1).

Ellis-Petersen 'Theaster Gates on the Nuts and Bolts of Life – all 30,000 of them', *The Guardian*. [Online] Available at: www.theguardian.com/artanddesign/2016/jul/14/theaster-gates-nuts-and-bolts-fondazione-prada-milan (Accessed: March 2019).

English Heritage (1999) *Conservation Plans in Action*, ISBN 1 85074 752 0, London: English Heritage.

English Heritage (2008) Conservation principles policies and guidance for the sustainable management of the historic environment for the sustainable management of the historic environment, report.

Evening Standard (2011) 'New Park Life: Whitechapel's Altab Ali Park', *Evening Standard*. [Online] Available at: www.standard.co.uk/arts/architecture/new-park-life-whitechapels-altab-ali-park-6368641.html (Accessed: March 2019).

Gunthorpe, K. (2017) *Delivering Public Engagement, Skills and Training–Harmondsworth Barn Case Study*, Historic England. [Online] Available at: https://historicengland.org.uk/images-books/publications/delivering-public-engagement-skills-and-training/heag150-harmondsworth-barn-case-study/(Accessed: March 2019).

Hackney, R. quoted in Wates, N. (1985) 'The Hackney Phenomenon', *Architects Journal*, 20th February: 47–61.

How, N. and Bell, N. (2018) *Heritage Schools CPD 2017 Evaluation Research*, York: Qasar Research. [Online] Available at: https://historicengland.org.uk/content/docs/education/exec-summary-heritage-schools-eval-2017-18/ (Accessed: March 2019)

Johnson, S. (1999) *Conservation Plans in Action*, Historic England.

Kracauer, S. (1963) *Das Ornament der Masse, Essays*. Frankfurt am Main: Suhrkamp. Italian translation M.G. Amirante Pappalardo and F. Maione, Napoli: Prismi, 1982.

Lichtenstein, C. and Schregenberger, T. (eds.) (2001) *As Found: The Discovery of the Ordinary: British Architecture and Art of the 1950s, New Brutalism, Independent Group, Free Cinema, Angry Young Men*, Zurich: Lars Müller Publishers.

Marini, S. (ed.) (2017) *Heritage. Orchestra Rehearsal*. Venice: Bruno.

Morris, W. (1877) Manifesto of the Society for the Protection of Ancient Buildings (SPAB), found in 'The William Morris Internet Archive: Works'. [Online] Available at: www.marxists.org/archive/morris/works/chrono.htm#date-1877-03-29

National Planning Policy Framework (NPPF) (2018) [Online] Available at: www.gov.uk/government/publications/national-planning-policy-framework-2 (Accessed: March 2019).

Nye, C. and Bright, S. (2016) 'Altab Ali: The Racist Murder That Mobilised the East End', *BBC News*. [Online] Available at: www.bbc.com/news/uk-england-london-36191020 (Accessed: March 2019).

Olmo, C. (2018) *Città e democrazia. Per una critica delle parole e delle cose*, Donzelli: Milan

Piepmeier (1980) cited in Kuhne, O. (2018) *Landscape and Power in Geographical Space as a Social-Aesthetic construct*, Cham, Switzerland: Springer Nature Switzerland AG, p. 51.

Piepmeier (1980) quoted in Kuhne, O. Landscape Theories: A Brief Introduction, Springer VS, p. 32.

Pinotti, A. and Somaini, A. (2009) *Teorie dell'immagine*, Milano: Raffaello Cortina Editore.

Pinotti, A. and Somaini, A. (2016) *Cultura visuale. Immagini sguardi media dispositivi*. Torino: Piccola biblioteca Einaudi.

Rainey, P. (2012) 'Digging for Dirt on the Hunchback King', *The Telegraph*. [Online] Available at: www.telegraph.co.uk/history/9497082/Digging-for-dirt-on-the-Hunchback-King.html (Accessed: February 2019).

Ritter, J.L. (1963) *Zur Funktion des Aesthetischen in der modernen Gessellschaft*, Munster: Aschendorf. cited in Proceedings/Anglistentag 1995 Greifswald, edited by J. Klein and D. Vanderbeke, Berlin: Walter de Gruyter GmbH & Co., p. 75.

Ritter, 1963 quoted in Huyssen, A. Twilight Memories: Marking Time in a Culture of Amnesia, Routledge, p. 263.

Robbins, D. (ed.) (1990) *The Independent Group: Postwar Britain and the Aesthetics of Plenty*, Cambridge, MA: MIT Press, p. 201.

Rosemberg, D. (2018) 'The Racist Killing of Altab Ali 40 Years Ago Today', *Open Democracy*. [Online] Available at: www.opendemocracy.net/en/shine-a-light/remembering-altab-ali/ (Accessed: March 2019).

Schlögel, K. (2011) *Marijampole, oder Europas Wiederkehr aus dem Geist der Städte*, Munich: Carl Hanser Verlag GmbH & Co. KG, Verlag.

Secchi, B. (2005) *La città del ventesimo secolo*, Bari: Laterza.

Semple-Kerr, J. (1982) *Conservation Plan*, seventh edition (2013) Australia ICOMOS publication. [Online] Available at: https://australia.icomos.org/publications/the-conservation-plan/ (Accessed: March 2019).

Semple-Kerr, J. (1997) *Conservation Plans in Action*, London: English heritage.

Simmel, G. (1971) 'The Metropolis of Modern Life', in Levine, D. (ed.), *Simmel: On Individuality and Social Forms*, Chicago: Chicago University Press, first published as *Die Großstädte und das Geistesleben (1903)*.

Simmel, G. (1903) *Metropolis and Mental Life*. [Online] Available at: www.blackwellpublishing.com/content/bpl_images/content_store/sample_chapter/0631225137/bridge.pdf

Smithson, A. and Smithson, P. (2001) *In' As Found: The Discovery of the Ordinary*. Edited by C. Lichtenstein and T. Schregenberger, Zurich: Lars Muller, p. 142.

Thackray, D. (1999) *Conservation Plans in Action*, Historic England, p. 57.

The Lord Hankey (1999) *Conservation Plans in Action*, Historic England, p. 109.

Walshe, P. (1999) *Conservation Plans in Action*, Historic England, p. 75.

Websites

Building Conservation. [Online] Available at: www.buildingconservation.com/articles/grants/heritage.htm

Chartered Institute for Archaeologists. [Online] Available at: www.archaeologists.net/http://publications.naturalengland.org.uk/publication/2134081

Fondazione Prada (2016a) *Two New Projects by Theaster Gates and Nastio Mosquito*. [Online] Available at: http://artdaily.com/news/88558/Fondazione-Prada-presents-two-new-projects-by-Theaster-Gates-and-Nastio-Mosquito#.XKIRz-szbyt

Fondazione Prada (2016b) *Theaster Gates: True Value*. [Online] Available at: www.fondazioneprada.org/project/theaster-gates-true-value/?lang=en

Heritage Lottery Fund. [Online] Available at: www.heritagefund.org.uk

Heritage Lottery Fund. [Online] Available at: www.heritagefund.org.uk/publications/hlf-annual-report-2017-2018

Historic England. [Online] Available at: https://historicengland.org.uk/

Historic England, Altab Ali, Tower Hamlets. [Online] Available at: https://historicengland.org.uk/research/inclusive-heritage/another-england/your-stories/altab-ali-park/

Historic England, Assets of Community Value. [Online] Available at: https://historicengland.org.uk/advice/hpg/HAR/CRB/

Historic England, Assessing the Value of Community-Generated Research. [Online] Available at: https://historicengland.org.uk/research/support-and-collaboration/research-frameworks-typologies/assessing-community-generated-research/

Historic England, Heritage Schools. [Online] Available at: https://historicengland.org.uk/services-skills/education/heritage-schools/

Historic England, Delivering Public Engagement, Skills and Training. [Online] Available at: https://historicengland.org.uk/images-books/publications/delivering-public-engagement-skills-and-training/

Localism Act 2011. [Online] Available at: www.legislation.gov.uk/ukpga/2011/20/contents

Mayor of London, Regeneration project: High Street 2012, Newham. [Online] Available at: www.london.gov.uk/what-we-do/regeneration/regeneration-project-high-street-2012-newham

MOLA *Community Archaeology at Altab Ali Park Community Archaeology at Altab Ali Park*. [Online] Available at: www.mola.org.uk/community-archaeology-altab-ali-park

muf architecture/art. [Online] Available at: http://muf.co.uk/

National Trust: People's Landscapes. [Online] Available at: www.nationaltrust.org.uk/features/peoples-landscapes-exhibitions-art-installations-and-events

Richard III, the King in the Car Park' History Documentary hosted by Simon Farnaby, published by Channel 4 in 2013 – English narration.

Venice Charter. [Online] Available at: www.icomos.org/venicecharter2004/

Village Design Guides. [Online] Available at: http://publications.naturalengland.org.uk/publication/2134081

Online dictionaries and definitions:

Merriam-Webster Dictionary, "engagement", https://www.merriam-webster.com/dictionary/engagement (accessed June 1, 2019).

Oxford Dictionaries, "ordinary", https://www.lexico.com/en/definition/ordinary (accessed June 1, 2019).

Oxford Dictionaries, "landscape", https://www.lexico.com/en/definition/landscape (accessed June 1, 2019).

Conclusion
So where is history?

The authors hope that the benefit from reading this book is to prompt a reconsideration of the prevailing technical emphasis of building conservation from a wider social perspective. Ideally the conclusions we draw will support the development of considered physical interventions in historic buildings and places that enable communities to recognise their own sense of custodianship and become engaged in it. The history of a building or place is more than the history of the professionals who directly repair and alter it – if history should be readable in our built environment, we need to ensure we know who it speaks to, how they understand its relevance and how our practice can contribute to that sense of inheritance.

> At its simplest, culture is itself a form of social capital. When a community comes together to share cultural life, through celebration, rites and intercultural dialogue, it is enhancing its relationships, partnerships and networks – in other words, developing social capital. Conversely, when a community's heritage, culture and values (in all their diversity) are overlooked, social capital is eroded, since it is often within these roots that the inspiration for people to act together for a common purpose can be found.
>
> (Stern and Seifert, 2009: 21)

If history is an armature for activity, then it is a jig to hold an action and not an end in itself. Historical events can be revolutionary and socially significant in shaping the present; equally the accumulation of the everyday can be significant in the way it shapes where we live. When undertaking to define a 'statement of significance' are we taking note of what physically remains, or what caused its condition? When we refine 'significance' into a colour-coded plan indicating what can stay and what can go, are we articulating a social history, or simply a chronology of building elements? When the objects of 'significance' are preserved and re-contextualised within a contemporary financial envelope, what do they continue to mean? When Viollet-le-Duc reinstated the sculptures to the façade of Notre Dame de Paris that the revolution of 1793 removed, do we read the full significance of the revolution that both destroyed and reshaped France through the absent statuary, or do we skip that bit and present a flavour – a refined, haute cuisine flavour, but flavour only, of medieval craftsmanship?

240

Through a number of case studies, we wanted to stimulate the discussion over the perceived and built significance of past materials, aware that the processes of 'heritage' signification involves operations of selection and communication besides the technical choices linked to the profession. If we conclude that heritage is 'made' and not inherited (Graham and Howard, 2008), and that heritage has to do with communication narratives, then memory "works by reinvesting places with new accretions of significance" (Kearns and Philo, 1993). Understanding the pivotal importance of observing cultural narratives must therefore constitute a vital part of heritage practice. Differing views that contribute to the signification of heritage have been revealed, and its value needs to be considered outside the leading narratives, seeing the social impact of material choices, the power of local histories and the resistances that they offer to neoliberal operations of city (re)building. Heritage is a resource for the present, but like any resource it can be shared or exploited.

1   *The engagement and knowledge of physicality of our surroundings, their substance and implicit social narrative does not preclude innovation and contemporary intervention, but simply surrounds it.*

The craft advocated by Morris, ICOMOS and the Charters should not be a brake on development but can be a means to engage and democratise not only the physical protection of buildings but their social and cultural advocacy. The Palacio Pereira offers an example of how an enlightened client, conservation philosophy and material significance are intrinsic to delivering a consistent approach to a complex restoration. Technical issues were thoroughly underpinned by constant reference to an approach to the existing that orchestrated the new – not the other way around. The strongest single detail within the Palacio belongs to Cecilia Puga and her design team, resisting the reinstatement of ornate plaster ceilings within the first floor but conceptualising the role that ornate ceilings offer to the definition of a space. The visual texture of the plasterwork was echoed in the supersized graphic use of a William Morris textile – a mark of respect for his contribution to the project, a visual equivalent of the 'splendour' required in the original government brief for the competition, and a startling act of contemporary design "that could in no way mislead" (Morris, 1877).

2   *An urban project involving matters of regeneration, conservation and renewal is not to be considered only the final outcome, but also as a resource to the same policies that generated it. The use of heritage practice as a vehicle for identity, cohesion and significance concerns buildings and places, but also who made them/use them/need them.*

Covent Garden and Battersea Power Station illustrate the power of social collectivity, but also reflect on the power of the free market that claimed the 'spirit of place'. In both cases, the community groups linked to these areas battled to defend their vision, questioning the (mis)use of the historic neighbourhood and iconic building to renew the area according to private interests. The concept of 'spirit of place' is often used by leading stakeholders as an overarching priority for a conservation project, it has even been included into the RIBA Plan of Work (Feilden, Conservation Overlay 2017), to explain a 'sort of' intentional adherence to original features. How, really, is 'spirit of Place' identified in RIBA Workstage 0? A Gazetteer of façades? A mapping of which doors retain their brassware or windows retain their original glass? The global chain-stores in Covent Garden retain all of these tangible signifiers. It could rightly be claimed that the 'spirit of place' here lies within the remaining local community that maintains the activities of the Covent Garden Community Association and still fights the authorities and potential developers for local identity, local access and local needs against the tide of "mediocrity" so clearly articulated by Jo Weir when she talks about the relationship between buildings and people, the unfolding continuity of action and the relational value that evolves within the environment.

3   *Despite preservation needs necessarily to deal with compromise when modifications are allowed, we need to be conscious of the fact that we are editing both material and social history, and that intervention has the power to highlight or erase part of the story, as any narrative would do.*

The installation at the Courtauld prompts a consideration of the depth of meaning present in the most enduringly ephemeral aspect of historic buildings – their surfaces. We say enduringly ephemeral as their recognisable presence seems to provide reassuring continuity – an asset for redevelopers – but at the scale of the surface itself history adds, obscures and erodes, leaving us with an actual record of human and environmental action rather than of the building itself. How we define what remains or what is reinstated is a detailed elaboration of core positions on heritage and significance. Conservation means 'to keep', yet to use is to wear and slowly eradicate. Buildings without use are monuments to the dead. The surface manifests the friction between human use and historical commemoration – the politics of negotiating the two requiring narratives that understand both technical value and social value to achieve an equilibrium. In a way, the National Trust attempted to define that equilibrium at Clandon Park, restoring the spectacle of 18th-century social theatre within the sequence of grand spaces, acknowledging the catastrophic events of 2015 in the retention and preservation of the burned surfaces of the shell in the secondary rooms. Treading the line between Viollet-le-Duc and Morris could end up pleasing no one, evidenced in the criticisms of the Georgian Society, but it is to the Trust's credit that it was willing to explore the detail of opposing philosophies in order to take its custodian role seriously. It can only be hoped that the quality of that exploration by the Trust and with its conservation professionals can be shared openly to inform our future practice.

4   *The concept of 'authenticity' can both support and undermine the relationships between craftsmanship and practices of renewal, fabric sustainability and intervention. Handle with care. Aesthetics is not simply appearance and functionality is not simply technical. Craft, manufacture and material specificity link with matters of social significance and appreciation.*

The St. Pancras case study focuses on a single material – terracotta – to explore the philosophies of producing heritage demonstrating that the linkages between the technical and the philosophical work both ways. The material embodies within its own history and the history of its manufacture a complex set of relations that bring aesthetics, politics, technology and social identity together. The material itself is never used in isolation, and as materials multiply, so too do the set of relations between them. The conservation work at St. Pancras required individual material strategies for terracotta, lead and stone and how they came apart in order to maximise their survival potential. The relationship between philosophical approach and technical care was articulated through lectures, a journal article and community events hosted as part of HLF funding, but on reflection even more should have been done to engage with a wider public on the importance of the building, the chronic effect of pollution on the fabric and by definition on public health. The health of our heritage becomes political almost instantaneously when significance is considered holistically.

By way of contrast, the treatment of terracotta as a sign of an idea rather than as a culturally loaded physical material at the Whitechapel Gallery allows us to reflect on how the 'spirit of a place' is manifest. Buildings exhibit their origins, they are the physical presence of a set of ideas and values that, in the case of the Whitechapel Gallery, shifted radically over time. The only constant across a century was the terracotta façade, which eventually registered its break with locality and community through its own materiality being co-opted as iconic art by an iconic artist. The two projects demonstrate the criticality of the use and misuse of 'craft' within a material process, and the relationship that the ideas of craftsmanship and originality have to cultural significance, locality and commodification.

5 *The study of fragments (intended as a plurality of materials and voices) can be considered a resource (Schlögel, 2011), a way to take a political position through reworked visions, and the city often offered critical materials for this operation. Rather than ultimate solutions, projects can be intended as open processes in approaching and dealing with heritage and place transformation.*

We deliberately concluded with some exemplary projects that intentionally address the social value of heritage, achieving a complex set of readings through engagement, rather than typifying or signifying value in technical terms. The reinvestment of the 'White Chapel' socially by utilising the practice of archaeology brought the children of Whitechapel's newest community in contact with the history of the place, their work becoming folded into the built elements that were collaged into the park, demarcating social spaces through traces of real and re-imagined 'archaeologies'. With the fragments unearthed by the children visible in the stratified walls the authors fabricated for the MUF architects' design, the tangible presence of past history is made evident, reinterpreted and appropriated. Together, a sense of ownership in the next generation of 'locals' is created. Theaster Gates' work has a similar archaeological underpinning, here working with the flipside of archaeology which is the disaggregation of a place, its cataloguing and museification of the 'as found'. This process of acknowledging the value of the ordinary – archaeology learns as much from a Roman waste pit as it does from a Roman palace – becoming a means of commemorating communal loss and prompting the acknowledgement of what capital makes, and then leaves behind as it becomes consolidated in ever fewer, more distant hands. Revealing the social agenda inherent within the spectacle of heritage was achieved through an exemplary project by the National Trust – 'The People's Landscapes', the intangible histories of direct action made visible through a curated set of site-specific interventions in buildings and territories.

6   *Alongside spatial changes come an interlaced system of norms and regulations,*
     promotion of social practices and policies which affect not only the way con-
     struction is enabled but also its social returns (Söderström, 2012). Too easily,
     however, they promote a univocal interpretation of heritage, excluding of the
     plurality of voices that ought to inform the reading of space.

We have seen how the charters themselves are records of a moment in time when
technical and professional direction was unquestioningly 'good for us', consequently
framing present benchmarks that provide unchallenged limitations to how communities participate in their own history. The lack of skills in engagement and participation
that heritage professionals are either familiar with, trained for or accredited in is a
consequence of this technocratic definition of conservation, one which built on only a
selected reading of what Morris and Ruskin had to offer. If communities are to have
a voice in the development of their historic environments, then re-layering this intellectual context is vital.

The authors advocate looking hard at the physical reality of heritage in order to
understand the connectivity between materiality, technique, culture and politics, and
propose that the interconnections between all of them create social capital. Through
the course of the research the connectivity across these themes and between the sites
under investigation started creating layer upon layer of connections, in a way exceed-
ing the original idea to develop a set of arguments that collectively cover a territory.
Instead, the case studies began to reappear within each other as the arguments took
shape – the redevelopment ambitions for Covent Garden displayed a nascent potential
for exclusion that became a highly sophisticated persuasion vehicle at the Battersea
Power Station; ironically the market that gave meaning to the social structure of 'the
garden' was relocated to Battersea, only to be removed again for the next reiteration of
the redevelopment agenda. Reflecting on the work undertaken at St. Pancras for a technical lecture to the SPAB, the position Morris took to terracotta opened up a critique
that informed the reading of Whiteread's Whitechapel installation. The loss of a social
mandate for the Whitechapel Gallery, unintentionally exemplified by Whiteread's intervention, took us back into the origins of the institution and its community purpose, the
exemplary work by MUF literally on the opposite side of the street was so close to the
original purpose of the Gallery and the reverse of what the Gallery has become – an
art-based practice founded on participation. The work of Theaster Gates proves that
this form of work is not an anomaly but a conscious practice with structured ideas and
clear intellectual accuracy. In turn, the exhibition 'This is Tomorrow' held at the Whitechapel Gallery in 1956 allowed us to focus our attention on the Smithsons' concept
of 'as found' articulated through their 'Patio and Pavilion' installation, to observe the
correspondences with Morris on the role of the necessary and value of the everyday.

The layered collage of information is both a methodology for the book and a methodology for the projects that manage to bring heritage into contact with people who have a
stake in that inheritance. If the book prompts practice to appreciate the value of understanding tangible heritage within a social context that can, through positive engagement, inform how change is managed for community benefit, then it has succeeded.

Bibliography

Feilden, H. (2017) RIBA Plan of Work 2013 Guide: Conservation, London: RIBA Publications.

Graham, B.J. and Howards, P. (eds.) (2008) *The Ashgate Research Companion to Heritage and Identity*, Franham: Ashgate Publishing.

Kearns, G. and Philo, C. (eds.) (1993) *Selling Places: The City as Cultural Capital, Past and Present*, Oxford: Pergamon Press.

Morris, W. (1877) *Manifesto for the Society for the Protection of Ancient Buildings.* [Online] Available at: www.spab.org.uk/about-us/spab-manifesto (Accessed: March 2019).

Schlögel, K. (2011) *Marijampole, oder Europas Wiederkehr aus dem Geist der Städte*, Munich: Carl Hanser Verlag GmbH & Co. KG, Verlag.

The production of heritage: biographies and thanks

Alan Chandler

A founding director of the architectural practice Arts Lettres Techniques with Luisa Auletta, I have worked consistently on the interface between contemporary design and conservation since 1993, when fabric-formed concrete casts weighing several tonnes were taken from the portico of Hawksmoor's St. George's Church in Bloomsbury to create a site-specific installation while studying at the AA. This early engagement with questioning material and heritage value has persisted, with expertise in conservation accreditation and award-winning projects in the UK and Chile maintaining a focus on how politics and cultural perception connect with material and philosophical conservation. Examining for the RIBA Conservation Register began at its inception in 2011, followed by membership of the Conservation Committee and Steering Group has allowed a perspective on the culture of professionalism, the criticism of which in this book should be balanced with a genuine respect for the knowledge and commitment of many professionals within the field, and an acknowledgement that the RIBA has made a genuine investment into conservation practice, supported by dedicated and intelligent staff within the organisation. The aim of the dissection is to discover what is missing, not what is wrong.

There are key individuals and organisations that deserve our thanks.

The following have kindly donated images and permissions to bring our text to life: The Prada Foundation in Milan for releasing images of the artworks of Theaster Gates; Ken Jacobson for kindly providing a copy of John Ruskin's beautiful 1849 daguerrotype from Venice; the National Trust for agreeing the use of our photographs of Clandon Park; the Covent Garden Community Group for opening access to documents from the events of the 1970s, the Society for the Protection of Ancient Buildings for a copy of an early manifesto and perspective of St. Pancras Church; Helen Howard for providing her scientific examination of the original decoration at Somerset House, and MUF Architecture/Art LLP for documents and images from Altab Ali Park. My colleagues and friends Alberto, Cecilia and Paula in Santiago de Chile merit a special mention, firstly for inviting me to participate in the reclaiming of the Palacio Pereira and then maintaining a supporting role as this incredible project has unfolded. Their support is gratefully acknowledged.

I would like to personally thank Luisa Auletta for enabling our practice to sustain its work in parallel to teaching and research, without which half the chapters in the book would be empty, and Michela Pace for extending and sharpening the scope of the entire book in what has been a great collaboration.

Michela Pace

A researcher at the Iuav University of Venice in the field of urbanism, previously working and collaborating with the Universities of UEL London, PoliTo Turin and PoliMi Milan, UH Hasselt, Tongji University Shanghai among the others, I studied the rising centrality of the 'heritage' rhetoric within processes of urban financialization worldwide, and the use of notions of memory, legacy, patrimony and tradition inside city marketing. Heritage, in particular, was observed in relation to real estate activities, the phenomenon of land privatisation and gentrification in Western and Eastern global cities. At the same time, as an architect, I deepened community-based research, collaborating with a different spectrum of partners and clients for the making of local projects.

These include local communities and school, councils and policymakers, international NGOs, charitable foundations and private clients. Merging the observations of 'heritage' promotion and protection at the global and local scale has in my experience the ability to disclose those mechanisms able to promote an idea of city, and the language and the rules able to distribute it. What is at stake is not only the concept of past and the power of history, but also our ability to imagine alternative futures.

Index

Note: Page numbers in italic indicate a figure on the corresponding page.

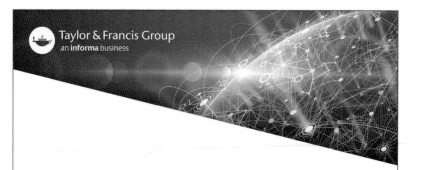